INTO THE CULTURE CAVE

Generator of Art, Community, Emotions and Ideas

Edited by Jörn Weisbrodt

LUMINATO FESTIVAL 10 YEAR

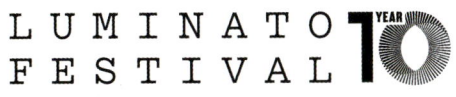

black dog publishing
london uk

CONTENTS

12	**Introduction** Jörn Weisbrodt	
16	**The Paradox of the Hearn** Jack Diamond	

THE IDEA
How to Go Forward Culturally by Going Way Back

24	**Into the Culture Cave** Jörn Weisbrodt	
48	**Cave Art and 'Cavemen'** Ian Tattersall	
58	**The Creative Force of Old Buildings** Richard Florida	
70	**Writings on the Wall** Georg Diez	
78	**The Théâtre du Soleil, or the Art of Assembly** Bruno Tackels	
88	**What Would Jane Do?** Michael Redhill	

STRATEGIES AND IMPACT
How to Start Moving

100	**Penetration, Unbuilding and the Future of Museums** Nicola Spunt in conversation with Alex Josephson and Charles Renfro	
120	**Why do Temporary Theatres Work?** Jerad Schomer and Clemeth Abercrombie, of Charcoalblue	
132	**Brave New Cultural World** Karen Brooks Hopkins	
136	**Departures from the White Cube** Kitty Scott	

THE REALIZATION OF THE IDEA
Exploring the Cave

145	**Gathering Citizens** Adrienne Clarkson	
152	**Toronto Needs the Hearn to Remind It of Itself** Shawn Micallef	
158	**Here Before the Hearn** Falen Johnson	
162	**A History of the Hearn Generating Station** Nicole Hurtubise	
168	**Don't Look Back I Back Look Don't** Clyde Wagner	
174	**Privy to Everything** Atom Egoyan	
182	**The Twenty-First-Century Concert Hall** Mat Schulz	
188	**The Coating Project** The Dietrich Group	
198	**Choir! Choir! Choir!** Nobu Adilman, Daveed Goldman and Steve Manale	
204	**A Canadian Dream** Rufus Wainwright	
212	**Snails and Chablis in Odd Places** Fred Morin	
214	**Escargots Bourguignonne Recipe** Fred Morin	
220	**Trove: A View of Toronto in 50 of its Treasures — A City as a Gallery of Art** Jörn Weisbrodt	
228	**Yes Yes Y'all @ Luminato** Sammy Rawal	
232	**The Weather's Getting In: The James Plays in The Hearn** Laurie Sansom	

EPILOGUE

242	**Yesterday was the Future** Jörn Weisbrodt	
249	**Biographies**	
251	**Acknowledgements**	
252	**Image Credits**	

Introduction
Jörn Weisbrodt

For 17 days in June 2016, the Luminato Festival transformed the Hearn Generating Station in the Port Lands in Toronto into the largest temporary cultural and community centre in the world. The Hearn is three times the size of the Tate Modern and fits the Statue of Liberty in it upright. It was decommissioned in 1983 and, apart from serving as a location for movie shoots for films such as *Robocop* and *Pacific Rim*, has been closed to the public. 100,000 people visited the Hearn and experienced large-scale exhibitions, theatre performances, classical, pop and electronic concerts, club events, sing-a-longs, talks, parkour workout sessions, drag queen shows, a high-end French bistro run by Canada's top chefs in the former control room... and no walls.

This book documents the festival and the 17 days that created a live proposal for the future of this building. But, more than being a mere documentation of an event that now lies in the memories of those who attended the festival, the book outlines an idea that was tried out at the Hearn for a radically new multidisciplinary cultural institution of the twenty-first century; one that is able to reflect the essential values of openness, inclusiveness and diversity, without which we are not going to survive as a democratic society. I call this idea the 'Culture Cave'.

I strongly believe that the three most pressing issues and challenges that we are facing this century are technological change, multiculturalism and global warming, and the speed with which these affect us. Nationalism, women's rights, minority rights, religious rights, gay rights etc were considered issues of the twentieth century; we assumed them solved, until recently when they started casting their shadows over our societies again. The causes of these issues of the twenty-first century might be buried deeper in the nature of human beings themselves: long-term fear of the other and short-term protection of one's own kind at all costs. Our cultural institutions should be organized according to principles that address the core of these problems in today's reality, but none of them are. Most institutions still mimic models that were invented hundreds of years ago. They struggle in retrofitting their buildings to contemporary artists' practices and to audiences who have completely surpassed them in what they regard as culture. We fail to see the beauty and opportunities that lie in the fact that people's motivation to consume culture today is no longer what they know, but to be with who you know. It is about gathering and creating community.

A first necessary step in moving beyond these old models is to stop segregating art from itself. Conventional multidisciplinary institutions, like the Barbican Centre, still separate in space and not in time. You can only see one thing during one visit. In the Culture Cave this rule is inverted. Inspired by the Neolithic cave, the earliest form of human shelter, everything happens in one huge space, but is separated in time. Audiences are able to experience the entire breadth of human activity and creativity without having to make choices.

Through the diverse voices in this book, a vision of a cultural institution emerges that breaks free from the traditional Western models that have colonized the entire world; that found their roots in the European Renaissance and have remained virtually unchanged since. The hope is that reading this book will be a similar experience to walking into the programmatic cornucopia of the Hearn: it is a book more spatial and three-dimensional than linear. Content overlaps, design and form are not absolutely consistent and seemingly unrelated things might be right next to each other—similar to how there were no divisions and hierarchies in the Hearn. It is supposed to stimulate, sidetrack, surprise and seduce the reader.

I walked into the Hearn for the first time on an extremely grim but sunny January morning in 2014 with Paul Vaughan, the custodian of the Hearn who became a dear friend. Looking at a rusty maze of steel beams that seemed to stretch towards an Escher-esque infinity, frozen puddles of water waiting for ice skaters, thick bundles of sunlight coming in through numerous cracks and holes in the walls, I felt like a prince having stumbled upon Sleeping Beauty and her castle. In 2014 we held our first annual fundraising gala in the space and, despite everyone's pre-emptive dust allergies months in advance (the building has a clean environmental bill), the evening was a huge success, with over 500 people parking inside the same space where, moments later, they dined and danced. In 2015 we added a two-day experimental music festival called Unsound Toronto to our exploration of the space. The following year, the entire festival was held at the Hearn. What happened in 2016, what thoughts and ideas inspired the festival and how it inspired the people and artists who came to visit and stay is what this book is about.

I am incredibly grateful to all the contributors. If it were hockey, people would speak of an all-star dream team. Every one of them has written an original text, created a new cooking recipe, drawing, short story or a comic strip. I tickled, ambushed and cajoled supporters and patrons who had become friends over my five years living in Toronto into supporting this book after so many had already been so generous in making the festival happen in the first place. I am forever grateful to them and hope that when they see this book they are proud of their gift.

These dear people are Mohammad and Najla Al Zaibak, Helen Burstyn and her family, Angela and David Feldman of Camrost-Felcorp, Wendy M Cecil, John Donald and Linda Chu, Helene Clarkson and the Max Clarkson Family Foundation, Janice Lewis and Mitchell Cohen, Tony and Lina Gagliano, the Haldenby family, Vahan and Susie Kololian, Eleanor McCain, Margaret McCain, Lynda and Jonas Prince, Jay Smith and Laura Rapp, Gretchen and Donald Ross, and Phil and Eli Taylor. Thank you to Anthony Sargent, who had just started as the new CEO of the Luminato Festival when I confronted him with this gigantic idea, for never doubting its value and importance for one minute; to the board of directors and to the entire staff of the festival, permanent and temporary; to all the artists who came and spent intermissions in construction-site trailers instead of dressing rooms; to our arts partners, without whom the Hearn would have been a lot less exciting; to our base jumpers who fired up the smokestack again and threw themselves off it for the opening; to all the volunteers, donors, corporate and government partners; to everyone at the wonderful publishing company Black Dog Publishing, in particular Duncan McCorquodale, who immediately said yes to making this book when he stepped into the building, Simon Arthur, our editor, and Clara Emo-Dambry, the designer. A glorious separate thank you to Clyde Wagner, our executive producer who worked harder than anyone I have seen on such little sleep and to Nicole Hurtubise who was not only my assistant at the festival but also on this book. Lastly to the incredible audience—young and old, of all colours and from all backgrounds—who not only attended, but who sometimes stormed the building, hoping to get a seat at Toronto's hottest restaurant Le Pavillon in the control room. Yes, I do forgive you for screaming at me and calling me unprofessional for being two minutes late opening the gates some days. It felt like the whole of Toronto was at the Hearn for 17 days and wanted it fired up again.

I see the book as a prism through which an idea gets split up into ever changing forms. It is loosely organized into four sections. It begins with texts focusing on ideas that inspired the concept of the Culture Cave, then moves on to everything that came before the realization of the festival, and, thirdly, what happened while the festival was running. Finally, the epilogue is a transcript of the speech I gave for the opening of the Hearn on 9 June 2016, dreaming that it was the opening of the finished Culture Cave 20 years in the future. Jonathan Castellino's beautiful full-bleed photos run through the entire book in chronological order. We dated them, creating a timeline from the day the first truck arrived to the day the last truck left. Smaller ancillary photos, plans and graphics are spread throughout.

I have always believed in the detour being the best way to get to where you really want to go. Without taking the first step you will never get anywhere. If the goal feels so overwhelming and you don't know how to get there, you'd better start moving immediately. If you don't, you certainly won't reach anything. A mathematics professor once said to me: "While a straight line connects two points in space, the most elegant connection between two points or dots is a curved line." Let's connect hundreds of dots elegantly with this book!

The Paradox of the Hearn
Jack Diamond

Once the epitome of rigidly functional design, now the locus of imagination and spontaneity, the Hearn is an exquisite paradox—a transformation from the classic to the romantic. Its heroic Piranesian scale, and the emotional response to its sheer size and complexity, is the canvas on which limitless possibilities of metamorphoses can be conceived.

It is the physical counterpart of a 6B pencil sketch, in which ideas suggest themselves that were not envisaged by the draftsperson, like seeing faces in clouds.

Transforming one artifact into another form is an accomplishment of the highest creativity, Picasso's toy car into a monkey, Ai Weiwei's assembly of chairs into a space-defining tower, even the conversion of an industrial building into an apartment complex, are just such metamorphoses.

The theatre, sculpture gallery and the restaurant in the control room of the Hearn during Luminato give magnetic expression to this potent phenomenon.

Beyond the accomplishments of the use of the Hearn as a locus for high art, whose possibilities are just beginning, it is also a manifestation of the shift of a provincial city to one of global significance. Such an enterprise was mounted on the hitherto unrealized sensibilities of the great city Toronto could be. And this is in spite of a governance structure that is woefully inadequate to the task of realizing the potentials of this emerging metropolis. Once again the arts have illuminated the way.

Sketches of the Hearn by Jack Diamond

24 May

THE IDEA

How to Go Forward Culturally by Going Way Back

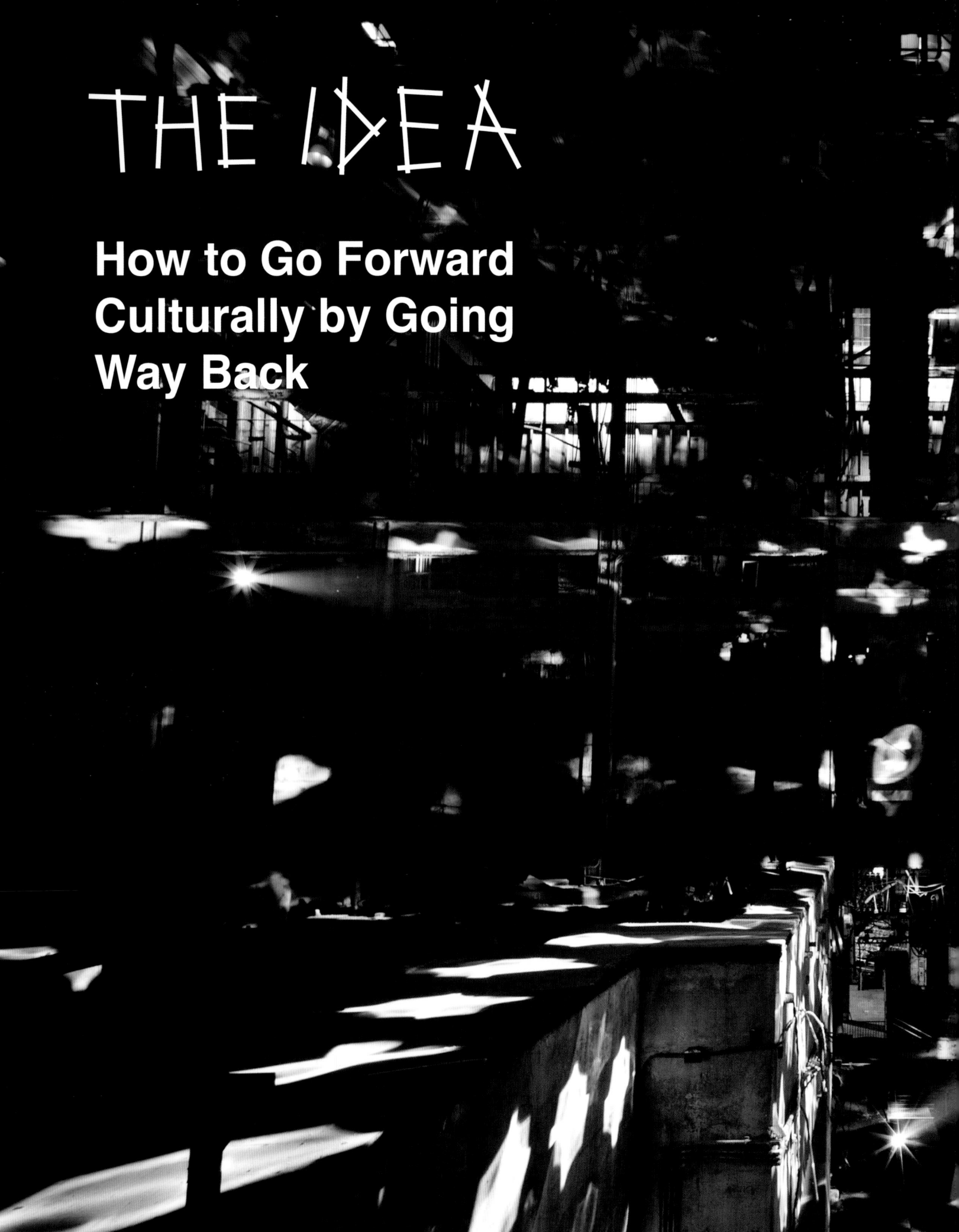

Into the Culture Cave
Jörn Weisbrodt

I. From the Neolithic Cave to the Culture Cave

A recent expedition into the Chauvet Cave in the Ardèche department of southern France revealed that visual artists emerged from the earliest human beings and communities about 35,000 to 40,000 years ago—many years earlier than scientists previously thought. Older examples of wall paintings might have existed but have not withstood erosion and other natural influences over the millennia. Interestingly enough, 'cave art', including musical instruments made out of vulture or mammoth bones, seems to have emerged around the same time, 40,000 years ago, in completely different regions of the world: Sulawesi in Indonesia, as well as the Arnhem Land in the Northern Territory of Australia.

Homo sapiens migrated from Africa to Europe about 100,000 years ago. Research shows that larger human communities seem to have developed throughout Europe at the same time as these paintings in the Chauvet Cave in the south of France were made. This could suggest that through the arts communities were able to form, as the arts offer a common spiritual platform, a reason for gathering, a way of interpreting, and therefore abstracting yourself from, the world, that makes communal living possible. During those days our ancestors shared the European stage with other hominins, namely Neanderthals. Scientists believe that Neanderthals produced little to no art, at least none significantly that would have lasted until today. In terms of other things that seem to differentiate us from the animal kingdom, such as building fires, cooking, clothing ourselves or creating tools, all the human species seem to have been pretty much the same. None of them survived except for our species. None of them except for us painted or made music.

Since Jane Goodall filmed chimpanzees using sticks to repeatedly poke out ants from a hole in the earth and teaching the skill to their offspring, we know today that animals also use tools—long-believed to be the differentiator between humans and other species. It was maintained that animals don't have consciousness; they don't have an experience of self. That wall has come crashing down as well. Animals do have consciousness; they can even recognize themselves in a mirror. Kathy, the main dolphin in the 60s TV series *Flipper*, could distinguish herself on the screen from her other female sub-stars or stand-ins Suzy, Patty and Squirt. She also clearly knew that it was not her on the screen who performed Flipper's famous 'tail dance', seemingly standing on the water, but a male dolphin, Scotty, who was brought in to perform the trick. She would react to the scenes on a TV screen that was propped up close to her water basin where she lived. She showed no interest when Suzy, Patty, Squirt and Scotty were pretending to be Kathy. When it was actually her on the screen she got excited and made noise. I doubt that any one of the millions of TV viewers saw the difference between Kathy, Suzy, Patty, Squirt and Scotty, but Kathy did.

Kathy committed suicide later in her career, by the way. It is doubtful she did it because she was depressed over the carelessness and lack of continuity that her character was treated with. She stopped breathing and sank to the floor of her small, enclosed water space. Dolphins breathe consciously; we don't. Mythologically and culturally, consciousness is something that is thought to be exclusive to man, but biologically it clearly is not. Human consciousness was 'born' when Narcissus fell in love with his own reflection in a pool of water. Now we know that Kathy could have swum in that water as well, aware of what Narcissus was doing; looking at his face from below through the surface of the water, just waiting for her own close-up.

The Chauvet Cave paintings are said to have ritualistic meaning. Neurologists have suggested that movement creates consciousness, implying that all creatures that roam freely develop a consciousness. You have to experience yourself in relationship to a changing environment. You have to react. Communication starts. The 'I' is born—

1 An early expedition into the Lascaux Caves, Montignac, 1948

although of course the 'I' of a crab is different from Descartes' "I think, therefore I am" of human beings. Recent studies have shown that even plants have a very sophisticated way of communicating with each other. The great Portuguese-American neuroscientist Antonio Damasio even thought about the possibility of plants who move towards sunlight, climbing plants who grow towards an obstacle, or beech tree branches rooting out once they touch the ground, having consciousness as they technically move and react to their environment.

If a certain plant is attacked by bugs, it starts producing a certain chemical or protein that will be absorbed by other plants and the whole community of plants start developing an antidote against the bug. I have seen this quite fascinatingly this year in our vegetable garden, where our zucchinis were attacked by bugs, and they actually managed to heal themselves. They formed a layer of scar tissue at the place of attack and protected themselves from rotting. Other zucchinis around them developed a tougher-than-normal skin. Now, of course one will argue that this is not necessarily 'language' but merely chemical processes that are triggered by certain impulses and therefore lead to certain chemical reactions. But on a neuronal level that is probably very similar to what happens in our brains as well. And, stunningly enough, some plants have thousands of different chemical substances with which they 'communicate' with other examples of their species and their environment. The average human vocabulary is significantly lower. The sophistication of whale sounds and languages, as well as those of many other species, are just beginning to be grasped. So what is the last bastion that only human beings are capable of inhabiting? What is it that no other living creature or substance has ever produced? In my opinion it is art.

Only we have created works of art that shift living organisms' relationship to nature from survival (which is what most species are after) to living; from something that is created solely for the purpose of surviving and procreating to something that has an additional meaning which we might call 'spiritual' or 'metaphysical', and which creates ritual or gathering. Yes, chimpanzees in zoos, who definitely have rituals and form social communities based on characters and individuality, have been known to produce 'paintings' if you put a canvas in front of them and dip a paintbrush into paint and put it into their hands, but there is no evidence that after they created them they treated these 'paintings' any differently to other objects. They would not gaze at them as we gaze at the oldest cave paintings or gaze at John Singer Sargent's *Madame X*. I would assume that our ancestors from 40,000 years ago would walk into the Metropolitan Museum of Art in New York and would see a direct line from their ochre, charcoal, bone and calcite cave paintings to these oil-on-canvas ones.

Art forms ritual and ritual forms community. Art is not a result of human existence or of the survival of our species. It is not something that came at a later point in our development as we became more sophisticated in terms of organizing our food supply, protecting ourselves from the environment and communicating better, and when we had some free time on our hands; it is right there at our origin, and at our independence and success as the only human species to continue living through the millennia. It is what distinguished us from the Neanderthals or any other human species before us, from any animal or plant that has ever survived and existed on this planet and probably ever will. It made us distinct from all living matter. We became superior in interpreting the world and the cosmos. Religion was born; science came a lot later. Through art we were able to give life a meaning. We were able to form larger communities that made us stronger. It is an evolutionary step that has nothing to do with the body of the animal that is undergoing evolution adapting in a more ideal way to the environment by making hands larger, beaks thinner, or the fur colour more invisible in its environment. Evolution steps outside of the body through art.

We know that art was produced even earlier than 40,000 years ago. We have records of simple abstract forms and patterns scratched into rocks. But, even earlier, forms might have been drawn into sand that the winds blew away, sticks arranged on rocks; there might have been dancing, chanting, singing and clapping. Performance, or any time-based art—art that is only created to last for a certain amount of time—is probably even older than painting or sculpture. And if not, we do know that they existed around

the same time as the paintings were created. We can assume that art was connected to rituals for thousands of years. It was intrinsically part of our ancestors' lives. I doubt there was a distinction made between decorative, applied and fine art.

The oldest musical instrument known to mankind is a flute made about 35,000 years ago out of the bones of a vulture whose descendants still roam our planet more or less unchanged. It was found in a cave. It is believed that the possession of these instruments gave our ancestors a strategic advantage over Neanderthals. They could communicate via long distances without necessarily revealing their identity or where they were. The sound of the flute could mimic nature, understandable to those who were communicating with each other but not to others; it was the earliest form of cryptology.

The Neolithic cave is the earliest form of permanent human shelter (it is literally a roof over your head), even though our ancestors would not yet settle down permanently in it and abandon their nomadic lifestyle. They simply could not afford to do that, as they had to follow animals and the fruit, roots and other plant material that became available for consumption at different times of the year in different locations. But they used caves regularly and repeatedly. They came back to the ones that they painted. The cave, as well as being used as a human shelter, and as a place for gathering and manufacturing, was also our first gallery, concert hall and theatre. This Neolithic multidisciplinarity and mixed-use concept is the foundation of the idea for the Culture Cave. The existence of the Neolithic cave is the model for the cultural institution of the twenty-first century.

II. From the cave to palaces, and the cultural institutions of today

Our cultural institutions today are incredibly varied in size, shape and form: from a community theatre and centre in Yellowknife in the Northern Territories to the Metropolitan Opera in New York, the Barbican in London, The Broad museum in Los Angeles, the Zaha Hadid-designed opera house in Guangzhou, the Centre Pompidou in Paris, the new Snøhetta-designed library in Alexandria, the Foster + Partners master-planned West Kowloon Cultural District in Hong Kong that also sits on reclaimed land, the Hamhung Grand Theatre in North Korea, the Minamiza Kabuki Theatre in Kyoto and the Jewish Museum in Berlin. We have designed and built contemporary art museums, shoe museums, train museums, war museums, holocaust museums, indigenous art museums, experimental theatres, Broadway theatres, opera houses, ballet theatres, contemporary dance theatres, children's libraries, university libraries, concert halls for classical music, rock venues, jazz clubs, arenas, underground clubs, open-air theatres… the list is endless. But they all have one thing in common: the genesis of our cultural institutions of today can be traced back to a few hundred years ago and since then nothing in their structure has significantly changed, even though our societies, our religious beliefs, our economies have. Louis XIV would still intuitively know where his place would be in the Snøhetta-designed opera house in Oslo: in the centre of the first balcony. He would see the stage from pretty much the same angle as he would in his own theatre, the Royal Opera House in Versailles (unless he was on stage performing, of course). It is the very same place where Norway's King and Queen, or prime minister, sit in Oslo today if they attend a performance.

Most of our cultural institutions were invented during the Renaissance and the feudal and aristocratic period in Europe. Of course, many new ones have been built by every generation, but all followed the old models. While 400 years ago there were no separate museums for chairs, design, ceramics, modern art, contemporary art etc, the DNA of the museum, of the theatre of today, is essentially still the same. Around the same time that the ancestors of today's cultural institutions were born, ritual was disconnected from art, thus losing its central role in our lives. Art was put into places that were specifically designed for it; applied art was separated from fine art. By seemingly giving it its own defined space, by creating art for art's sake, we have inadvertently banned it from the centre of our lives: cutting its roots and leaving it to slowly die.

Europe is currently in its most recent phase of colonialism, which is a cultural colonialism. We build European models of cultural organizations all over the world, with Western-style museums and opera houses in China and the Middle East, such as the Guggenheim Abu Dhabi, the Louvre Abu Dhabi, NYU Abu Dhabi and the Dubai Opera, to name a few recent examples. The opera house in Manaus, the Teatro Colón in Buenos Aires and

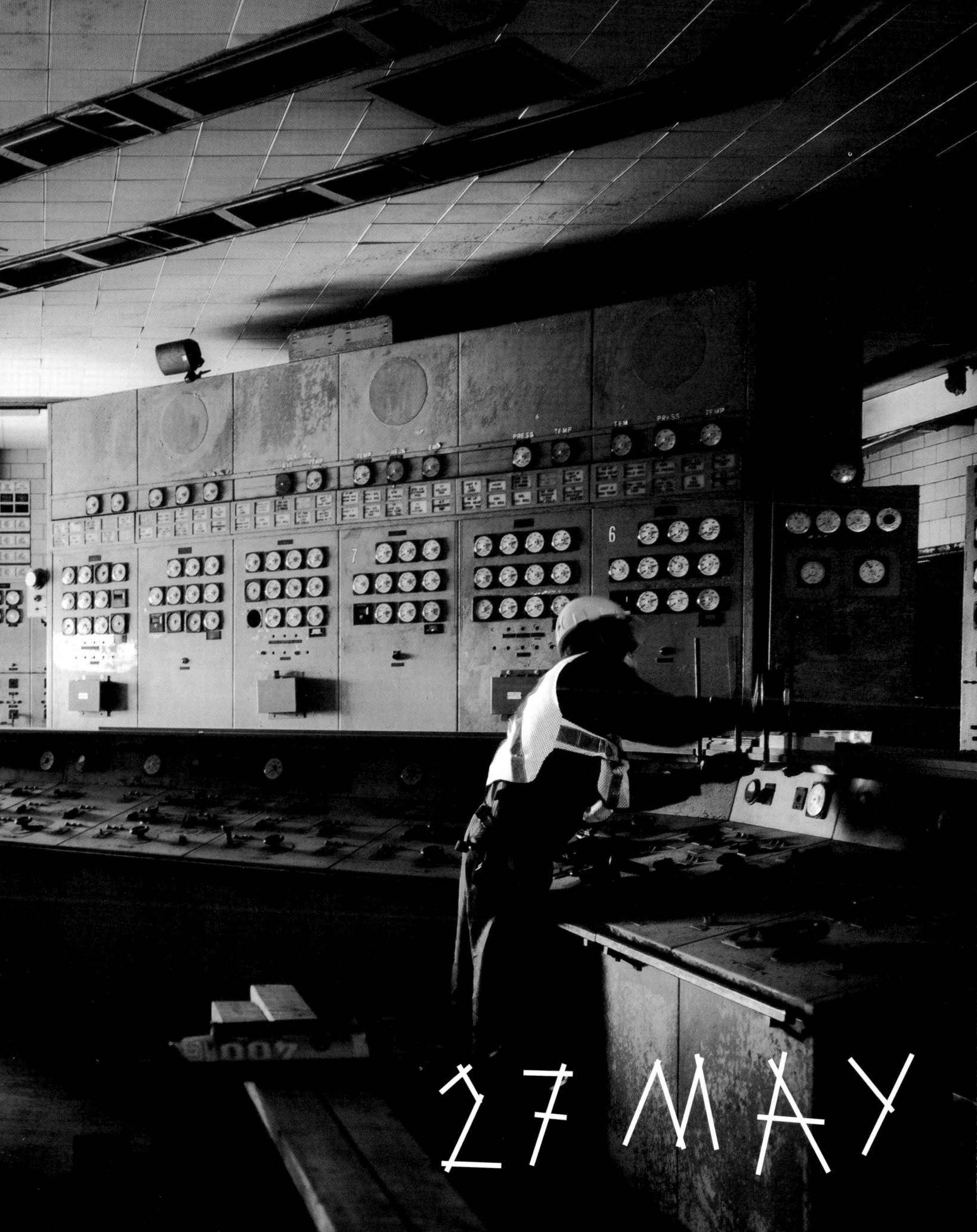
27 MAY

the Museo de Bellas Artes in Havana are actual colonial examples of how Europeans exported their culture and their forms of cultural organizations across the world, paralyzing the development of any new cultural institutions.

Over hundreds of years, not much has changed in the way we preserve and show art. Of course curatorial discipline and conservation have become more rigorous, and lighting and technical stage equipment more sophisticated. But in the most fundamental ways—how the audience interacts with art, how they experience it, how they can consume and access it—nothing has changed, even though our societies have vastly changed. Except for the fact that audiences have to make more and more choices as more and more cultural and creative niches get their own versions of the hundreds-of-years-old models of the museum, the theatre, the concert hall. And, as shown above, we continue to build the same models over and over again, just giving them more spectacularly designed skins.

But we have hit a point were the niches and disciplines that institutions have carved out are becoming too small, where institutions cannot react to social changes anymore—just like an animal who is too finely adapted to a certain environment will die out with the slightest shift in its microclimate. Today, as opposed to 400 years ago, we separate culture more and more. Everything is in a different place. You cannot go to an exhibition, a concert, a nightclub and an opera in one day. It is physically not possible. In the old days, the monarch did not even have to leave his palace. Of course, unlike back then, culture is accessible to all people today—although that is somewhat an illusion as well. One could almost be tempted to say that fundamentally nothing changed for 400 years but things have become a lot worse and less convenient.

In addition to the fact that a lot of our culture happens in different spaces at the same time (almost 90 per cent of the performing arts start between 7 and 8 pm; museums all have more or less the same opening hours), transportation has become a huge issue in many major cities and people are less willing to leave their neighbourhoods. For many New Yorkers, Brooklyn is still almost a different country. For Torontonians, after 6 pm when commuters are home, there is hardly any osmosis between the inner city 416 or 647 and the suburban 905 area codes. In São Paulo the rich commute with helicopters to get from one place within the city to another. In the highest capital city in the world, La Paz in Bolivia, which stretches over 750 altitudinal metres, people tend to stay within their range of altitudes, with the rich living lower and the poor higher up (more oxygen for the rich). If highways 10 or 405 in LA are congested, performances at Royce Hall at UCLA are half empty.

Most festivals in the world were founded after great crises. Many festivals were founded as a reaction to the cultural devastation of the Second World War, and as a symbol of growing national identity. Prague Spring Festival and Bregenzer Festspiele were founded in 1946, the Edinburgh Festival in 1947, the Festival Aix-en-Provence in 1948, Wiener Festwochen, Berliner Festwochen and Berlinale in 1951, Bergen International Festival and Perth Festival in 1953, documenta in 1955, Lincoln Center and Santa Fe Opera Festival in 1956, and Spoleto Festival in 1958, to name a few. Others like the Ruhrtriennale and the Manchester International Festival were created to be vehicles of social and economic change in cities that needed to find a new direction of growth in the post-industrial world. A lot of festivals celebrated a post-dictatorial reality in their countries, like Santiago a Mil, which was founded in Santiago, Chile, a few years after Pinochet stood down, or the Lake of Stars Festival in Malawi, less than ten years after the first multi-party elections were held. The founding of the Luminato Festival in Toronto was a reaction to SARS, a viral epidemic in 2002 and 2003 that basically shut down the city. But even festivals, which are not as bound to institutions and buildings as most cultural models, are mostly monothematic and often make use of seasonally vacant cultural institutions, thus often giving a more out-of-the-ordinary spin on their product, but not really rethinking the model of how culture and art are presented, consumed and experienced.

Giovanni Battista Piranesi's "The Gothic Arch" from Imaginary Prisons, c 1749–50. Background: 3D rendering of the interior of the Hearn.

III. Attempts at changing the cultural institutional model and the birth of the Culture Cave

The social upheaval of the late 60s had an effect on how culture was being thought of. It led to the construction of new institutions that tried to celebrate a new openness and social and cultural reality, like the Centre Pompidou, which turned the architecture of a museum inside out. The guts and skeleton of the building are literally on the outside. Richard Rogers and Renzo Piano turned the idea of architecture inside out, but did they equally turn the idea of a cultural institution inside out? The Pompidou was founded to combine different art forms under one roof: the visual arts, through the Musée National d'Art Moderne; music, through IRCAM, a brainchild of Pierre Boulez; and the literary arts, through the Bibliothèque publique d'information. The idea was born largely out of necessity, as all of these institutions needed new homes. One of its main achievements, ushered in by its founding director Pontus Hultén, was that it did not think about projects in a geographically exclusive way. A project by the Pompidou did not necessarily have to take place at the Pompidou. This was a more radical idea in those times than it is today, where institutions, like documenta in Kassel, create satellites in cities such as Kabul or Athens to become socially relevant. But even today artists struggle if they propose a project to an institution completely outside of its building or main location. Hultén's decentralized idea was later institutionalized by creating branches in Metz and Maubeuge (and later in Malaga), basically giving birth to the idea of franchising cultural institutions, which has led to Guggenheims and Louvres all over the world. One is led to think that cultural decentralization—as noble as the idea of bringing culture to 'the people' might initially sound—is truly the worst version of cultural imperialism, forcing a culture that does not come from the midst of people onto them. This mistakes a symptom for the cause. The cause is that our institutions are fundamentally wrong in how they preserve, and therefore isolate from our lives, the arts.

What the 60s and 70s then produced was the idea to spread more of the same flawed institutions into so-called underserved regions or neighbourhoods. All the satellite institutions of the Pompidou that were built in exactly these regions have given up on the idea of multidisciplinarity, which was the one hopeful new element, and which seemed to be so much at the heart of the founding of the original Pompidou in Paris, focusing instead only on the visual arts. Even in Paris, the different departments are hardly communicating and are organizationally very much separated. Through its architecture the Pompidou was supposed to signal an openness, to welcome audiences. One did not need a ticket to enter and experience large parts of the building. The entrance was through the top after going up large escalators that got rid of the normal idea of the street-level lobby that only allowed for a glimpse into the building. Here you could be literally on top of it without even paying. In 2000, the decision was taken that visitors could only enter the spectacular escalators at the Pompidou if they carried a ticket. The Pompidou became a fortress like all the other cultural institutions founded by aristocrats before.

On the other hand, stepping into the Cartoucherie, the home of Ariane Mnouchkine's Théâtre du Soleil in the outskirts of Paris, is like stepping into a place that is as familiar as home. The great writer Anna Deavere Smith described best, in my opinion, what the essence of a cultural institution founded today should be. She said "radical welcome" is the main quality that a cultural institution of the future needs to have. A "soft radical welcome" is how I would describe the Cartoucherie.

The Théâtre du Soleil found its home in a baroque bullet and gunpowder factory. The main door to the lobby is very modest and one only really finds it as a bee would find the entry to a hive: there is a constant trickle of people coming out of and going into a hole in the building. You show your ticket when you pass through this little opening. The box office is located in a small outbuilding. Once you are inside the Cartoucherie you are 'one of us'. When I went for the first time, I was shocked: Ariane Mnouchkine herself stood in the door and punched our tickets. It wasn't a stunt for just a few minutes; she did it for every single one of the members of the audience. We were coming to her place. Never had I felt so welcomed in a theatre. Inside, the lobby looks like a taverna on a market place in the late, lazy afternoon sun from a Fellini movie. The company has prepared food, mostly soup with or without meat that tastes simple and delicious and gets served from behind a counter. Towards an area in the back there is an open space under the bleachers of the theatre that

is situated in the adjacent hall. There you see the actors getting ready for the show, putting on their costumes, make-up and wigs. There is no attempt to create the illusion of theatre. The artists do not try to hide and only appear on stage in costume and make-up, as if they are the real characters that they portray. You see what it takes to get there and how it all comes down. The director, the creator of the theatre, is not the invisible god or puppetmaster behind the stage-creation, but a public figure who, more like a circus director, greets everyone at the entrance. There is no illusion, no "anaesthesia", as Brecht might say; but there is so much atmosphere, so much wonderful, stimulating "scent and perfume".

Brecht revolted against the illusionistic theatre that tried to lull the audience and dictate its thoughts and feelings. He invented a theatre that is aware of itself, that is rational, critical and self-reflective, that reveals its mechanisms and therefore the mechanisms of the world it describes. It is an anatomical approach to the human body and soul. Mnouchkine's theatre is all of the above, but she brings back the fine clothes, the feathers, the skirts, the flowing scarves, the atmosphere and the perfume. She takes the same ingredients as Brecht and prepares them French-cuisine-style. Mnouchkine's approach to theatre clearly comes from a countercultural and communist movement. The Théâtre du Soleil was founded in 1964. She and the members of her company were often seen protesting on the street. In 1995 she entered a month-long hunger strike to protest France's failure in Bosnia. She says, "Utopia is not something which is impossible; it is something that has not been done yet."

Another important cultural institution was a product of the social changes of the 60s. The Barbican, although officially opened in 1982, was conceived over a decade earlier as a utopian vision to transform an area in London that was devastated by bombing during the Second World War. Again, culture was supposed to heal the wounds. It was also a new approach in terms of a cultural institution: it was not only a centre for the performing arts, but also included a gallery, restaurants, public spaces, the Guildhall School of Music and apartments (part of the Barbican Estate) in one large cultural complex, all designed by one architectural team in several stages.

The Barbican is maybe the one place in the world that comes closest to the concept of the Culture Cave as a generator of art, emotions, community and ideas, as it combines living, learning, visual art and the performing arts. Yet, while there are distinct spaces for the different art forms, there is almost no fluidity between them. The school, the library, the theatre, the movie theatres, the concert hall, the exhibition space: all are separate entities within the larger complex. They are designed so that visitors can experience one art form without disturbance. Schedules are not coordinated and do not encourage the attendance of multiple events in one visit. One can summarize the organizational formula of this multi-arts venue as follows: individual events are separated in space and not separated in time. Everything is close by, so it gives a sense of heightened activity, but the diversity can hardly be enjoyed at once. Most performances start around the same time (7 to 8 pm), which prohibits visitors from meandering between art forms. You have to choose whether you attend a concert, play or other performance. The gallery closes at 6 pm so you would have to come over two hours earlier to see art and a performance in one day. 'Cross-pollination', a word that is so abundant and overused on the artistic creation side today but, realized so little, is not encouraged among visitors. The way the Barbican is programmed is geared towards one visit of one event at one time. The audience has to make a choice: "Do I go to see a play, or do I go to a concert, or do I go to see an exhibition or a movie?" But the audience cannot do everything at one time. The Barbican solves the problem of bringing all the arts closer together, of creating one destination, but it totally fails to go the final step to actually give the audience the freedom to be able to experience it all during one visit. It clings to the old idea that performances need to be presented in autonomous, undisturbed spaces, separate from the outside world, with audiences conditioned not to make any noise.

The idea of the Culture Cave is to flip the formula of "separation in space, and no separation in time" on its head. We don't separate in space; we separate in time. There is no institution in the world that has ever attempted this, because it is a rule that started with the birth of cultural institutions and has become even more rigorous over the centuries, as the performance space and the exhibition space became more and more segregated and sacred, or maybe even hermetic. As mentioned, separation or segmentation is one

1. Young visitor in the Turbine Hall at the Hearn
2. Ariane Mnouchkine protesting in Paris, 1981
3. A woman playing a Paleolithic flute, and a vulture. Video still from *Raptor's Rapture* by Allora & Calzadilla
4. The foyer of the Cartoucherie in Paris
5. The Panel of the Lions in the Chauvet Cave, c 32,000 BCE
6. Horse drawn carriage at the Hearn
7. Cleaning the Hearn
8. Bike racks at night at the Hearn
9. Luminato Festival volunteers

of the guiding principles of our culture. It is the result of the autocratic, aristocratic leader making the decisions. It is about the individual who does not want to be disturbed during the consumption of art, who wants to experience art in the highest form of refinement possible, and we think we need absolute quiet for that. These institutions force us to attempt to escape the world while consuming art. The Culture Cave wants you to be in it.

A porcelain museum is an institution that is attractive to a very small circle of individuals—the same applies to a print museum, to a design museum etc. All of our cultural institutions are only geared towards small segments of the population. It is not a surprise that cultural institutions are in a crisis, because they have segmented their audiences more and more without being inclusive. You cannot have one without the other. The Culture Cave is for the people. It is conceived with a heterogeneous, diverse, multiethnic, multiracial, multisexual and gender diverse group of people in mind, of varying (from none to total) cultural sophistication. Our societies are increasingly getting richer in minorities. This is an irreversible movement. The Culture Cave tries to reflect and incorporate this diversity into its institutional DNA. It is not retrofitting, like so many organizations of today, in order to stay relevant.

Unlike all other Western cultural institutions, the Culture Cave is not conceived with the idea of one ideal visitor in mind. For the Salzburg Festival, the ideal visitor would be someone like former German president Richard von Weizsäcker, an incredibly sophisticated, well-read and educated cultural person, and most likely a layman musician (a "Kulturmensch", as Thomas Mann—another ideal visitor—would say). For the Manchester International Festival, for example it would be someone like Caroline Vreeland: a tastemaker. They only appear if something is of a zeitgeist and sizzling. They are not bound to any art form or other forms of entertainment. It just has to be hip, new and cool. For the opera, the ideal visitor is still the monarch.

There is no single way of experiencing the Culture Cave in one visit as it is not geared toward an ideal visitor and there are multiple choices that a visitor can make at any given time. At all other cultural institutions, visitors have to make one choice and then stick to it, otherwise their visit ends.

IV. From the Culture Cave to the Luminato Festival at the Hearn Generating Station

The Hearn Generating Station is a unique industrial ruin in the world. It is three times larger than the Tate Modern, it is larger than the Colosseum in Rome, larger than Lincoln Center, MoMA, the Brooklyn Academy of Music and the New York Public Library combined. It sits on Toronto's waterfront in very close proximity to downtown Toronto in a gigantic industrial wasteland in a city that is one of the fastest growing and most multicultural cities in the world. Its smokestack is the only other structure in Toronto apart from the CN Tower that you see from across the lake on good days. For decades, nobody from the public has ever been there. There are probably very similar topographic and geographic reasons why we chose the Hearn today as a location for making and showing art and why our ancestors chose the Chauvet Cave to make some of their most beautiful works of art—why these ancient artists came back for generations, over and over again, adding new images to the collection on the rock walls of this earliest art museum, learning from earlier works of art and inventing movement, early forms of perspective and three-dimensionality. Today, probably every architecture student, architect and urbanist in Toronto has dreamt about what the Hearn could be; many have illegally entered it and taken pictures. Nobody had done anything significant there until June 2016. Now hopefully we can keep coming back in the future.

Developers and city officials already know that in 20 years about 50,000 people will live in the Port Lands, the man-made island in Lake Ontario that the Hearn proudly sits on. It is an area in the city of Toronto that hardly anyone has heard of, and even fewer people have actually been to. It is physically so close but mentally so far away. This has changed.

The Hearn is an ideal location to try out the concept of the Culture Cave, of art and culture without spatial separation, just separation in time. It is a gigantic structure that is of an overwhelming post-industrial beauty. Its decayed beauty is a bonus but certainly not integral to the concept of the Culture Cave. There is a gigantic difference between the idea of the Culture Cave and places like the Armory in New York or the Jahrhunderthalle in Bochum. They stage their spaces as spectacular backdrops to their program and make the space the main player. They treat the space like a new building, and in most cases what they do in these buildings are old ideas, artistically and institutionally, it's just the backdrop that makes them appear new. The Culture Cave is not about a seductive surface but it is about a giant, empty volume. The Hearn is a space the likes of which hardly anyone has ever set foot in. It is so big that space actually never became an issue in the conception of what we were trying to do there. We always had more space than we needed. We could build a 1,200-seat theatre, a 2,000-seat concert space that turned into a 5,000-person-standing-room music stage, multiple galleries, workout spaces, exhibition spaces, community spaces, multiple restaurants and many more things, without running into space problems. In addition to that, it was space that was not culturally, economically or ideologically coded. It was uncharted, unexplored territory. It was a discovery. This abundance of uncoded space is of course a luxury in most large, economically prosperous Western cities. It is the determining factor, though, in moving most of the great cities in the world forward. This kind of free and open space has been the number one catalyst for creative explosions in global cities, from Montmartre in Paris after the 1871 uprising of the Paris Commune which drove out 'normal' citizens from the area, to SoHo in the 60s in New York, which let artists live and work in abandoned manufacturing buildings, or the post-Wall Berlin of the 90s which, basically overnight, opened up massive amounts of abandoned and empty spaces in the most central parts of town. It is one of the secrets that developers and city planners do not understand: that artists do not like developed spaces. You cannot build space for artists. They build it themselves.

The DNA of the Luminato Festival developed over time—unlike, for example, the Salzburg Festival, the Manchester International Festival or the Centre Pompidou, where it seems that the DNA was created first and then the institutions, its structure and programs built around it. The code for the Salzburg Festival, which has defined everything since the three artists Hugo von Hofmannsthal, Max Reinhardt and Richard Strauss founded the festival in 1920, was: from the best, for the best. They were only interested in the best performers, directors, designers etc, and the festival was catering to the best audiences: a cultural, educated Western European elite. Nothing in Salzburg has really changed since. For Manchester it is equally easy to define the genetic code: interdisciplinary creations and world premieres. Manchester is based on the idea of initiating new artistic collaborations and everything you see there is a first. It is a simple and quite ingenious formula.

On the other hand, the Luminato Festival was founded without a clear identity, but towards the end of the first decade of its existence it seemed to reach puberty and its true shape started to form more definitively: adventurous art and ideas in adventurous spaces. What the festival was best at was setting its audiences off firstly on a mental adventure through the artistic projects that it presented or created, but secondly also on a physical adventure, on a discovery or rediscovery of the city through the arts. While festivals like Salzburg Festival have very established venues, Luminato was at its best and most precise when it discovered new places and occupied territory that had not been touched by art. Yet, while the Air Canada Centre was the home to a participatory orchestra mob that spontaneously brought together 500 people playing Bizet's bolero, and a 1980s Via Rail train car replica in someone's basement in Vaughan, a far away suburb of Toronto, was used for an artist-chef collaboration taking audiences on a

journey through food and music, not every location could be an adventure, as concerts, plays and other performances often still needed some sort of a theatre.

An early concept of Luminato was to spread across the city, to engage and partner with as many communities and other arts organizations in the city. Part of this strategy was to actually appease other cultural institutions whose leaders felt that a festival was not needed and sucked up cultural and financial oxygen in the city. 'If you sleep with them, they cannot hate you as much' seems to have been the initial approach. One might also call this a 'partial cultural Stockholm Syndrome'. The founding idea of the festival was to change the way people see Toronto by being present everywhere in the city. Unfortunately, it is a myth that festivals can change how people experience a city the size of a major metropolis such as Toronto, New York, Sydney, Paris, Berlin or Hong Kong.

The Greeks invented festivals in Europe. One of the earliest ones was the Dionysia, which consisted of two parts: one in the countryside and one in the city. The festival started out in the more rural Eleutherae, which ceded its independence to become part of the Athenian Republic, then imported the festival into its capital. For the urban part, all citizens, mostly men (the presence of women at these events is still under debate) had to attend the performances of tragedies and satyr plays that were written for the festival each year. Cultural life had taken over everyday life for five days. This would be impossible today. The 'rural Dionysia' was more of a pageantry, with re-enactments of the arrival of Dionysos, wine and singing contests. Plays that were premiered at the city Dionysia the year before were sometimes reperformed in Eleutherae. Even the Greeks knew that in order for a festival to take over the life of a city like Athens you had to make attendance compulsory, otherwise it was better to do one in a smaller city, where you had to travel to attend and lose your mind. It would be a dream to send every citizen of Toronto to the festival, but probably an unrealistic one. Wagner founded his festival in a small Bavarian town called Bayreuth, which becomes one with the idea of the festival during the summer performance months. The festival takes over the town. The same happens in Salzburg, in Glastonbury, in Tanglewood, in Matsumoto, in Spoleto, in Guanajuato, in Coachella, in Stratford-upon-Avon (both in the UK and in Canada).

The idea to radically change the entire mental and physical geography of the Luminato Festival—to reverse the motion of spreading out into the city and instead concentrate everything into one location at the Hearn—came in October 2015. It solved a large number of problems and questions in one go. First of all, we had created the ultimate adventurous space and therefore found the purest expression of the festival's DNA. Nobody had ever been at the Hearn before. A few movies were shot there—using the Hearn mostly as a futuristic or apocalyptic set—families of raccoons, a family of coyotes and a falcon lived there, but families with kids and their grandparents had not had access to the Hearn since it was decommissioned in the 80s. Would anyone come? How were people going to get there? These were the most common suspicious questions we received. Having one's own venue meant that the festival had total control over the audience experience: we did not need to work with anyone else's front of house team. But there was also nothing to rely on, no built-in audience.

The 2016 Luminato Festival at the Hearn can be understood as a sketch or blueprint of the idea of the Culture Cave. As outlined above, 'Culture Cave' is the name for the concept of the cultural institution of the twenty-first century that goes back to the first permanent human shelter and artistic space where art gives birth to community. The Hearn was alive for 17 days, whereas hopefully the Culture Cave will become a permanent living reality at some point in the future. Three inspirations that shaped the realization of the Luminato Festival at the Hearn Generating Station are:

- Jane Jacob's dogma that "new ideas must use old buildings"
- Ariane Mnouchkine's hierarchy-free theatre company Théâtre du Soleil
- Cedric Price's and Joan Littlewood's Fun Palace (thinking about architecture in terms of process and events in time rather than objects in space)

Openness was the guiding principle that was applied to the architecture, to the audience, to the program, to the institution itself. The Culture Cave is a space without walls.

1 Inverted trees growing upwards: Natalie Jeremijenko's *Tree Logic* at Mass MoCA
2 Inverted gravitropism: tree growing downwards in a cave in Baia, Italy

The audience is constantly aware of everything that is happening in the space. At the Hearn, the space was always open. Even though a performance was going on, audience members could come in and walk freely in the space, visit the exhibitions, or go to the restaurant. One could compare it to how people navigate their computer and online access, having multiple windows open at all times, meandering back and forth between them, listening to a video on YouTube while writing a text and chatting with friends. Joni Mitchell said in an interview that as a child her teachers criticized her for always colouring across the edges. This is what the Culture Cave does; it colours across edges, it smears the boundaries, it creates a bit of a glorified chaos. It is difficult to explain this to artists who are used to performing in silence or having their work exhibited in white, finite spaces. But in essence it is what art is about. Art is about transgression and transcendence, crossing human, behavioural, physical, spiritual and mental borders, repeatedly telling a different story about who we are in our environment, taking us out of the world and putting us into it in a different way, thus asking the question about our place in the world and in the cosmos over and over again and giving it ever new answers. This approach can already be observed in the earliest art known to us. It puts us in perspective with nature, which immediately, of course, also cuts us loose from nature, as independent, thinking beings. Therefore, progression and development can happen. Art is not about locking up works in a white cube or a soundproof concert hall and basically forcing the audience to suppress their bodies.

1

If we want to make culture an essential part of people's lives in a multicultural society, where it is impossible to indoctrinate people with a single narrative of what a country's culture should be, it is necessary to open up our institutions and let people understand that they are welcome all the time. Regular cultural institutions function like a binary code: you are either on or you are off. You go to a museum to see an exhibition, you go to a theatre to see a show, and you leave. There is not much else to do. The minute you enter the front lobby you are on; you are in the experience. That is terrifying for a lot of people just like it is terrifying for a lot of people to walk into a high-end luxury store just to browse, because, sure enough, after ten seconds some far-too-well-dressed-for-his-or-her-salary shop assistant comes up to you and asks you if there is anything particular that you are looking for. If you are that person walking into the store and it is obvious that you have never even worn any of the brand's clothing or would ever buy any of their articles, that experience gets even more frightening. Normal cultural institutions are like those stores. You are immediately confronted with everything inside, and a lot of people are unable or unwilling to expose themselves to that kind of an attack. At the Hearn, entering into the building, into the cultural space, was gradual and without any obstacles. You could partake as little or as much as you wanted. You knew it was always there, but it was never imposing itself. You had a choice and it was not about high or low art, loud or quiet, big or small, intellectual or not, uplifting or exhausting... it was all these things.

While above it is made clear that the idea of the Culture Cave is one about openness to the people that is aimed at tearing down cultural and artistic barriers, the institution in itself also has to exercise openness and actually function as a host to other institutions. If it is about creating a meeting place for audiences and artists, it should also be a meeting place for other institutions of all kinds. This was practiced at the Hearn in a very dedicated way. Over 25 other Torontonian cultural, community and entertainment institutions were invited to present their own program under their own institutional banner inside the Hearn. These ranged from students from Ontario College for Art and Design (OCAD) to established entities such as the Toronto Symphony Orchestra or Tafelmusik (a Toronto-based baroque music ensemble), from Yes Yes Y'All (a queer, hip-hop, multiethnic dance party), Choir! Choir! Choir! (a choir sing-along event) and Monkeyvault (a parkour workout studio offering special classes at the Hearn), to the Institute for Canadian Citizenship (ICC), Joe Beef (my favourite Canadian restaurant) and Team FX (a group of Canadian base jumpers throwing themselves off the 700-foot-high smokestack on opening night), to name just a few. So the Hearn actually addressed for the very first time the idea of collaboration with other institutions and groups in the city in a much more comprehensive way than could have been achieved in previous years. Twenty-five participated—many more were asked but for various reasons couldn't participate. For the first time,

1 Entrance to Qafzeh Cave, Israel

the collaborations of the festival did not seem to be selective, other institutions did not feel threatened or left out, everybody was welcome in the vast space. There was enough time and space for everyone. Ticket revenue was given to these so-called arts partners, making them complicit in marketing their events and shows, which brought their audiences into the Hearn, mixing people who would never cross paths and reaching a diversity of audiences one single institution would never be able to reach. A queer Iranian-Canadian youth from The Beaches at the Yes Yes Y'all party would not go to a play about Scottish kings from the fifteenth century, but these two events were back to back, and the different audiences criss-crossed while coming and going; some were seduced to stay on, interested to see what happens next. Over half of the 100,000-person audience of the entire festival did not buy a ticket for a particular event, but came to see the free exhibitions and the space. This openness needs to be constantly pushed further and further for the institution to stay vibrant and relevant. In a time where shopping malls purchase theatre production companies, as they understand that they need to bring in arts and culture to stay relevant, we have to constantly expand the inclusiveness of the Culture Cave. We certainly cannot lose the fight for survival of the arts and culture to shopping malls.

A place like the Hearn must not become simply a venue, hosting various events from rock concerts and conventions, to fairs and other cultural offerings. It sounds almost contradictory to say this, as the main guiding principle of the Culture Cave is its openness to all creative expressions and its inclusiveness. We have to look closer at the nature of a venue compared to the idea of the Culture Cave. A venue is a mere shell that is filled, emptied and refilled, whereas the cave is a shell that is constantly filled and overflowing. It is a fountain. A venue is a cultural space without a soul, without an identity. It can swallow any cultural product one after the other. A venue can have character, or a particular look, and its character is used to create an attractive backdrop for what you put in there. But it doesn't have curatorial integrity. With every event it does, the venue appeals to a different segment of the audience. The Culture Cave appeals to all by letting content co-exist. Radio City Music Hall is one of the most spectacular venues in New York City. The Air Canada Centre is a beautiful venue. Both of them have character and it is wonderful to go and see something there that one loves, but one could not say what their identity is or what they stand for. There is no cross-pollination and mixing of audiences happening. You do not go to see a Coldplay concert if you are not a fan, just because you saw Kendrick Lamar at a certain venue and loved the experience. You do not go to see a Broadway show because of the Broadway theatre that it is performed in. Audiences do not build; they get exchanged in a venue. The regression from institution to venue is a tiny one and so easy to make in one direction. As Faust experiences himself, unfortunately the return—putting the soul back into a lifeless vessel—is almost impossible. It would be easy to fall for the superficial beauty of the post-industrial space of the Hearn and come up with a mixed-use of culture, entertainment and sports. Venues treat these uses in succession as renters want spatial exclusivity. Everything the Culture Cave does is additive. It is like a medieval market place. You can buy, see, experience, hear and smell everything there. It is the most wonderful, human and natural chaos. It is like the origin of life itself.

The Culture Cave is all about seduction: seducing people to cross lines that they did not cross before. Lines are made invisible in the Culture Cave. At the Hearn we have only scraped the surface; so much more can be done to create a true gathering place for people around the arts. There were a lot of ideas that remained unrealized. A campground was supposed to allow people to actually live at the Hearn, just like our ancestors would have temporarily cooked, slept and lived in the entrances to the caves. It was not possible as the site was deemed a construction site and people were not permitted to sleep there (welcome to the beauty of red tape!). Sports and physical activity, in addition to cultural activity, could have been explored more. Conceptually, these were alluded to with the inclusion of the parkour workout courses that were offered and sold out throughout the run. Openness also means that the way the Culture Cave is activated, the way different spaces are used, needs to change all the time. It is a space that is permanently temporary. The 17-day residency at the Hearn was a live proposal for the future of this building. Our residency outlined one version of what this could be, but, like a kaleidoscope that contains a limited number of colourful pieces and creates an infinite number of patterns, the Culture Cave can find an infinite amount of expressions if all the pieces that constitute it are kept.

V. From the Hearn Generating Station to the Culture Cave in the future

The Culture Cave has to be an institution that incorporates all forms of human activity. Bridging the gap between sports and culture is almost impossible as the spatial needs are different—but mostly they are just so different in our minds, because history has separated our body from our mind over centuries. At the Hearn, due to the massive dimensions of the building, it would be possible to combine these two. Gigantic climbing walls designed or decorated by artists could be constructed. Roller or ice skating rinks could be built next to the theatre and adjacent to galleries, letting parents drop off their kids at the rink while going to an exhibition or vice versa. The Culture Cave is the first institution that serves the mind as well as the body. A school should be housed inside the Culture Cave building a curriculum out of the activities of the Culture Cave itself, not separating education from what is being taught.

The Culture Cave is the anti-Guggenheim-Bilbao. The Guggenheim Museum, Bilbao, feels like the architectural expression of Hans Christian Anderson's "The Emperor's New Clothes". It gives a very old idea new life, a new dress, but ultimately it just creates a different armour around what is inside. Nothing has changed. It is a new opiate to make us forget that museums are still the vaults of aristocratic rulers (today they are just called 'patrons'). The Culture Cave is not about architecture. Caves are not about architecture: they were built by nature without design, yet they're breathtaking, elegant and beautiful; they weren't engineered, yet they are gigantic, stable and impressive.

The Hearn today is a building that transformed itself through decay. It became open for interpretation. Any construction measures that lead to a greater permanence of the building must not be of an architectural or design-led nature. Architecture and design calcify space: they make it impossible to interpret space in a different way, to change it, to let it artistically rot, build up or blossom. Cedric Price describes the Fun Palace as architecture in time and not in space, as process. This was radical when he proposed it. Although never realized, his drawings reveal that he imagined an architectural toolkit for the inside, a matrix of elements that could be moved and reconfigured. He wanted to play God. He wanted to create the building blocks for us to design worlds with. After playing with it for a time it would have become limiting and boring, just like a child moves on from wooden blocks and Lego to other, more refined toys, products and, lastly, ideas. Temporary spaces have the longest life. An artist starts with emptiness; therefore, that is how we start at the Culture Cave. In order to get a step further from the Fun Palace to the Culture Cave we have to take away the toolkit that Price installed in the space. We cannot predetermine anything.

Cultural institutions have been a driving force in the development of kinetic architecture. Unfortunately most modular spaces of the past have often experienced, very soon after their construction, what most people experience with older age: you just want to move less, you get comfortable. The Schaubühne in Berlin—a massive and impressive theatrical space that can be reconfigured to combine all three theatre spaces in one gigantic, beautiful space—has not been used as such for the longest time. Jean Nouvel's kinetic facade of his Institut du Monde Arabe (which was supposed to change shape, creating ever-new interpretations of Islamic tile patterns, thus harnessing the amount of sunlight that penetrates the building) does not function properly anymore. Ludwig Mies van der Rohe designed hanging, moveable walls for the upstairs of the Neue Nationalgalerie in Berlin, which were soon abolished after the opening. The Nakagin Capsule Tower was designed to create modular apartment spaces from capsules that could be hung into two vertical towers like Brussels sprouts and combined or taken apart for larger or smaller living spaces. The building has fallen into disrepair and a large proportion of the capsules are not used for apartments anymore but are storage. Residents have moved out, as life there was not practical. The Culture Cave is a shell, it does not have a program, it does not offer a toolkit, it does not offer a grid or a framework. It is absolutely empty and therefore can be refilled constantly.

American entomologist and biologist EO Wilson said, "The real problem of humanity is the following: we have Paleolithic emotions; medieval institutions; and god-like technology." On a current world-political level that might be absolutely true, and easily understandable. The idea of leaders like Assad, Putin, Kim Jong-un and others being capable of launching nuclear weapons, cyber attacks, gas attacks or biological warfare is absolutely frightening. However, I would say the real problem is that we have forgotten our Paleolithic roots and don't do enough for our Paleolithic emotions. We have created a world full of institutions and technology that does not leave room for these experiences anymore, for a Paleolithic approach to nature and community that would let us incorporate our creator-like inventions into our emotional tapestry. The Culture Cave could be a space where these sides of our existence are brought together. It is the amalgamation of the aspects of the problem in one space that might solve the problem.

Architects dreamt, and continue to dream, of creating performative, kinetic or modular architecture, spaces that can be changed and reconfigured by the humans who live there. They do not realize that the best way to achieve this is by not creating architecture at all. It is the same misconception that leads developers and city planners to think that they can plan spaces for artists and creative people. They create their own space, and when they have a new idea, they create something radically different, tearing down the old. Architecture is about creating walls, doors and floors. Ultimately it is about creating support and shelter for the human body. In order to give a platform to liberate artistic imagination and give artists the right environment, we cannot create the spaces for them. We cannot make the boundaries for them. They need to do that themselves. So, the more we leave them alone, the more we let them seek—the less we rule and build, but let them rule and build—the better. And this is where the two worlds—the outside world of the community and the inside world of the artist—come together; where the inside of the artists becomes the experience of the community. Because the Culture Cave, the cultural institution of the twenty-first century, has no walls, artists can build and rule throughout the entire building, and community can gather throughout the entire building. Artist and audience are no longer separate but part of one whole. The artists in the Neolithic era would venture deep down into the caves, far away from the entrance, far away from the world, far away from light, to create their astonishing interpretations of nature, and life within nature, on a grandiose scale. Their people, their tribes—everyone including their children—would follow into the darkness of the caves to see the world reborn through the eyes of their artists. We can easily imagine today how cavemen and cavewomen felt 40,000 years ago seeing these cave paintings for the first time, as we have all stood in front of a work of art, seen a performance, listened to music and been shaken to our bones. We are still looking at art with the same eyes, listening to it with the same ears, smelling it and feeling it with the same senses as our Neolithic ancestors. We have all been at the bottom of that cave. Now we just have to find it again and rebuild it for the twenty-first century.

1 Couple kissing in front of the Grand Staircase at the Hearn
2 The felled Golden Spruce tree, Haida Gwaii, British Colombia
3 Buckminster Fuller's Project Toronto, as part of Scott McFarland's photo series *Trove*
4 The Hearn in the winter of 2014
5 Bees
6 Cement truck in the Hearn
7 The Hearn seen from the top of the smokestack
8 Baroque violin soundcheck in the Hearn in the winter of 2016
9 *Apocalypsis* by R Murray Schafer, staged by Salā Lemi Ponifasio at the Luminato Festival in 2015

...stival List

...: The Key Will Keep the Lock / James II: Day of the Innocents / James III:...
...aime, Sunn O))), The Bug ft Flowdan & Miss Red, Alessandro Cortini, Roly...
...ly Body Tattoo and Godspeed You! Black Emperor / Rufus Rufus Rufus...
...ox / Tafelmusik / Song of Extinction—Music in the Barns / Beethoven:...
...stra / Regent Park School of Music / Apocalypsis Listening Party / Choir!...
...s / JACKMAN GALLERY Trove: A View of Toronto in 50 of Its Treasures /
...Jlin, RP Boo, Waclaw Zimpel, T'ien Lai, Olivia, Aurora Halal, Ancient...
..." A Study on Effort—Sharing Spaces Productions / Doggie Show—Bath...
...e Party—YTB Gallery / Fábrica de Ritmo—Battle of Santiago / Canadian...
...TURBINE HALL OCADU Prescience Exhibition / YTB Gallery Exhibition /
...rich Group / Circa 1948—TIFF, NFB and Stan Douglas / Michel De Broin:...
...nds Pop-Up Studio / TALKS James Play Talk with Laurie Sansom / Rise...
...lture, and Place-making in the City / Trove Talks / monumental Talks /
...Audiences / ON THE MOVE Off Limits Zone—DLT / The Hearn Trail / 66...
...OUTSIDE Pierre Huyghe's Untilled (Liegender Frauenakt)—Art Gallery...
...SMOKESTACK B.A.S.E. Aerial Services—Team FX /

Cave Art and 'Cavemen'
Ian Tattersall

Our species, *Homo sapiens*, is, as far as we know, unique in possessing a creative imagination. This unprecedented capacity was acquired subsequent to the first appearance of anatomically modern humans in Africa (around 200,000 years ago), because only at about 100,000 years ago do we begin to find archaeological evidence of behaviours that were clearly more nuanced than any ever before exhibited by a hominid. Both the first anatomical *Homo sapiens* and related big-brained species, such as *Homo neanderthalensis,* were undoubtedly complex and resourceful beings, but they left very little, if any, evidence that they mentally recreated their exterior and interior worlds in the way in which people do today.

The earliest intimations of the modern sensibility come in the form of ochre-stained marine shells that were pierced for stringing into bracelets or necklaces. Bodily decoration of this kind is, or was, characteristic of all historically documented modern human societies, but it was rare, if present at all, among earlier human species. By 80,000 years ago, this initial evidence for the evolution of complex 'symbolic' cognitive processes had been joined, again in Africa, by the production of geometric engravings that almost certainly encoded symbolic meaning. Complex, multi-stage technologies that transcended the purely intuitive, and that almost certainly demanded symbolically mediated forward planning, also appeared at around this time.

What had happened? Well, symbolic information processing depends on the brain's physical ability to share information between various different functional regions. And the anatomical circuits necessary for this were almost certainly established in the fairly radical developmental reorganization that led to the emergence of our species as a distinctive anatomical entity. The subsequent trigger that drove the adoption of the new cognitive process was most likely the spontaneous invention of language (I like to think by children at play), in a small African isolate of the infant species *Homo sapiens*. Language is, after all, the ultimate symbolic activity, depending as it does on the generation and recombination of a vocabulary of intangible symbols representing objects in the outside world.

Yet those early African archaeological intimations of cognitive modernity are basically proxy indicators, from which we have to infer the presence of modern thought. They are not directly emblematic of fully fledged modern symbolic minds. For an unequivocal demonstration that the modern human sensibility had arrived, we have to await the first representational art, which appeared at around 40,000 years ago. That art was so breathtaking in its power and sophistication that it is impossible to imagine it was produced by humans who were not entirely our intellectual equals.

Since 1879, when the first cave art was discovered at Spain's Altamira, it has been assumed that early rock art was a local European phenomenon; indeed, by now such art is known from literally hundreds of caves in France and Spain and marginally beyond. Recently, however, representational animal art at a site on the Indonesian island of Sulawesi has been dated to around 40,000 years ago, making it roughly contemporaneous with the earliest dated European cave decorations. The strong implication is that the two regional traditions of representational rock art had a common origin even earlier, most likely in Africa, out of which symbolic modern humans began to spread at somewhere around 80,000 to 70,000 years ago.

Still, a small area of northern Europe has yielded nearly all of the very early art known. Possibly this geographical distribution is an artifact of preservation and/or cultural bias, since the art is found principally in limestone regions of France and Spain. In this geological environment underground caverns readily form; certain settings within deep caves have proven conducive to the preservation of art; and in northern Europe a tradition happened to develop of decorating such places. That tradition endured an almost unimaginably long time, from around 40,000 to 10,000 years ago.

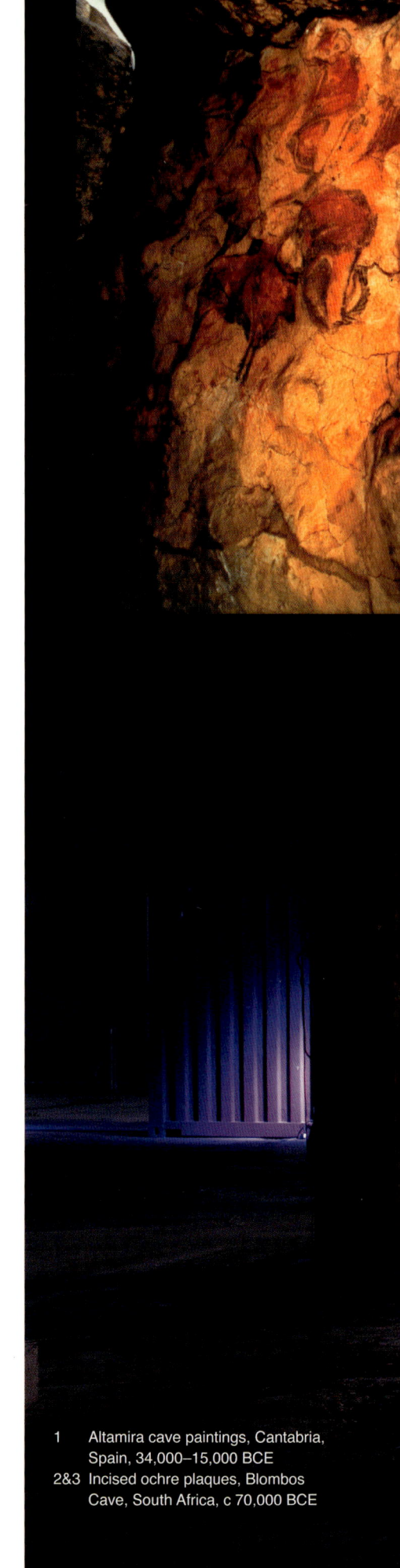

1   Altamira cave paintings, Cantabria, Spain, 34,000–15,000 BCE
2&3   Incised ochre plaques, Blombos Cave, South Africa, c 70,000 BCE

Art made deep within caves has a better chance of persisting over the millennia than art made in cave entrances and rock shelters. But there are plenty of indications that the Cro-Magnon modern humans of Ice Age Europe (named for a place at which their remains were found in the mid-nineteenth century) often decorated the latter as well, despite the far less propitious conditions for its preservation.

The tradition of European cave art began almost exactly coincident with the arrival of *Homo sapiens* in the subcontinent. That arrival also presaged the disappearance of the resident *Homo neanderthalensis*, a large-brained hominid species with deep roots in western Eurasia. New genomic information suggests that there was some minor intermixing between the two species, but, although the Neanderthals may thus have contributed a few genes to the modern human genome, they rapidly became extinct as a distinctive anatomical entity. The exact reasons for Neanderthal disappearance are unknown. Most plausibly they mainly involved competition between the two species for economic resources—though, given what we know historically of human behaviour, it seems unlikely that there was no direct conflict.

Whatever the case, there is little reasonable doubt that the first European artists were members of our own species: people possessed of mental processes that were at least as complex, murky and subtle as our own. Biologically, this allows us to see Ice Age art through the same eyes as its creators, but culturally these early artists were undoubtedly very different from any modern people, making the images they bequeathed much harder for us to place in context.

Around 40,000 years ago, Europe was experiencing the build-up to the Last Glacial Maximum (which occurred roughly 18,000 years ago). Winters were typically long and bitterly cold, and summers were short and cool. Still, microclimates differed substantially from place to place, and most of the art was made in relatively sheltered and favourable areas of southwestern France and northern Spain. At this stage in human history all humans were still hunter-gatherers, living off the bounty of nature and moving across the landscape as dictated by the constantly shifting local abundance of resources.

Settled life was still far in the future, but this does not mean that human societies of the last Ice Age in Europe were not highly complex—the cave art itself is enough evidence that they were. In addition, there are plenty of independent archaeological indicators that European societies in this period were diverse and flexible, not only in their beliefs, symbolic systems and technologies, but in their forms of economic organization as well. At one site in western France, it is estimated that during the winters some 30,000 years ago, several hundred people gathered in one long rock shelter that served as a veritable factory of decorative beads made from mammoth ivory. At other times of year, those same people would have split up into smaller bands that ranged widely across the landscape in search of sustenance.

Such flexibility of economic arrangements was possible because for hunting and gathering peoples cold times were not necessarily hard times. When the climate warmed up—as it periodically did—forest moved in over the landscape, offering relatively meagre resources to foraging humans. In contrast, when the climate cooled the forest was replaced by steppic grasslands and tundras on which vast herds of mammals grazed, offering early hunters an infinity of opportunities. Indeed, it was following around 12,000 years ago, when the climate began to warm and the polar ice cap to shrink, that the great hunting cultures started on their final steep decline. The great tradition of cave art finally disappeared a couple of thousand years later.

We often think of the hunter-gatherers of the last Ice Age as 'cavemen'. But this is a hugely mistaken designation. Evidence of the Ice Age Europeans' activities is most often found in cave entrances and rock overhangs, simply because these are the places in which preservation was most likely. Almost certainly, the Cro-Magnons actually spent most of their lives camping out in the open, as dictated by the resources—plant and animal—that were available for them to exploit in any particular place and season. Relatively rarely did they ever penetrate the dark depths of caves, which were for the most part difficult and unfriendly places that they only visited for special reasons.

In contrast to deep caverns, cave entrances and rock shelters were favoured for residential purposes when they were available. Such spots provided natural shelter from

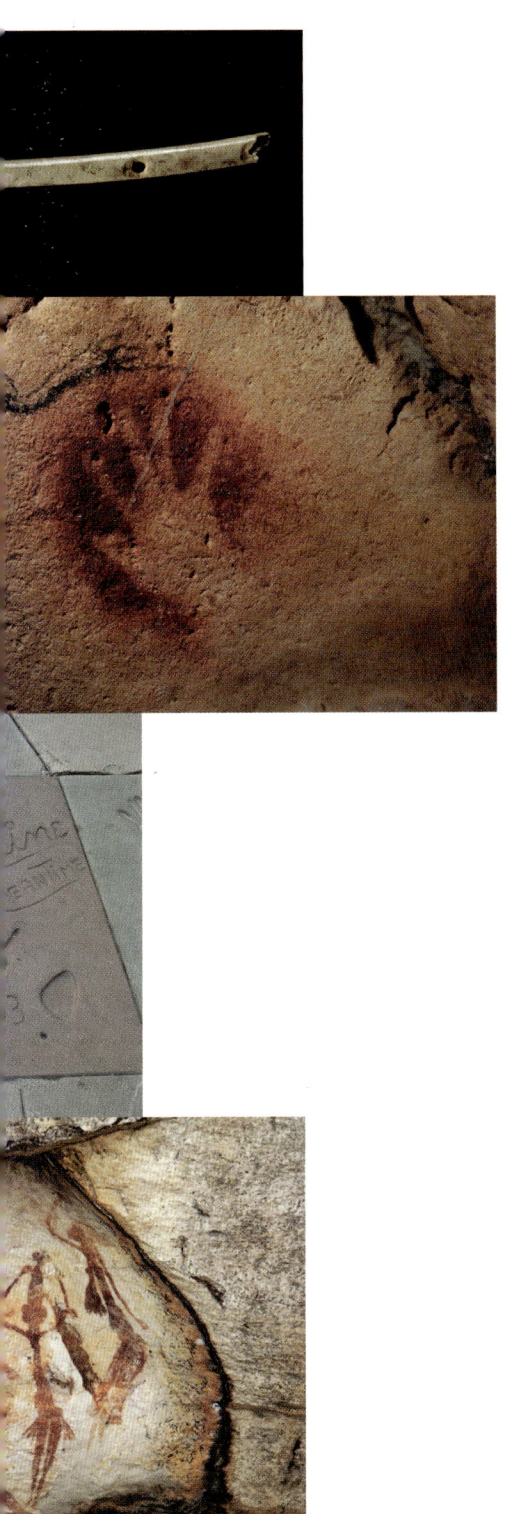

1. Oldest musical instrument in the world: a bone flute from southwestern Germany, c 42,000 BCE
2. Red ochre hand stencils in El Castillo cave in northern Spain, c 37,300 BCE.
3. Handprints on Hollywood Boulevard in LA, California
4. Bradshaw rock art in the Kimberley Region of Western Australia, thought to be from at least 17,000 BCE

the wind and rain, yet they were light and airy and allowed the smoke from campfires to dissipate easily. Particularly prized in those cold times were south-facing caves, which were naturally warmed by the sun.

We know from a few exceptionally well-preserved sites that the Cro-Magnons decorated the walls of the rock shelters and cave entrances where they lived. But while such decorations—engraved and/or painted—have rarely survived the millennia, the same is not true for the abundant 'portable' art that the Cro-Magnons made. In certain periods, these people abundantly embellished everyday utensils—spear-throwers, harpoons, bone points, plaques of various kinds—by carving and engraving them, often exquisitely. At many sites multitudes of such artifacts have been preserved, along with animal bones and stone tools, in the stratified archaeological deposits that formed from the detritus of their makers' day-to-day existences.

Wherever it was lived, in rock shelters or open-air camps, Cro-Magnon life was drenched in symbolism. The cave art these people left behind embodies only a tiny proportion of their symbolic activities—though evidently a very important part. Deep cave interiors are dark, uncomfortable and potentially dangerous spaces, and they were probably visited—by the light of burning torches, or of 'lamps' made by burning animal fat or marrow cupped in hollow stones—only on special occasions or for the most special of purposes. Apart from the art itself, there is certainly not a great deal of evidence for prolonged human activity deep inside caves.

Still, it seems the Cro-Magnons may not have found these dark underground spaces as intimidating as we tend to nowadays. One indicator of this is that they clearly took young children deep into the caves, as indicated by the occasional diminutive footprint in the mud of a cavern floor, or marks on the mud coating of deep cave walls made by tiny fingers.

The clear distinction the Cro-Magnons made between the exterior and interior parts of caves may be reflected in the fact that, even when inhabiting the entrance of one cave, they might do their art in another. The intimate cave of Covalanas in northern Spain is, for instance, believed to have been decorated some 20,000 years ago by people who actually lived in the porch of the much larger cave of El Mirón, a few hundred yards down the hillside. And the people who painted wonderful bison, horse and ibex images deep within the large cave of Niaux, in the French Pyrenees, are thought to have camped in the fairly cramped entrance to the small cave of La Vache, a couple of miles away.

What is more, inside the caves the Cro-Magnons decorated, the exact places chosen for artistic activity seem to have had special significance. Often the artists ignored apparently excellent painting surfaces that were easy to get to in favour of spots that often involved very uncomfortable scrambling for long distances underground, and were very difficult to access. Indeed, it's possible that the locations themselves were just as special to the artists and to their audience as the art itself. Exactly what was done there—besides the creation of the art itself—is anyone's guess. These decorated places deep in caves are often referred to as 'sanctuaries', which is as good a term as any, since it implies that they were of special significance without specifying the nature of the activities that might have been carried out there.

The art that the Cro-Magnons made, whether large-scale or tiny, engraved or painted, portable or mural, exterior or deep cave, was clearly integrated into a much larger spiritual and cultural context. As ancient as the first statuettes and paint marks on walls are the earliest musical instruments: vulture-bone flutes, which modern flautists have played to haunting effect. And the Cro-Magnons also improvised: at one cave in France, you can sit in the darkness listening to a recording of xylophone-like music produced by banging a broken-off stalactite against thin calcite 'draperies' hanging from the wall. It is an unforgettable experience and replicates what Ice Age people are known to have done in the exact same spot 18,000 years ago.

If the Cro-Magnons played music and wore jewellery—as we know they did from the vast quantities of beads, pierced teeth and pendants they left behind—we can be pretty sure that they also sang, danced, wore make-up and told long and complicated stories just as we do. What's more, although they did not have writing systems as such, the Cro-Magnons did keep track of events and kept tallies using notations pecked into bone or antler plaques.

THE IDEA—How to Go Forward Culturally by Going Way Back

To summarize, the 'cavepeople' of the last Ice Age actually led lives that were based mainly out on the open landscape, and that were, in their own ways, every bit as complex as our own. However, it is also clear that they lived those lives in technological, cultural and environmental contexts that were vastly different to anything we know today. Those undocumented cultural disparities, in particular, make it highly unlikely that we will ever know exactly what drove the Cro-Magnons to create astonishing art in the most difficult and inaccessible of places, or what that art meant to them.

Of course, a few generalizations can be made. The sheer abundance of beautifully observed Ice Age animal representations strongly implies that the Cro-Magnons' art in some way reflects their beliefs about their own place in nature; such factors as the selectivity in species depicted, and the wealth of geometric and other abstract signs associated with the animal images, make it clear that those beliefs were structured in a highly complex fashion. What is more, the very fact that the tradition of cave art endured over some 30,000 years—even as several different 'cultures', as recognized from artifacts, came and went—suggests that there was something deeply enduring about the Cro-Magnons' relationship to their environment over this vast lapse of time. It is hard to venture beyond these rather unsatisfying speculations with much confidence—although there is no shortage of those willing to try.

The bottom line? Anyone who has ever had the privilege of seeing the immensely powerful animal art of Lascaux, Altamira, Niaux or Chauvet, will be fully aware that it is the product of a sensibility entirely equivalent to our own, and of its extraordinary ability to reach out over the millennia and viscerally transfix the viewer. These complex images present us with a host of imponderable questions, but it would be wrong to allow our inability to answer many of them to frustrate us. Because Ice Age art is, above all, art to be experienced, rather than art to be explained.

1&2 100,000-year-old shells containing ochre pigments, Blombos Cave, Cape Town, South Africa

31 May

The Creative Force of Old Buildings
Richard Florida

"New ideas must use old buildings." The great urbanist Jane Jacobs—who was born in Scranton, moved to New York City and lived in Toronto's Annex for the last decades of her life—had many memorable sayings, but that's my favourite. It's worth quoting it in its full context:

> Chain stores, chain restaurants and banks go into new construction. But neighbourhood bars, foreign restaurants and pawn shops go into older buildings…. Well-subsidized opera and art museums often go into new buildings. But the unformalized feeders of the arts—studios, galleries, stores for musical instruments and art supplies, backrooms where the low earning power of a seat and a table can absorb uneconomic discussions—these go into old buildings…. As for really new ideas of any kind—no matter how ultimately profitable or otherwise successful some of them might prove to be—there is no leeway for such chancy trial, error and experimentation in the high-overhead economy of new construction. Old ideas can sometimes use new buildings. New ideas must use old buildings.[1]

1 Jane Jacobs, Toronto, 1968
2 View of the Port Lands from the top of the Hearn smokestack looking north
3 View of the ship channel in the Port Lands from the top of the smokestack
Background: floor plan of Hearn with outline of the Coliseum in Rome superimposed

What does this mean? In short, that if you want your city to be the kind of place that incubates new and innovative ideas, songs, paintings, cuisines, politics, technologies and, yes, new high-tech startups and business models, the people that you are counting on to create all those wonderful things need an abundance of flexible, adaptable and affordable places to live and work. The production of new ideas requires real cities, with diverse, authentic urban neighbourhoods, filled with lots of old buildings.

That's the story of the death and life of Ontario Power Generation's gargantuan RL Hearn Generating Station. The Hearn, as it's locally known, is located in the formerly industrial district of the Port Lands—an industrial wasteland now primed for rebirth and renewal.

Around the turn of the last century, the wetlands around the mouth of the Don River overflowed with waste and raw sewage from nearby slaughterhouses and distilleries. A breeding ground for cholera, the city rerouted the river and filled in the marshes. As Toronto's manufacturing economy boomed, the site became the epicentre of its most noxious uses. Smokestacks rose up, belching effluents into the air; vast tank farms sprouted up like mushrooms, leaching toxins into the ground.

The Hearn's smokestack towered above them all. At 215 metres high, it was the tallest structure in Toronto until it was surpassed by the CN Tower when it opened in 1976. Some 600 people worked in the Hearn's interior, which is often described as 'pharaonic'. It is capacious enough to hold 12 Parthenons or one Statue of Liberty, either standing upright or lying on its side.

The building's coal-burning generators were first fired up in 1951, when Toronto's economy was booming with manufacturing and industry. But that manufacturing boom was short-lived. In the 1980s and 90s, Toronto, like so many other Great Lakes cities, entered into a new and troubling phase of 'deindustrialization'. As more and more of the city's factories shuttered, the utilities that filled the Port Lands gradually fell silent. Though the Hearn continued to make electricity through the 1990s, less and less of its capacity was used; by the turn of the twenty-first century, its great turbines had been stripped out, sold for scrap, and the building was abandoned to the elements. As Christopher Hume described it in the *Toronto Star* in 2010, its remaining shell "feels more geological than architectural; it has open spaces, outlooks, frozen ponds and even its own indoor cliffs…. The equipment long gone, the interior is a Piranesian maze of columns and beams."[2]

This monument to Toronto's vanished industrial past became a harbinger of its creative, post-industrial future when in 2014 it was chosen to house the Luminato Festival's annual fundraiser, and in 2015 the first Toronto edition of the Unsound Festival. Then, for two and a half weeks this past June, Luminato, Toronto's annual global multi-arts festival

dedicated to performance, visual art, music, theatre, dance, magic and more, temporarily refurbished the space for a variety of performances, and included a bar, restaurant and club. Thousands flocked into its cavernous spaces to socialize in its pop-up cafes and restaurants. Rufus Wainwright recreated Judy Garland's 1961 Carnegie Hall concert and led a 1,500-voice choir in a rendition of Leonard Cohen's "Hallelujah"; drag queens and show dogs strutted their stuff at a surreal dance party. I was there and it was amazing. I saw families, cyclists and Torontonians new and old alike making their pilgrimage through the industrial wasteland of the site. The Hearn was generating power again: the power of human creativity on the urban landscape.

Then-director Jörn Weisbrodt (he stepped down in July 2016) told me that the decision to hold Luminato in the Hearn "came out of a lot of thinking about what is a cultural institution of the twenty-first century and how we can create a cultural institution or cultural statement that reflects the diversity of this city". Though temporary, the Hearn's transformation was part of a larger, permanent reshaping of the city in which arts and culture are used to reimagine existing and new urban spaces and function as active drivers of the city's overall growth and development. Seen in that light, the Hearn was not just a striking venue for the festival, an old building gussied up and repurposed to fulfill a new use. While retaining its old industrial soul, it celebrated and enabled a future for the city powered by creativity.

In other words, the creative and innovative impetus, whether it is art, music, performance or technology, comes from the clash and clamour of real people in real neighbourhoods in real cities.

In the gilded heyday of the industrial age, arts and culture institutions were things that cities 'purchased' to celebrate and advertise their wealth. An opera house, a museum or a grand monument were visible proof of a city's (and its donor class's) success. When urban manufacturing cities began to wane in the mid-twentieth century, arts and culture were seen as a means of reversing their failing fortunes. Build it, the thinking went—commission a starchitect to design a fancy new museum, or go all-in with a full-blown cultural district, like New York's Lincoln Center, fully loaded with a symphony hall, an opera house and a ballet—and tourists, businesses and real estate development will come. But, while such amenities do make cities look and feel like they have hit the cultural big leagues, they don't make them any more creative or innovative.

Jane Jacobs warned us about this way back in the 1960s when she decried the wrong-headed ideas of urban planners who bulldozed rundown, but still viable, neighbourhoods and replaced them with sterile housing projects. Too many city leaders and placemakers still believe that the surest way to renew a city is to create new destinations for tourists and suburban shoppers—and to do it from the top down, with publicly subsidized megaprojects. That is what the late Rob Ford and his brother envisioned for the Port Lands and for Toronto's waterfront writ large—giant new malls and amusement areas, even a Ferris wheel. Distressingly, that is what countless other cities have done too, destroying the very fabric of old buildings and authentic urban neighbourhoods that propelled them in the first place. But, by the simple gesture of opening up the Hearn and allowing Luminato to re-inhabit it, Toronto planted the seeds of something much more vital.

A vast body of empirical research, including my own, shows that neighbourhoods that are thicker with working artists and cultural creatives have higher rates of innovation and economic growth. After the Wall fell, Berlin looked to its artists to help revitalize its economically depressed Eastern half. It was artists, not city builders, who revitalized New York's down-and-out Lower East Side. In Toronto, artists and musicians helped lift up stretches of the city along Ossington and West Queen West, turning them from areas that Torontonians once avoided to destinations for shopping and nightlife. High-tech companies are streaming into those bohemian neighbourhoods too, in San Francisco's Mission District, Lower Manhattan and Toronto's own Queen Street.

In my book *The Rise of the Creative Class,* I identified the rise of a new class that spans arts and culture, science and technology and the knowledge-based professions. With more than 40 million workers—nearly a third of the workforce—it's the driving force of our time. It's an increasingly urban class, as we've seen in the striking back-to-the-city movement of the past couple of decades.[3]

Cities are, of course, where the creative class flourishes and always has. And they are where three kinds of creativity—technological, entrepreneurial and artistic and cultural—come together.

The reality today is that creativity is not just an artifact of economic growth but a key factor in what actually drives it. My own research finds that neighbourhoods that are thick with working artists and cultural creatives—that score highly on my 'bohemian index'— have higher rates of innovation and economic growth. Research on the United States, Canada and Sweden shows that arts and cultural occupations, as well as science and technology and business and management, are what power innovation and economic growth.[4] Arts and creativity are not something that cities and nations gain when they develop economically and become rich; they are things that help power their innovative prowess and economic development to begin with.

This connection between arts and urban economic development goes back a long way. Archaeologists and anthropologists have found that our earliest civilizations emerged in the densest communities and settlements, where humans developed the first rudimentary tools and cave paintings.[5] The presence of baroque opera houses in German cities played a key role in the attraction and retention of talent and the presence of high-quality economic growth, according to a detailed study, even centuries after they were built.[6] "Proximity to a baroque opera house is a strong predictor of a region's equilibrium share of high-human-capital employees", the study's authors wrote, adding that "it is the local level of high-human-capital employees who value their proximity to a baroque opera house that shifts a location to a higher growth path". Arts and culture, in other words, are so much more than the proverbial icing on the cake.

Adrian Ellis, director of the Global Cultural Districts Network, argues that successful cultural districts are powerful policy tools:

> For planners they can help build community and social capital; for sociologists they keep at bay the forces of anomie; for economists, they incubate and inculcate creativity, and draw those fickle high-net-worth tourists; and for the politicians and the semioticians alike, they signify and calibrate complex aspirations and identities. But they are difficult to get right, and expensive and politically embarrassing to get wrong.[7]

Few cities are regarded as "great" or even "liveable" without a significant cultural presence. "A successful cultural district is not one that is built", he adds, "but one that, once built, thrives and animates the city or region that it serves."

Arts and cultural organizations do contribute significantly to city economies. A 2015 study examined the effects that arts organizations with annual budgets of over $2 million have on the attraction of high-human-capital talent in more than 100 American cities and metros.[8] Metros with just one type of performing arts centre saw a 1.1 per cent increase in knowledge-class employment between 2000 and 2010; those with two types of performing arts centres saw a 1.5 per cent increase; and those with all three types saw a 2.2 per cent increase. Big metros, like New York, Los Angeles and Chicago, with their numerous symphonies, ballets and opera houses, saw the greatest gains. New York attracted by far the highest share of knowledge-class jobs (64,100) and income ($5.7 billion). Behind New York was Los Angeles, with 41,700 new knowledge-class jobs and more than $3 billion in income. Both Chicago and Washington DC generated more than $2 billion in knowledge-class income, while cities like Atlanta, Dallas, Houston, Miami, Philadelphia and San Francisco each generated more than $1 billion. Even smaller metros with just one or two performing arts organizations racked up considerable gains: Austin, Nashville, Cincinnati, Providence, San Antonio and Sacramento each generated more than $200 million in knowledge-class income during this same period.

Arts and culture aren't magic bullets, but they closely correlate with strong local economies. The Knight Foundation's Soul of the Community study, a survey which I created with the Gallup Organization some years ago, found that "three main qualities attach people to place: social offerings, such as entertainment venues and places to meet; openness (how welcoming a place is); and the area's aesthetics (its physical beauty and green spaces)".[9] Arts and culture are a critical part of that fabric.

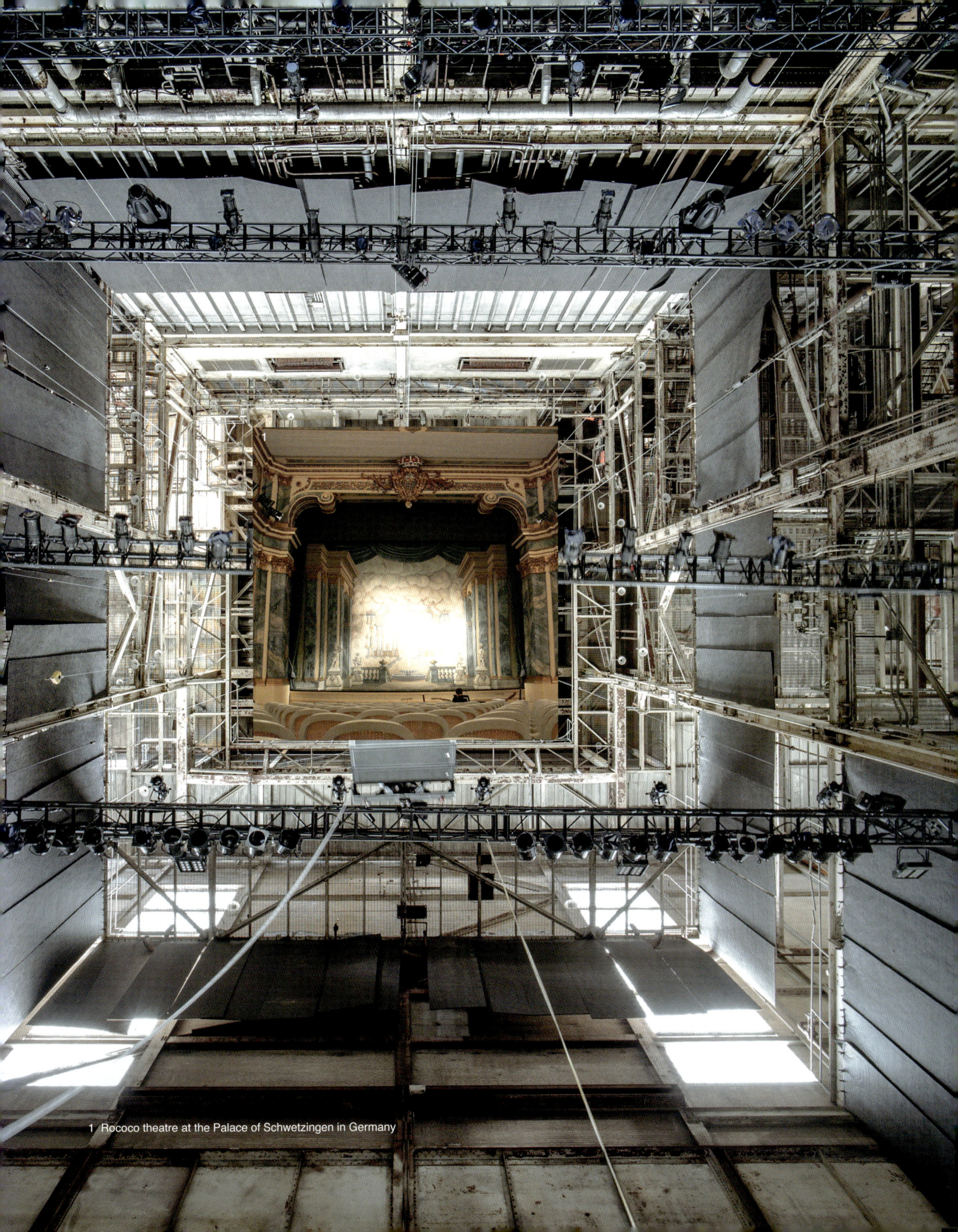
1 Rococo theatre at the Palace of Schwetzingen in Germany

Background: Elevation of the Statue of Liberty inside the Hearn

A recent study by McKinsey identified thriving cultural sectors as essential to making cities great.[10] And another study by AEA Consulting noted that, across the globe, more than two dozen new cultural centres, with museums at their core, are set for construction in the next decade. These projects are projected to cost more than $250 billion.[11] This investment can be transformative or it can fizzle ineffectually and never quite catch fire. Or, to put it more bluntly, city builders need to get out of the way and let these neighbourhoods develop organically. Too much of an emphasis on developers and development can hurt the process. It works best when arts and culture are not imposed top-down on a city's fabric, but emerge organically and naturally from it, as with Toronto's Hearn and its Port Lands.

Thankfully, these places are no longer seen as blights on the skyline to be torn down. Cities now recognize the cultural and economic power embedded in old industrial sites like the Hearn.

Yet, there remains a tendency to go too far the other way, making these spaces over until their original purpose is no longer discernible. But you don't have to go from zero to 100 immediately. As developers look for unique ways to capitalize on existing civic assets—people, landscapes, buildings, vacant land and industrial spaces—it will be vital to offer spaces that bring meaning and opportunities to visitors and locals alike.

The creative and innovative impetus, whether it is art, music, innovative new technologies or world-changing business start-ups, comes from the clash and clamour of real people in real neighbourhoods in real cities. The desolate old industrial buildings and poisoned brownfields of Toronto's waterfront—like the abandoned industrial lofts of New York City's SoHo in the 1970s, the bombed-out ruins of East London's Docklands in the 1980s, or the empty factories in Brooklyn's Williamsburg and Bushwick in the 1990s—is where creativity happens.

In fact, these places have generated so much economic value that they have become hyper-gentrified and artists and creatives are being priced out. High-tech companies have come streaming back to urban bohemian neighbourhoods—the places that artists and creatives initially pioneered and brought back to life—with large high-tech clusters emerging in and around downtown San Francisco. The competition for space in these neighbourhoods has become fierce, and the artists and creatives who initially spurred that growth are now being pushed out, victims of their own success.

"If the 1 per cent stifles New York's creative talent, I'm out of here", musician David Byrne warned in 2013. New York City's incredible economic success, he wrote, was threatening to become its cultural undoing. "Most of Manhattan and many parts of Brooklyn are virtual walled communities, pleasure domes for the rich", he continued. "Middle-class people can barely afford to live here anymore, so forget about emerging artists, musicians, actors, dancers, writers, journalists and small business people. Bit by bit, the resources that keep the city vibrant are being eliminated."[12] As the world's super-rich have rushed into these same neighbourhoods, an even more vexing phenomenon has occurred that Simon Kuper of the *Financial Times* has dubbed "plutocratization".[13]

I call this 'the new urban crisis'—less a crisis of urban failure, like the original urban crisis back in the 1960s, and more of a crisis of the back-to-the-city movement, runaway gentrification and urban success.[14]

Toronto is suffering from its own new urban crisis too. The city is increasingly unaffordable for all but the very rich. It has been divided into what my University of Toronto colleague J David Hulchanski calls three separate and very unequal cities: a shrinking band of old, sturdy, middle-class neighbourhoods which once defined the city as "Toronto the good"; a small band of advantaged, downtown, core neighbourhoods filled with the elite and the economically advantaged; and a much larger span of disadvantage across the city and suburbs alike.[15] This third Toronto is the Toronto that spawned the backlash championed by Rob Ford, who emanated from the anxiety, anger and fear of those left behind by the city's urban revival.

If the city is to continue to grow and remain affordable (or become affordable again), the Port Lands are a natural place to do that. They, and the waterfront writ large, are big enough to be a new city within an old city, which can be grounded in reusable, flexible and authentic urban ruins like the Hearn.[16]

Lighting up the Hearn was a culmination as much as a new beginning. But before the

Port Lands can become a kind of creative hub—a new city within a city—more substantial investments in transit and other vital infrastructure that will allow it to be fully integrated into the physical fabric of the city are required. In this sense, the Hearn and the Port Lands must be part of Toronto's next chapter of city building.

Creative city building is central to the city's future. Dense and interactive connectors, cities—with their diverse, teeming neighbourhoods and jumbles of old and new buildings—are the true economic and social organizing units of today's creative economy. They bring people and ideas together, providing the platform for them to combine and recombine in myriad ways, spurring artistic and cultural creativity, technological innovation, entrepreneurship and economic growth. The arts can no longer be put in a separate basket from technology and business. Creativity of all kinds is not an artifact of growth in the post-industrial city, but its principal driver.

What is next for the Hearn? It could become a permanent cultural institution where ideas, art, artists and audiences come together. But, to my mind, while the space can and should be used 12 months of the year for all sorts of things, the infrastructure itself must be left alone. It should be the heart of a new city, built around old industrial buildings on Toronto's waterfront. Toronto was once an industrial city, built on the backs of immigrant workers from all over the world. Standing inside the Hearn, I couldn't but think of how much blood, sweat and tears was poured into its walls—both during its construction and then as a working power station. Buildings need to retain their souls, and keeping the Hearn as it is doesn't erase the past, it celebrates it.

Now the Hearn has the potential to catalyze creative urban vibrancy that can help reanimate the Port Lands, Toronto's waterfront and the city as a whole. It is an invitation on a grand scale to 'turn on the Hearn' and, in doing so, to turn on the city once more.

That's not to say that re-energizing the space, remaking the Port Lands, or preparing Toronto for its next urban future will be easy and straightforward. Like all aspects of city building, it will be hard. But what is hard is what is worth doing. The future is ours to make, and it surely requires old buildings like the Hearn as its central axis.

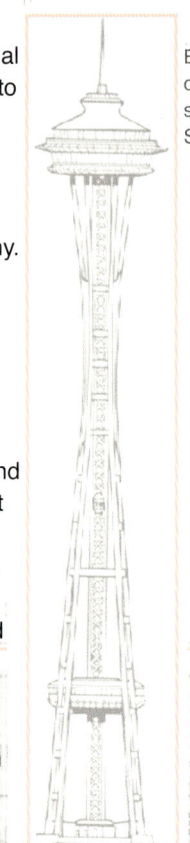

Background: Size comparison between smokestack and the Seattle Space Needle

1 Jacobs, Jane, *The Death and Life of Great American Cities*, New York: Random House Digital, 1961.

2 Hume, Christopher, "Hume: Powerful Reasons to Keep the Hearn Station", *The Toronto Star*, 27 December 2010, https://www.thestar.com/news/gta/2010/12/27/hume_powerful_reasons_to_keep_the_hearn_station.html, accessed March 2017.

3 Florida, Richard, *The Rise of the Creative Class: And How It's Transforming Work, Leisure, Community and Everyday Life*, New York: Basic Books, 2002; Richard Florida, *The Rise of the Creative Class: Revisited*, New York: Basic Books, 2012.

4 Florida, Richard, Charlotta Mellander and Kevin Stolarick, "Inside the Black Box of Regional Development: Human Capital, the Creative Class and Tolerance", *Journal of Economic Geography*, vol. 8, no. 5, 2008, pp 615–49.

5 Richerson, Peter J, Robert Boyd and Robert L Bettinger, "Cultural Innovations and Demographic Change", *Human Biology*, 81, 2–3, 2009, pp 211–35; Stephen Shennan, "Evolutionary Demography and the Population History of the European Early Neolithic", *Human Biology*, vol. 81, no. 2–3, 2009, pp 339–355.

6 Falck, Oliver, Michael Fritsch and Stephan Heblich, "The Phantom of the Opera: Cultural Amenities, Human Capital, and Regional Economic Growth", *Labour Economics*, December 2011, pp 755–766, http://www.sciencedirect.com/science/article/pii/S0927537111000650, accessed March 2017.

7 Ellis, Adrian, "Successful cultural districts are powerful policy tools", *The Art Newspaper*, 1 July 2013, http://old.theartnewspaper.com/articles/Successful-cultural-districts-are-powerful-policy-tools/30007, accessed March 2017.

8 Nelson, Arthur C, Casey J Dawkins et al, "The Association Between Professional Performing Arts and Knowledge Class Growth", *Economic Development Quarterly*, December 2015, http://edq.sagepub.com/content early/2015/12/04/0891242415619008.abstract, accessed March 2017.

9 "University of Miami Blends Placemaking and Entrepreneurship in Third Place Project", *Knight Foundation*, 16 April 2015, http://www.knightfoundation.org/articles/university-miami-blends-placemaking-and-entrepreneurship-third-place-project, accessed March 2017.

10 Bouton, Shannon, David Cis et al, *How to Make a City Great*, McKinsey & Company, 2013, http://mckinsey.com/global-themes/urbanization/how-to-make-a-city-great, accessed March 2017.

11 "The Bilbao Effect", *The Economist*, 6 January 2014.

12 Byrne, David, "If the 1% Stifles New York's Creative Talent, I'm out of Here", *The Guardian*, 7 October 2013, http://www.theguardian.com/commentisfree/2013/oct/07/new-york-1percent-stifles-creative-talent, accessed March 2017

13 Florida, Richard, *The New Urban Crisis*, New York: Basic Books, 2017.

14 Florida, *The New Urban Crisis*, 2017.

15 Hulchanski, J David, *The Three Cities Within Toronto: Income Polarization Among Toronto's Neighbourhoods, 1970–2005*, Toronto: Cities Centre, University of Toronto, 2010.

16 Pett, Shaun, "A Multi-Billion Dollar Development Is Transforming Toronto's Waterfront and the City's Cultural Life", *The Guardian*, 8 August 2015, https://www.theguardian.com/travel/2015/aug/08/a-multi-billion-dollar-development-is-transforming-torontos-waterfront-and-the-citys-cultural-life, accessed March 2017.

Writings on the Wall
Georg Diez

Think of the cave as your future. And you will see the present in a different way.

Think of the cave as a possibility. And you will learn more about human nature, growth and decline.

Think of the cave in terms of belonging. And you will realize that what feels most alien to you might just be home.

The cave was the beginning, they say. The cave was the origin. But what is that supposed to mean? When does a beginning end? What has to happen? And what is the purpose of declaring something ended?

What does it mean to cut yourself off from who you were? And who is to say that you no longer are that person?

In other words, the cave offers a space for reflection on the very path of how we got here. The cave is not a mirror. The cave is not a metaphor. The cave is a specific form of reality. It is not different from us, not different from today, just distinct.

The cave is a way to think about the beginning. It is an alternative reality and still very concrete. There is a specific history of the cave as a place for culture; the beginning can gather meaning.

So, if time has changed its direction, as the philosopher Armen Avanessian says, together with his colleagues of the accelerationist movement, and we are governed by events that will only happen in the future, then the past is the real future. This is what everything leads up to.

I do not mean to sound dystopian. It can sound just this, of course. "The human psyche naturally rebels against the idea of its end", the writer Roy Scranton explains in his book *Learning to Die in the Anthropocene*.

Avanessian and Scranton share this term 'Anthropocene'; they are both thinkers of the end of humanity—in order to make humanity work, in order to make it better, in order not to give in to the pressures of a present that has become so total, so all-encompassing, so totalitarian in many ways that to escape the false necessity of chronology is an act of anarchism worthy of any terrorist.

So, time and the Anthropocene. Avanessian is taking his insight, among other things, from the way technological capitalism is wired: future bets can destroy the real present, whole countries can go under, the financial crisis has shown that these are dangerous instruments, and any algorithm bears the seeds of the future which is being used to modify the behaviour in the 'now sphere'. We know what you want before you know it yourself.

Time thus becomes a commodity. Time in itself is used to make a profit. To turn time around might be a way to upend the way the mechanism of money works.

If the arrow of time is turned around, our imagination no longer pushes ahead. This is a problem, on the one hand, because you need a sense of a future to develop a sense of responsibility for the present—or, better yet, a utopian approach to change.

But it is also, in a way, liberating to take away the uniformity of time moving in one direction. If time goes backwards, and we go with time, then the way ahead is our own history. We live in it, we try to hold on to it. Where we are from is where we are going to.

The cave is in that sense the most radical form of a past that lies ahead of us. The cave becomes a space of longing. The cave is where we want to be because it is what is meant to be.

It is not Eden. There never was an Eden. But the cave becomes a place with additional meaning. This should not be kitsch. It could be kitsch. But it is real. It is the focus of a loss. It is the secret of survival.

The philosopher Achille Mbembe once told me that we have to learn from the poor, from the patterns of poverty, from the logic of the disenfranchised, in order to understand our future.

1 Anders Krisár, *Untitled*, 2014–2015

1

1 "Cave Painting" by Banksy, 2008.

I did not get his point until a few years later. He had seen the decline that I had seen: Western dominance falling and faltering, metaphysically and intellectually—a process that is still going on.

But he lived in South Africa. He had grown up in Cameroon. And he had understood what it meant. When need becomes reality progress is just another word for very much to lose.

All these things are present in the cave. This is our fascination with it. These people seem to know us. They are not like us. They are like us.

So where does that leave all that has happened? Was it all in vain? What is the meaning, if there is any?

You won't find the answer in the cave. But you will find it on the way to the cave. And then you enter the cave. And see. And change. And stay.

Because the cave is a place for transformation. It is not a closed space, it is not a shelter. It is storage and cathedral. It is school and den. It is a monastery for the many.

History unwinding. The undoing of time. As we race back through history, as we fall through it, like Alice, in a way, we can watch ourselves die and not die, live and not live.

This is freedom.

If we imagine the cave, we imagine the future as the past. The cave, on the other hand, is when the present began, if you believe that we live in the 'Age of Man', the Anthropocene, an epoch of its own, with its own triumphs and tragedies. Man shapes the earth and subdues her. She might succumb. Man will die.

This is the reality you have to accept today. The biologist Eugene F Stoermer and the Nobel Prize-winning chemist Paul Crutzen coined the term Anthropocene in 2000, and it has gained more and more plausibility as the consequences of global warming and the potentially catastrophic future become ever more evident.

Roy Scranton asks: When did this epoch start? With the Industrial Revolution around 1800, or with the first atomic bomb in 1945, or rather with the dawn of agriculture 12,000 years ago?

The Anthropocene has its very specific story of domination and destruction. It has its morals and lack of them. It has a hubris which is kin to mankind. And if we want to survive as a species, says Scranton, we first have to learn how to die.

We have to go down the path together, and as a species we might well go back to where we came from, to reflect, to relive, to communicate with a different history. If we want to learn how to die as a group, as the 'Family of Man', we have to go to the cave to bury ourselves and see how we can rise again, differently.

You don't hide in a cave. You live in a cave. You live there because you cannot live anywhere else. There is an existential truth to the cave. It is the other side of nothingness.

"Carbon-fueled capitalism is a zombie system, voracious but sterile. This aggressive human monoculture has proven astoundingly virulent but also toxic, cannibalistic, and self-destructive", writes Roy Scranton.

"Humanity's survival through the collapse of carbon-fueled capitalism and into the new world of the Anthropocene will hinge on our ability to let our old way of life die while protecting, sustaining and reworking our collective stores of cultural technology.

This is the cave. It is cavernous. It folds into the present. It is a place of learning. It is a place of absence. It is a strange notion.

The future. The past. Writings on the wall.

The Théâtre du Soleil, or the Art of Assembly
Bruno Tackels

> I think any theatre company worthy of its name must be a school. Why? Because it is on a search. And searching with someone who is a little better than you is always the best school.
>
> I would have liked to stay in school forever. I didn't say high school. I said school. School is a particular view of happiness. I think if we managed to see life as school, we would be much happier. I sincerely believe that, and even more so as I grow older. Unfortunately, it's not always easy. But I would like to be able to. And for the next show, and the one after that, we will once again have to go back to school.[1]

It is July 1995, the Avignon Festival. The Théâtre du Soleil is presenting Molière's *Tartuffe*, in itself a magnificent take on fundamentalism. We have just learned in the newspaper about the discovery of a mass grave at Srebrenica in Bosnia-Herzegovina: 8,000 Bosnian civilians slaughtered in cold blood by nationalist Serb militias. In shock, the artists at the festival, who have already written the 'Avignon Declaration', come together to decide what to do. How does one respond to the greatest genocide perpetrated in Europe since the end of the Second World War?

We attend the performance of *Tartuffe* in the Théâtre du Soleil exhibition grounds of the Avignon Festival. The place has been transformed, like markets that metamorphosize deserted lots. The immense cement parking area is taken over by caravans and a restaurant with innumerable tables that occupy the space, crowned overhead by coloured garlands delineating the festival.

And yet, on this night, the atmosphere is tense. The challenge is to find a way to pressure Western governments into getting the UN to insist that the resolution demanding the retreat of Serb troops finally be enforced. Sometime during the night, Ariane Mnouchkine, François Tanguy, Maguy Marin, Olivier Py and Emmanuel de Véricourt decide to go on a hunger strike over the month of August. It will last 27 days. I still remember the vital energy emanating that evening from Ariane and the actors of Théâtre du Soleil, a communal home, vibrant and open, centred on its art, but ever vigilant about the world outside.

That night in the parking lot of the exhibition grounds of the Avignon Festival, transformed into a garden of delights, I am given a truly political lesson. I discover utopia, in the act, carried out by flesh-and-blood beings ready to put their lives in danger to save others. I now understand that utopia is not the instantaneous flash I had always thought it to be, that disintegrates as soon as it emerges, an event that disappears in the very energy that makes it erupt. How is that possible?

The Théâtre du Soleil takes utopia in a whole other direction, adopting Théodore Monod's maxim: "Utopia is simply what has not yet been tried."[2] Utopia should not be understood as an impossible dream, but as a possibility that has yet to be realized. So it is that every workday at Théâtre du Soleil contributes to realizing this possibility, working at what is not yet, or is only barely, real.

This is what I witnessed from the beginning of that August as I accompanied the hunger strikers in their battle—a militant artisan convinced this was utopia, a real one. And so it was. The Cartoucherie movement became an indispensable partner, with ties to all the main actors in the conflict—even at the Élysée Palace, where the new president Jacques Chirac was not prepared to wholeheartedly don François Mitterrand's Serbophile garb. Over that month, a swarming group of some 50 activists ended up in the school of life. We worked hard, fought hard and learned a lot.

The Cartoucherie is a big house. But unlike most houses, it is an open rather than private space, viscerally devoted to the public. Its main objective, the company's lodestar, is to do everything possible to welcome an audience who have left their homes to spend time with others. This is the crucial challenge, and everything about the Théâtre du Soleil is designed for people to come together for a brief moment in their lives with justifiably high expectations. Because of its nature, the theatre is one of those rare places that still allow for celebration. It calls it out with all its might, requiring little rituals to be constantly invented on and off stage. Celebrating is inscribing oneself in time and honouring that which teaches us, making every occasion in life an opportunity to come together in revelry. It is seeing the festive as an ideal in-between space linking life and art; two extremes that need constant reassembly. It is the occasions we choose together: an actor's birthday, the fifth staging of the show, a saint's name day, a wedding, a birth, the twentieth day of the hunger strike against the Bosnian war—everything in the lives of the actors at Théâtre du Soleil calls for celebration. It is a brief time out; rare moments difficult to explain to those not there; fragments of utopia in the flesh and blood of all who assemble. It is virtually impossible to transmit the magic present at these moments of celebration; a very ordinary magic that lights up faces and makes one feel like sharing, listening, giving to others; a subtle metamorphosis that lifts the soul and liberates the body.

One summer evening, I have an experience that perfectly exemplifies the power of celebration. I have come to see students from Manufacture, a school of performing arts in Lausanne, participate in the Festival of Schools organized at the Cartoucherie by François Rancillac and the Théâtre de l'Aquarium. After the show, jubilant and full of energy, the students, along with Oskar Gómez Matta, who directed and conceived the show, organize a little picnic in front of the theatre.

While talking on the terrace of the Tempête, I can't help but bring up the Théâtre du Soleil and its art of daily celebration, and muse about the spontaneous way we imagined our picnicking 'festival' in the middle of the Cartoucherie devoid of revelry moments before, while on the other side of the wall, 50 metres away, the men and women of the stage had, for 42 years, never stopped showing us to what extent celebration is at the heart of our lives, as wearisome and difficult as they so often are. I don't see how we can love theatre and call on people to come together to hear the stories we want to tell them without thinking about the conditions under which we receive them. And I keep on wondering: how has this art of celebration, so prominent among 'theatre people' a decade ago, now so thoroughly abandoned our stages and theatres?

As we head home at the end of our impromptu picnic, a Swiss friend tells me, "You know, I'm amazed at being here. I've never been to the Cartoucherie... and never seen a Théâtre du Soleil performance...." I tell him it would be crazy to go past the Soleil without seeing the theatre and suggest we make a detour before continuing home.

Fifty metres to the left, then left again, and there it is: light. Between the trees that line the aisles of the Soleil, multicoloured lamps illuminate the overpopulated round tables. A veritable feast of chicken legs, grilled sardines, mixed salads, stuffed potatoes, vegetables, wine, sorbets, Catalan-styled flambéed coffee.... We suddenly pass into another dimension. Maurice, all dressed in white, elegant down to his fingertips, greets us. "Welcome! Grab a plate and help yourselves; there's more chicken coming. Make yourselves at home." And we're propelled into the magic of the Soleil, like Tintin sliding down the waterfall that leads him to the Inca treasure, in the Temple of the Sun.

Ariane is serving wine when I greet her and introduce the evening's visitors. I tell her these young actors have never been to the Cartoucherie and that I wanted to show them the mythical place, unaware there was a party underway. She welcomes them with her hands full of glasses, serves us wine and invites us to take a plate and eat with everyone. Maurice returns and tells me, "Tonight, as we do every year, we're celebrating the day of St John the Baptist, which happens to be the summer solstice." Behind him, a big pile of wood waits to be lit. When night finally falls on the longest day of the year, some of the actors ignite the bonfire. It's St John's fire. As the bright flames shoot up, one of the actors jumps, making scissor-like movements right over the blaze. Other jumps follow in quick succession.

After ten minutes, a circle forms of almost 100 people watching each other leap. The actress Shaghayegh Beheshti explains to us that in Persian tradition you jump over a fire saying, "I leave you my yellow", meaning "health", and then say, "I take your red", meaning the fire's energy—a kind of ritual metabolism that marks the start of a new cycle bringing the harvest and the fruits of one's labour; a basic and vital principle of exchange. Everyone jumps over the fire once, twice, three times; jumping alone, in

1 Théâtre du Soleil in the Cartoucherie in Paris from the outside with small entrance to the left
2 Ariane Mnouchkine rehearsing with the Théâtre du Soleil at the Cartoucherie

pairs, three at a time, some very close to the blaze, with a pose, a leap, a gesture. The performance goes on, lit up by the vivifying flames…. On the other side of the garden, under the trees, Maria is flambéing coffee while Maurice plays guitar. Another group forms around them. Then comes the sorbet, dozens of pots spread on a big table. Always big tables at the Soleil—a signature unit of measurement.

Eve comes to say hello and I introduce my Swiss friends. "Would you like to see the house?" It is a house that manages, profanely, to evoke the beauty of a cathedral. "Welcome to our home." And we're off on a trip through the aisles of the Soleil. There are many sacred things in this house. Here are its heart and lungs: the stage of the theatre that lights up the Cartoucherie, that gives us the power so difficult to find in ordinary life. "If we don't preserve within us a little bit of the treasure of childhood, there can be no belief, enchantment, enthusiasm—enthusiasm is anything but stupid; childhood is the ability to be enthusiastic, to be taken over… by the gods…."[3] The stage provides this space for freedom and, for this reason, is the alpha and omega of everything that happens in this place. It generates the power that comes from life and work mixed together, bringing a resurgence of a form of phalanstery. A place that is open to the world because it welcomes the whole world, both on stage and in the audience.

The spirit of the Soleil is never far from the ideas expressed by the utopian, early socialist thinker Charles Fourier, though it is troubling to note that, like the Cartoucherie itself, the term 'phalanstery' has military roots.[4] 'Phalanx' refers, in Greek, to a rectangular military formation, which makes it hard not to think of these buildings in the Vincennes woods. But how to organically arrange the elements needed for collective living? This question, posed by Fourier in the nineteenth century, is precisely the one taken up by the Théâtre du Soleil two centuries later (although they never apply its underlying theory dogmatically). Troupe leader Ariane Mnouchkine has always been very wary of philosophical theories that seek to insinuate themselves directly into the world. Thought is born of communal experience, and the way we envisage it together, including our disagreements. Because the troupe is a place of immense differences, but also of shared treasure, it is a collective that dreams itself into being, reinventing itself each day and in every performance. The power of the Soleil lies in its invention of a unique tool, one based on collective power, that has enabled it to build an economy exempt from the laws of the market that is also free from the injunctions of the state when these do not serve the purposes of art and its requirements. The political power of the Théâtre du Soleil comes from this living community, wholeheartedly engaged in the work of art.

Contrary to popular belief, the Théâtre du Soleil does not operate under the sole authority of Ariane Mnouchkine. While the troupe clearly bears her artistic signature, it remains a place of debate, exchange and even confrontation—a community of individuals. And it is the stage, in the end, that decides, because theatre is and always must be a 'permanent school'. Ariane Mnouchkine is one of those artists who is not afraid of the truth, and who finds a way, through the school, to keep on searching for its ineffable principles. Thus this wonderful definition of the actor:

> The actor, like the artist, is an explorer; someone who, armed or unarmed, and more often unarmed than armed, advances through a very long, very deep, very strange and sometimes very dark tunnel, and who, like a miner, brings back pebbles: among these pebbles, he has to find the diamond, and cut it. I believe that is what actors call the 'adventure'. In any case, it is what I call adventure. Descending into the soul of beings, of society, and coming back; that's the first part of the adventure.[5]

Heiress to the great Russian masters, and Vsevolod Meyerhold in particular, Ariane Mnouchkine has always seen the theatre as a kind of laboratory, another way of describing adventure and the quest for diamonds. This is why we go back to the great texts, because from them we learn for future. This is the spirit of the famous internships organized by the Soleil open to young artists from all over the world. And it is this neverending quest for the origins of theatre that inspires the incredible adventure of a 'nomadic school', a utopia transmitted in acts that travelled the world between September 2015 and February 2016. This singular experience shows the extent to which art must always live up to the demands of the quest and all the explorers who precede us.

After the *Macbeth* adventure, it is once again urgent to question everything and wipe the slate blank before embarking on a new creation. From Santiago de Chile to Pondicherry, India, with stops at Oxford University and the Bergman Foundation on the island of Fårö, Sweden, Ariane and a few colleagues worked with hundreds of young actors and actresses, recharging the stage until they could bring in the whole troupe, fresh from the nomadic school, to begin rehearsals in India at the very place that was the 'cradle' of the theatre.

The capacity to always start over from scratch has assured the troupe's unusual longevity, along with the phenomenal energy each of its members devotes to the common endeavour. On the theatre's facade during performances of *Ephémères*, above the famous door always ritualistically opened by Ariane as she greets every spectator, three words have been painted, as they are on all of France's town halls: liberté, égalité, fraternité. Or, the art of assembly.

1   "La troupe-école du Théâtre du Soleil", interview with Guy Freixe, *La Filiation Copeau, Lecoq, Mnouchkine: Une lignée théâtrale du jeu de l'acteur*, Montpellier: L'Entretemps, 2014.

2   Monod, Théodore, *Révérence à la vie: conversations avec Jean-Philippe de Tonnac*, Paris: Livre de poche, 2002.

3   Mnouchkine, Ariane, in the film by Catherine Vilpoux, *Ariane Mnouchkine, l'Aventure du Théâtre du Soleil*, Agat Films & Co, ARTE, 2009.

4   The term 'phalanstery' refers to a self-sustaining utopian cooperative community as planned by Fourier.

5   Extracts from interviews with students from the Conservatoire National Supérieur d'Art Dramatique (CNSAD) and the Ecole Nationale Supérieure d'Arts et Techniques du Théâtre (ENSATT), 2008, Reprinted in Béatrice Picon-Vallin's *Ariane Mnouchkine*, Paris: Actes sud papiers, 2009.

1&2   Ecole Nomade [Travelling School] by Ariane Mnouchkine and members of the Théâtre du Soleil in Pondicherry, India, 2015
3   Performance by Théâtre du Soleil in Pondicherry, India

What Would Jane Do?
Michael Redhill

1

I'm looking at Jane Jacob's face in Cervin Robinson's famous picture of her taken in the White Horse Tavern in New York City. It finds her at the very beginning of her meteoric rise, sitting at the bar and leaning forward while she listens to a man whose back is to us. In one hand she holds a cigarette with a single puff left in it; the other hand is wrapped around the handle of a beer mug. She's the only woman in the bar. It's 1961 and Betty Friedan is still writing *The Feminine Mystique*.

Jane Jacobs is about to publish *The Death and Life of Great American Cities* and change the way people think about urban economies and communities. In her lifetime, she'll start a pile of fights and win most of them, raise three kids (one of whom seems to be sitting beside her at the bar), get arrested in 1968 for protesting an expressway and move to Toronto to spare her sons from the draft. She'll live to 89 and publish nine more books along the way.

But at this moment Jane is bantering, a half-smile on her lips and her eyes wide open behind her lenses. Her discerning but skeptical expression was one of her facial presets. She listened intelligently. You can see that in the picture, as well as also her openness: you know she's paying attention—filtering, filing, ready to deploy facts and stats from her vast depository—because if you're wrong, she's going to tell you. And she's going to enjoy it.

Jane Jacobs died in 2006. I only met her once, in 2001, when we did a panel together at the University of Toronto. She was fighty and charming, although diminished in her body, and her wide-open eyes were smaller behind thicker lenses. In my mind, I see a particular pose of hers, one she assumed sometimes when talking to another person face to face: one hand in front of her chin, index finger pointing at the other person, keeping a beat with her points as she made them. All of this with a wide smile on her face. She seemed to be constantly smiling—sometimes in triumph, sometimes in rue, often in fellow feeling. Also, she wasn't above twitting you if you deserved it.

She'd become an *éminence grise* by the end of her life, and the adulation, you could see, was not for her. She patiently signed my book, one among probably a hundred she signed that night. No indecipherable scrawl either. In an unshaking hand, she signed each book with her full name; the two 'J's looping high over her signature like a pair of raised eyebrows.

The Toronto she'd lived in for over 30 years had in part been moulded by her ideas, if not preserved by them. It's disturbing now to imagine an expressway running through Chinatown, the Annex and Forest Hill Village, among other old neighbourhoods, but it almost happened. The Spadina Expressway had been in the city plan since 1943 and was supported by successive provincial and city governments. Jane didn't stop the expressway alone, but she provided the movement with its bullhorn. (The Spadina Expressway was cancelled by the government of Bill Davis, in 1971. The part that was built—now called Allen Road—terminates at Eglinton Avenue.)

Ten years have passed since her death, and in 2016 she would have been 100 years old. Jane's influence continues to grow. There are Jane's Walks held in cities all over the globe—walks to explore and observe cities. There have been walks in Córdoba, Amsterdam, North Vancouver, Jerusalem and Durham, North Carolina, to name only a few. And this year alone has seen three books with Jane's name on them: a selection of interviews, a collection of unpublished essays and a biography.

One reason she's still such a vital presence, especially in Toronto, is that the problems she identified in her books remain unsolved here. She loved her adoptive city, but the Toronto she left in 2006 is, in large measure, not the same one we live in today. To be sure, long-term Torontonians have witnessed comprehensive changes to their city in the last 50 years. It took a generation to revitalize the Railway Lands behind Union Station,

with the CN Tower appearing in 1976, SkyDome (now Rogers Centre) in 1989 and, signally, the refurbishment of the Toronto Carpet Factory in 1995, which was the first major reclamation of nineteenth-century industrial buildings in Toronto, and which touched off the resurrection of Queen West. (But, curiously, not Parkdale just a titch further to the west. Be careful where you put your overpasses and your rails! As Jane herself said, some types of physical boundaries become psychological ones. There was, she said, quite literally a wrong side of the tracks.) Some of the changes wrought between 1965 and 2006 fundamentally altered our skyline and breathed new life into downtown neighbourhoods. But those years of building have nothing on the last decade.

By the end of 2006, Toronto had mostly recovered from the economic impact of the SARS crisis three years earlier. The city's reputation as safe, and especially clean, had been reinstated, and people began to arrive again—and not just tourists. People were coming to stay. People had always come to Toronto to stay, but in the past a large percentage of them were coming from other parts of Canada. These folks often arrived grumpy, disliking even the *idea* of Toronto, and complaining that economic necessity had forced them to come. You don't hear that kind of apologia from new residents of Toronto anymore, though. The majority of new Torontonians have come from all over the world and they're very happy to be part of a forward-looking, truly twenty-first-century city.

During this decade-long influx, new neighbourhoods have continued to appear in old downtown, like Liberty Village and the Distillery District. Other neighbourhoods have been resurrected, many of them also at the fraying edges of nineteenth-century Toronto: The Junction, Lesleyville, Regent Park and Ossington are just four of them. Each has been revitalized by an influx of restaurants, services and youth, and the sidewalks are alive with people supporting local merchants and acting as "eyes on the street"—as Jane called the act of natural surveillance that neighbourhood residents perform unconsciously. That is to say, they keep their eyes out, and in cities where the street life is as abundant as Toronto's, the sidewalks become self-policing.

Growth at this rate for downtown neighbourhoods is a marvel, but the dark side of it is a continued lack of housing and infrastructure to support the increasing human load. Hence the condo boom, hence the waffling on the fate of the Gardiner Expressway, hence traffic jams on Sundays, as well as the strain put on public transit and the premium on rental housing.

Currently, the city is trying to deal with some of this population bulge by spreading further east along the waterfront, starting with the Sugar Beach/Pan Am Games development at the foot of Lower Jarvis Street. This, and the new modernist zone called River City, are a collection of works in progress that, at the time of writing, are still not meaningfully connected to other parts of the city. But people are flocking to put their deposits down on the forthcoming towers.

It's been at least a decade since the view of the city's skyline contained less than a dozen cranes. Now 50 or more stand at various heights, as condominium after tower after corporate headquarter thunders upwards. The new buildings crowd the Gardiner Expressway below Front Street, almost enclosing the raised highway in a tunnel made of two-, three- and four-bedroom suites starting at $750,000.

This is the view you get when you drive into Toronto, which you invariably do from the west: a seemingly two-dimensional tableau of very tall buildings pasted onto each other.

Old Ideas in New Buildings
1   The new Tate Modern annex by Herzog and de Meuron, 2016
2   'Bird's Nest' Olympic Stadium in Beijing by Herzog and de Meuron, 2008
3   Harpa Concert Hall, Reykjavik, by Olafur Eliasson, 2011
4   Guggenheim Museum, Bilbao, by Frank Gehry, 1997
5   CCTV Headquarters in Bejing by Rem Koolhaas, 2012
6   Bibliotheca Alexandrina, Alexandria, by Snøhetta, 2002
7   Galaxy SOHO in Beijing by Zaha Hadid, 2012, which was illegally replicated in Chongqing (image shows the original building; the rights for the image of the copy were too expensive)

5 JUNE

Cranes loom over it all like pins on a map. When I see what's happened to Toronto in the decade since Jane's death, I often wonder: what would she make of it all? I wish I could drive her in along the Gardiner Expressway and show it to her. Get off at Bathurst and drive her down to see the new tunnel to Billy Bishop Airport. Better than a bridge perhaps, but still nothing like the Harbour City she once imagined for that parcel of land across the harbour mouth.

"Money and stupidity will have their way", I hear her grumble in the passenger seat. "Keep going. I want to see the rest of it."

2

"Take me up Yonge Street", says Jane Jacobs. "That should tell a tale." I drive east to the foot of Yonge, and turn left at the Toronto Star Building. She rolls down her window and fall air fills the car. She fiddles with the radio. "Did they totally wreck the CBC yet?" she asks, dialling past one unsatisfactory station after another. I find Radio 2 for her and it's early enough in the day that it's still playing classical. "Leave it", she says.

I follow the ebb and surge of northbound traffic. She watches what she thinks is called the Hummingbird Centre, but which changed names (again) in 2007. For now, it's the Sony Centre. The Hockey Hall of Fame slips by on the left. Not much has changed north of Wellington, but when we reach Dundas Square she rolls up her window, wrinkling her nose. I ask her if it's the smell of pot smoke that's offended her.

"No, I hate this instant Times Square", she answers. "Like it came from a kit! It's what Mel Lastman did in North York. One day it was a sleepy hamlet with a local library and a hundred-year-old hardware store, the next it was a mall a mile long. Sudden change in established communities is very destabilizing."

"Yonge and Dundas wasn't an established community when they started on all this in 1998", I tell her. "Yonge and Dundas was pizza slices and Sam the Record Man. There were and still are tonnes of people down here. Spending money, mingling. All ages."

"Sam the Record Man", she mused.

"Gone now. Ryerson University demolished it and built their student centre on its footprint. Look—" I drive past the new building, an ice cube looming over the street with a huge atrium opening off the corner entrance. She seems to approve, but then she's lost in thought, watching the passing show. The sidewalks are teeming. When I cross College Street, her jaw falls open. Huge swathes of both sides of Yonge Street have been demolished—the buildings torn out, vistas to the east and west revealed.

"Downtown is for condos", she snarks. "And what are they doing *there*?"

She's pointing at the empty facades of nineteenth-century buildings facing the street. Houses, originally. Their yellow- and red-brick facades have been sandblasted and cleaned up, but there's nothing behind the windows except for an empty pit that goes down 30 feet. "I think that's what you call a compromise between the historical board and developers", I tell her. "It's just lip service."

"It treats those fine old buildings as if they were ornaments."

"Sometimes it works. I like the streetscape you come across inside Brookfield Place at the foot of Bay Street. You think you're walking into a modern building, but then inside there's this row of old stone houses, their steps and front doors… it's pretty incredible."

"If architecture is a form of entertainment to you, then I suppose it would be." She shoots me a semi-affectionate glance. "Take me up to the Annex. I want to see my house."

Albany Avenue is a beautifully treed street above Bloor. Number 69 is on the east side. I park across the road from it. "Nice to see some things aren't changing", she says. "Someone has repainted."

Kids ride by on bikes with colourful ribbons streaming from their handlebars. She watches her house silently, lost in thought, and I don't want to disturb her. "Sometimes that house was full of people day and night", she says at last. "One person would leave and three more would arrive."

"What for?"

"Oh, strategy meetings, dance parties, dinners. Girls would show up during the school year to ogle my boys. It was a house full of energy and talk. I can almost hear the voices."

I let her listen to them. Having read about who Jane knew, and who came to seek her out on Albany Avenue, I can only imagine the voices she can hear. "All right", she says. "Take me to a couple of these new neighbourhoods you're going on about. The Port Lands you said?"

"The whole eastern waterfront of Lake Ontario is changing. There's Sugar Beach and River City—which is calling itself Toronto's 'Lower East Side'—and some of the last factory land on the waterfront is being revitalized."

"Well then, we don't have all day."

We buckle up and head south again. I ask her, "What's different now about Toronto than, say, the 1970s and 80s, when you were putting down roots here?"

"Oh gosh, now you're asking me to think back. When we first moved here, it was just starting to loosen up. I like to think all the Americans who arrived at the end of the 60s helped add some spice to the proceedings! Don't laugh, you couldn't get a draft beer on a Sunday in 1969. And I was once stopped for jaywalking! Can you imagine? I was still a New Yorker when I got here—I couldn't see the advantage in going slow or taking the long way."

That reminds me—"Oh, speaking of which", I say, "let's take a longcut through Regent Park on our way to the lake. You should see what's happening there."

"I shudder to think. Luxury bungalows?"

"They've torn out most of the neighbourhood and they're replacing it with mixed housing, including affordable housing and geared-to-income rental units. There's a new aquatic centre, and green space not fenced in by buildings. New restos—fast food and slower food."

I slow down on Dundas past Parliament and we come alongside the growing redevelopment. "Well, this is much more hopeful", Jane says. "As long as they're not shooing out the previous inhabitants."

"I think they've cut two thirds of the affordable housing and the rest is going to be market units. The idea is full-on mixed-use, and self-sufficiency as a neighbourhood. But it's going to take 15 years or more to complete."

"It seems cruel to reduce the number of income-geared units, but when it was all income-geared it became a ghetto and no one paid much attention to it. Just let it fester. Real diversity means everyone lives together, rich and poor, walking the same streets, watching out for each other. A rising tide lifts all boats, you know what I mean?"

"It's insta-village, though, like you were calling Dundas Square. And I drive this stretch a lot and I still don't see a concentration of people on the sidewalks or in the greens. How long do you think it might be before people take to this as a functioning neighbourhood?"

"A long time probably. More than 15 years before the seams disappear. Where else is this happening?"

"At the bottom of this street", I tell her, turning right on River. Within a minute, we arrive in River City, a new clutch of buildings nestled in the pocket of land made by King Street, the Don River and the Eastern Avenue overpass. The first two of three phases are finished. Phase One is a dark, imposing building that ranges south down Trolley Street and looks like a huge dresser with all of its drawers hanging open. Parallel to Queen Street, the northeast wing of Phase One extends toward the Don, where, at its full extension, it appears to be collapsing 'just a bit', as if frozen in mid-demolition. Behind it, Phase Two is a trio of boxes made of glass and smooth panels, struck in contrapuntal white. It has an industrial energy to it, harkening back to the area's manufacturing past. It looks like a machine designed to turn out perfect examples of something.

"That's nifty, that one there", says Jane. She likes Phase Two. "But apart from the Tim Hortons, where are all the services?"

"It's only steps to Queen Street."

"It feels cut off from the world around it, penned in. But it'll knit into its surroundings with time. Like Regent Park."

I'm not crazy about this phase of the city's architecture, AutoCAD-influenced meta-buildings. "I think these things look like 3D computer renderings. You can sense someone moving the architectural elements around on a screen."

"The new is always frightening, Michael. But the people who live here will feel like they're part of something. They'll be pioneers."

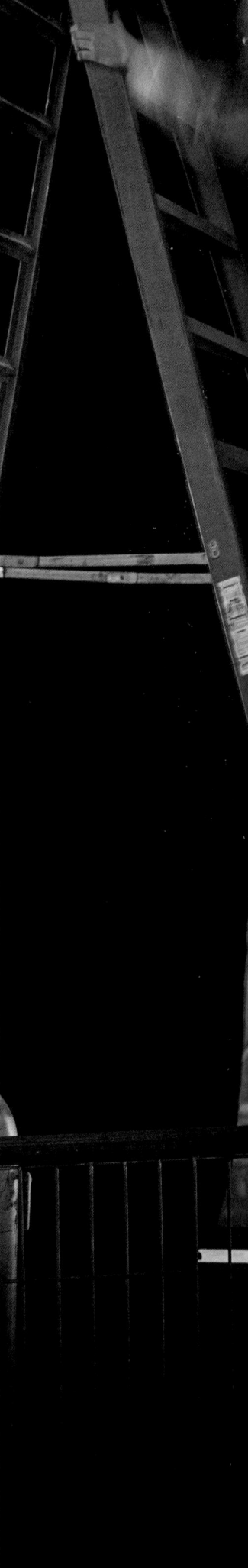

"Let's go to the lake."

I return to Jarvis and then head down to Sugar Beach. We cross beneath the Gardiner for the second time. The underside of the expressway looks like it has psoriasis. "I gather they're not cleaning this thing up or tearing it down?" she asks.

"No. Council voted to keep it. It's like a wire in a tree—the city just keeps growing around it."

"Burying it makes more sense, but no one thinks of a legacy for the future anymore. Anything that's going to take longer to complete than your term of office isn't worth your time!"

We come to Sugar Beach, where I explain to Jane how the Pan Am Games were held in Toronto in 2013 and all of this stretch of the lake—going basically to the Don River—was developed. "It's a work in progress", I tell her. We drive slowly past the Corus Building to the hoardings of the Bayside development, which promises still more condos, office space and retail opportunities. The skeletons of at least five new buildings are rising on either side of Queen's Quay East. I ask her what she thinks of the way Toronto has continued to obscure its own view of Lake Ontario.

"Well, that's been going on about 60 years now. Why stop at Yonge Street?"

"It's like you have to make a plan if you actually want to see the lake. Or pay through the nose to live in a lakeview property. There's still a part of the city where they don't seem to plan on blotting out the lake. Down by Unwin Avenue."

I continue along Lakeshore to Cherry Street and continue south. We cross over the channel, into Toronto's Port Lands—one of the final frontiers of undeveloped downtown.

"Have they already started building condos on Cherry Beach?" she asks.

"Not yet. But in five years, who knows? There are acres of land here currently being used as parking lots for school buses or storage places for mounds of gravel." We're driving along Unwin now. I go past the soccer fields and unkempt forest to the abandoned Hearn Generating Station. "Wow", says Jane, as it comes into view.

"Have you ever seen it?"

"No. I knew it was here. Much bigger than I thought."

The Hearn is a colossal, if not monumental, building of red brick. Its eastern aspect—the actual front of the Hearn—is a three-storey layer cake of brick and windows, 90 of them in three horizontal rows. Behind it and towering above it stands the generating station itself, 55 metres high and containing 650,000 cubic metres of space. Afternoon and evening light would have poured through the vertical bands of glass cascading down its front.

We park, and Jane and I get out of the car and stand in front of the massive structure. "It looks like a giant typewriter from another planet", she says. We go in the front doors and walk through to the huge, empty station building. The turbines that once generated electricity are gone, as is much of the salvageable metal that was left here when the plant closed in 1983. The gantries remain high above the turbine row, stilled forever on their rails. The only metal left in the place are the steel catwalks and stairways.

Jane is grinning. "She's a wonderful old hulk, isn't she?"

I recount its afterlife: how various provincial governments made plans to bring it back into service one way or another, although, in the end, none of them did. Movie productions and TV shows used it on and off through the years, and Toronto's Luminato Festival set its tenth season inside the Hearn, in 2016. She walks ahead of me, listening and nodding. My voice is swallowed up in the huge volume of space above us. "There's been talk of converting this into a three-pad hockey arena."

"That would be a waste." She's standing on the cracked concrete floor with her hands on her hips, craning back to look up. "You could fit the Statue of Liberty in here. Maybe even the Taj Mahal." She brings her eyes back to me. "This could be a cultural landmark for Toronto if it were handled properly. Something as grand as the Tate or the Pompidou."

"It could house a massive theatre complex", I suggest. "Or a brewery."

"Nonsense", she sniffs. "There's enough beer to go around. It should be a destination for Torontonians as well as visitors, and something that enriches and keeps changing."

"What about making it the new planetarium?"

"Maybe. Or a museum of some kind. A museum of Toronto."

"That's come up a few times, but no one ever pulls the trigger."

"It could be all of those things, for goodness' sake—it's so vast! It's just begging to be spruced up and set spinning. But whatever the city does with it, it'll decide the tone of whatever neighbourhood might spring up around it over time. But! Will it be a strip mall with the Hearn Indoor Waterpark at one end? Or a new community along the lake that can boast it's situated beside a world-class children's museum, say, or a First Nations cultural centre? How high is it again?" she asks, breathless.

"55 metres."

"It would be interesting to go way up there and look down."

"I hate to point this out, Jane, but you're a ghost. You can do whatever you want."

"I did whatever I wanted when I was alive, too, young man." She lifts one foot like she's going up a step, and then the other, and stands about 18 inches above the floor. "Well, how do you like that", she says, "You're right. You're good for something after all!"

Then she goes straight up, all the way to the roof. "Wonderful!" she calls down to me. "It looks like the ruins of a dead civilization."

"Let's hope it doesn't come to that!"

She zips around the concrete pillars, stopping to inspect a detail here, a view there. "I'd say there's hope for this town. You're still managing to live together and the city centre is alive. People are going to want to come here for a long time, to live, to visit, to learn from the city. So don't screw it up."

Thus spake Jane Jacobs, I think. "Are you coming down?" I ask her. "Do you want a lift to… um…"

"Oh, I can find my way back. You get on with your day."

"This was really interesting for me. Maybe we can do it again some time."

"Oh dear, probably not", she replies. "I'm very busy these days. The afterlife is *full* of committees and my desk is piled high. There's talk of paving paradise."

"With a parking lot?"

"You got it. Go on then. I'm going to explore a while longer."

Jane Jacobs waves goodbye to me and exits through a wall 40 feet in the air. I return to my car.

New Ideas in Old Buildings

1. Climbing garden in the former steel mill in Duisburg, Germany
2. Sasha Waltz & Guests performing in the Palast der Republik—the former parliament of the German Democratic Republic and a musical theatre in Berlin, Germany
3. High Line in New York by Diller Scofidio + Renfro
4. Apartments in the Jaegersborg Water Tower in Copenhagen, Denmark
5. The Pyramid at the Louvre in Paris
6. Workshop for *Overture* for *KA MOUNTAIN AND GUARDenia TERRACE* in Robert Wilson's loft on 147 Spring Street in SoHo, New York
7. The Salina Turda salt mine in Romania
8. Second-World-War bunker in Berlin, former location of a hardcore techno club, Bunker
9. Snow sledding in the 'Bird's Nest' by Herzog and de Meuron (or, how a new building with an old idea turned quickly into an old building)
10. John Bock's *Medusa* in the Magazin building of the Berlin State Opera
11. Cupola of the Reichstag in Berlin, with visitors and windows into the assembly hall of the German parliament, by Foster + Partners
12. Bobbi Jene Smith's *A Study on Effort* at the Hearn
13. The Schaubühne am Lehniner Platz in Berlin

THE IDEA—How to Go Forward Culturally by Going Way Back

Penetration, Unbuilding and the Future of Museums
Nicola Spunt in conversation with Alex Josephson and Charles Renfro

Culture is around us more than ever before. In museums—the numbers of which have skyrocketed in past years—in houses, in concert halls, in warehouses, on the streets, in the woods, in the desert, by the ocean, on our phones. It costs a lot to see it. Or it costs nothing to see it. You have to make a special trip to find it. Or you chance upon it on your daily routine.

While the typologies of contemporary art and performance remain rooted in the classics of cultural history, there has never before been a more expansive period of art- and culture-making in both space and time. Never before have so many different modes, methods and materials been invoked. Never before have so many publics been engaged. And for those of us who believe culture is more than just entertainment—that it inspires greater understanding, tolerance, connection, empathy, love—and are lucky enough to be tasked with helping to create the spaces where it unfolds, our objective is to make the experience as full and inviting as possible.

But how does one actually do that? How do architects and designers think through all the combinations and permutations? Are cultural presentation venues, like museums, in crisis? How does one predict the unpredictable? And further to that, how can buildings or structures be designed to anticipate the things we don't yet know?

These were some of the questions that were prompted and emerged during a conversation between Alex Josephson (AJ), Nicola Spunt (NS) of PARTISANS and Charles Renfro (CR) of Diller Scofidio + Renfro on a rainy September afternoon in Toronto a few months after the PARTISANS team had completed the design and its execution for the Luminato Festival at the Hearn in June 2016.

1&2 Reinterpretations of Price and Littlewood's Fun Palace by PARTISANS
Background: Floor plan for the mezzanine of the Hearn

NS: Jörn's vision for Luminato's residency at the Hearn was to create "a cultural institution without walls". Can you talk about where PARTISANS looked for inspiration to help achieve that vision?

> AJ: For us, the most obvious place to start was Cedric Price and Joan Littlewood's Fun Palace scheme. It's the Holy Grail of monumental modular architecture for arts and culture. We riffed on some of those ideas in sketches and renderings to get the inspirational juices flowing. Romantically speaking, the Fun Palace, like the Crystal Palace in London and the Exposition Universelle in Paris, are the large-scale ephemeral projects that all architecture students study and dream about. But in practice, when you're in the trenches figuring out how to make a behemoth like the Hearn work and account for all the moving parts, you have to consider really brass tacks stuff: people have to eat, drink, walk, go to the bathroom. A stage has to be set up; there are acoustic properties that have to be dealt with. You're really dealing with the belly of a beast and letting the guts of the site drive the decisions as opposed to coming in with some grandiose design vision.

>> CR: When I visited the Hearn I was struck by how it seemed to harken back to certain Situationist principles, Deleuze, and this idea of tactics versus strategies. I imagine you guys were looking for tactics, for ways to work in cooperation with the building and for the opportunities it gave you instead of bringing a pre-existing concept of what it should look like or what it should do.

> AJ: Totally. In cooperation with the building and in cooperation with others like Charcoalblue, the Luminato production team, the City. At PARTISANS we get excited

1 Hearn Theatre rendering by PARTISANS
2 Music Stage rendering by PARTISANS
3 The Hearn Theatre
4 The Hearn Theatre Fly Tower
Background (opposite): Elevation of Turbine Hall

by projects that require us to think about how to actually make the improbable possible. The Hearn was definitely one of those projects. It took a village.

NS: Just how cooperative was the building, though? Your team only had seven months to come up with and execute a plan for a dilapidated, decommissioned coal plant that ranks as Canada's largest enclosed space. How did PARTISANS set about approaching the task?

AJ: It was actually very unglamorous. It was like, okay, how do you deal with the rules and regulations that would even allow people to access a space that is otherwise forbidden according to modern zoning and building codes? It was all about egress. We created a plan for how people could get in by figuring out how they could get out. But we approached the overall design like it was a macro-scale game of architectural Jenga. The intention was to honour and enhance the raw beauty of the Hearn while maximizing flexibility for programming. Dozens of shipping containers were needed to get equipment in and out of the building, so we took that cue and turned it into a tactic. Shipping containers became our Jenga pieces for carving out distinct spaces that created intimacy and functionality, and building blocks for designing a state-of-the-art shipping-container theatre with Charcoalblue that would fit in a space that was previously designed to house a giant boiler. This was our ode to the Fun Palace. It was about the architecture of a multi-arts event, something akin to anti-architecture because it needed to be ephemeral. It wasn't about finding permanent solutions, but using the permanence of the old building to drive ways of hacking it to get it to do something it was never intended to do. We needed to leverage the form to create a platform for the performances.

NS: This idea of 'anti-architecture' makes me think of the Hearn in terms of an 'unbuilding'—an approach that deconstructs, so to speak, conventional architectural moves and forms to yield, like you say, a platform. It's less about building something up and more about sheering it down to discover what it can offer and how it can be repurposed.

CR: Yes, I like this concept of unbuilding, or an unbuilding, which I think has everything to do with the creation of experience. What makes something like what happened at the Hearn or in other temporary situations or found spaces so special has to be, by definition, about the experience, and not about the thing itself. Our appetite for experiences like Luminato at the Hearn is part of a backlash against the isolation wrought by technology, which is a really obvious statement to make. But the kinds of events that bring people together and orchestrate a collective experience have new meaning in this day and age.

NS: When describing his vision for the Hearn, Jörn would invoke the famous Jane Jacobs quote: "New ideas must use old buildings." Found spaces like the Hearn or the Park Avenue Armory thrive as venues for temporary arts and culture programming. What is it about found spaces that continue to hold us in their thrall? Is it nostalgia? A backlash against technology? The juxtaposition of history and contemporaneity?

AJ: Honestly, they're convenient. I think we underestimate the sheer convenience of foundness. It's ready-made architecture.

NS: But the Hearn wasn't super convenient...

AJ: It was a challenging space, yes, but if you have the stomach for pushing the political process through to ensure access, it's more convenient than building from scratch. Also, you're not beholden to a single patron with these spaces. Jörn's programmatic freedom within the Hearn allowed the Luminato team to bring

STRATEGIES AND IMPACT—How to Start Moving

together some pretty unconventional bedfellows, which is part of what made the festival so wonderful.

CR: There are the logistical advantages that you just mentioned, like the fact that you don't have to bother to make a shell. It's there for you so the initial expenses are less. But it's like when you listen to bands that do remakes of classic songs. There's something about the juxtaposition, the clash, the violent reinterpretation of a space through its re-inhabitation, usually with a program that was not the intended use—it's naughty. It's naughty to go into an old building and make something new. It feels sexy.

AJ: Yes! It feels like you're doing something a bit bad, like when you smoked your first cigarette, drank your first beer, had your first kiss. It always happened in an alley or somewhere more secret. It didn't happen at home or in an art gallery…

NS: It never happened somewhere comfortable…

AJ: Nope.

CR: I GET WHAT THIS IS! It's penetration!

NS: Oh my god, it is!

AJ: Haha, it totally is.

CR: It's penetration. That is what the found space offers. You're inserting yourself into a foreign body.

NS: It's funny because this idea of naughtiness resonates with one of PARTISANS' core philosophies: beauty emerges when design misbehaves. Alex, how would you connect this notion of 'misbehaviour' with the Hearn?

AJ: When we talk about misbehaviour it isn't really about a question of behaving badly. We situate it in the context of resistance and play—political resistance or resistance to the status quo on the one hand, and the play or inventiveness required to come up with strategies and designs that allow us to push that status quo on the other. PARTISANS penetrating the Hearn was itself disruptive to the way conventional architecture is practised, at least here in Toronto. Fundamentally, most studios would not have done this kind of project because it's not architecture. But if you think about it in the bigger picture, what's the difference between activating or penetrating this old space and building the pyramids? I mean, obviously that's a hyperbolic comparison, but the Hearn affected thousands and thousands of people, if not the entire collective consciousness of our 'B' city…

NS: Beta city…

CR: The test city! I love it!

1&2 Cedric Price, *Fun Palace: interior perspectives*, c 1964
Background: Hearn site plan

104   Into the Culture Cave

AJ: Sure, yes, our beta city. My question is: If there'd been a patron and we'd tried to build our version of the Fun Palace, would it have reached and affected people to the same extent? Would there have been an internationally renowned chef from Montreal working Le Pavillon and getting all his Toronto restaurant buddies to pitch in? Would people from across the city and the country have come together in the same way? I say no. It was a way of penetrating or disrupting traditional architecture. We didn't just push permits; we helped change the way people experience the fundamental aspects of a performing arts centre.

CR: So one thing I would say about penetration itself isn't an entirely new concept. In recent years, the tech industry has been fond of using the word 'disruption'. People are so proud of themselves for using that term, but I don't think it's quite what we're talking about here. Penetration suggests an outside body that you then work with, but more importantly, it's temporal. I mean the sex act is really like Bakhtin's carnival. You don't have carnival all the time. You have carnival on occasion. You have sex on occasion. You have Luminato on occasion. And it's that time-based excuse to get together that supercharges the whole experience. And I think that what you guys did is you just let everything sweep in there. I loved how dangerous it felt! People get excited about a limited time event and that's a huge part of the appeal of a festival like Luminato.

NS: Absolutely, although more often than not architecture is obsessed with the fantasy of permanence, with legacy as a function of time-worn brick and mortar. In 2002, Diller Scofidio + Renfro created a Swiss Expo pavilion called The Blur Building. Charles, can you talk about what it's like to design something that's intended to be ephemeral?

CR: The Blur Building was one of our first internationally known projects. It represented two sides of our practice: one side that's grounded in the art world, which I think is fundamentally about revelation and creating experience, and the other in the architecture world, which is about making a thing that structures an experience. The Blur Building was about those two things coming together. The thing itself was a performer. It was a cloud; it kept changing and shifting and moving. You put on a raincoat and could go into it, but you didn't know what to expect—you couldn't see anything when you got out there. There was nothing to see or do in this building that was supposed to be an Expo pavilion. And then they loved it so much that they asked us at the end of the Expo if they could save it and keep it going. And we said no. We said: it has to be taken down; its lifespan is this six-month period and that's it. And it must live in memory only. It must remain a lived experience. It's like a Tino Sehgal piece. You don't record a Tino Sehgal piece; you don't install one in a museum to be there in perpetuity.

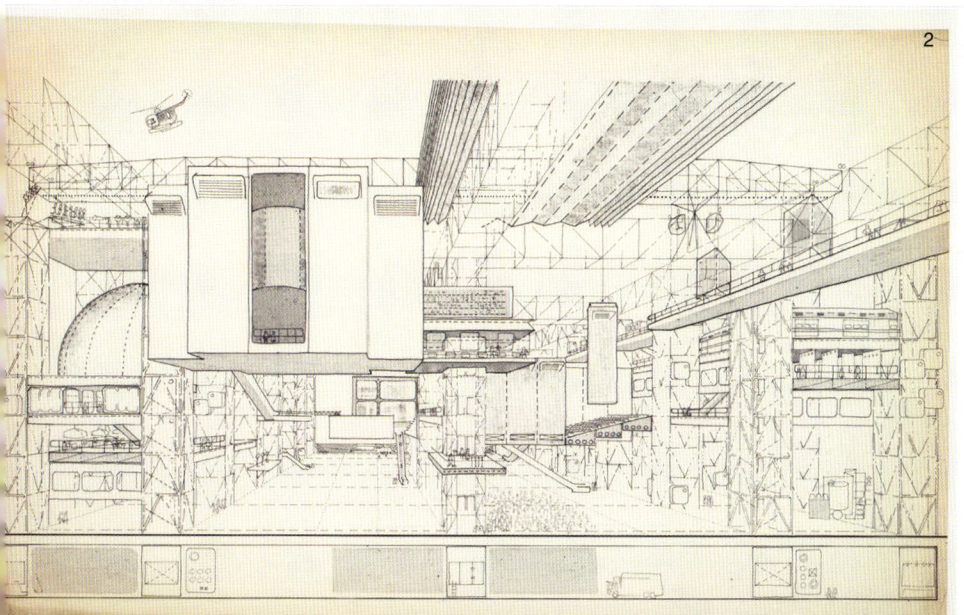

2

AJ: One of my favourite Diller Scofidio projects was the drill destroying the drywall slowly at the Whitney. For me, that was so perfect. It was the ultimate deconstructionist architectural art installation. The banality of drywall, the shackles it puts on us. And for that exhibition to just destroy that wall—I loved that.

CR: Well that was a real 'meta' project because it was essentially like slapping the hand that feeds you. We were given

1 Aerial view of The Blur Building by Diller Scofidio + Renfro
2&3 *Mural* by Diller Scofidio + Renfro at the Whitney Museum of American Art

a retrospective at the Whitney, and to have the one site-specific piece we made destroy the rooms we were given for the exhibition.... You know, we were behaving in a bad way. But actually also behaving in a good way by acknowledging the importance of the museum as an infrastructure.

AJ: Fundamentally, we're all just trying to do thoughtful work. But you've come full circle because now you guys are making the museums...

CR: We get a contract, and just like everybody, we need to get paid. We want to put good thought into every project we take on. Life isn't worth living if you don't push it. I mean, I think that way about everything. Even when we went to lunch at Bar Raval today, I scanned the menu and thought, I want everything on the menu. Except for the eggplant because I'm not an eggplant person. But I really do want to experience everything and want to push the experience in the work we do, and I think you're operating in the same way.

AJ: I hope, I don't know. Do you know when you're doing it?

CR: You know you're doing it when you get scared, when you can't sleep at night.

NS: Museums like Bilbao, the Guggenheim in New York, or the ROM here in Toronto are sometimes criticized for their flashy, overly robust designs. Is it the case that architecture sometimes competes with or distracts from the art it's intended to display?

CR: No doubt that that's the balancing act or the needle that we have to thread in thinking about architecture as a container for art or as an armature for constructing an experience that we call art. But I'm starting to feel like 'museum' as a term should actually be banished.

AJ: I think you're right.

CR: We need to come up with something else. Like the Hearn... that wasn't a museum. Mostly there was performance going on and there was some art. But I think we need to ask ourselves: What is art these days? Art is multidisciplinary, art is multimedia, art is multi-temporal...

AJ: There's penetration within art!

CR: Yes, you can even do double penetration! And that's when it gets really exciting when you're afraid you're going to 'bust' the suspension of disbelief. But you asked the question, what is the role of the container...?

AJ: To get filled.

CR: To get filled doubly! But all joking aside, what is the container's role in housing art? One of the things we struggle with as people who make spaces for the presentation and production of culture is we have no idea where it's going. There have been general trends, sure. If you look back 20 years, 50 years, 100 years, there are certain things you can say have happened: art has gotten bigger, art has gotten louder, art has gotten faster, it's gotten more dimensions, it requires more space, it's gotten more expensive. All of these vectors will continue to evolve. But at a certain point, isn't the human body the limitation or the thing that establishes the relationship we have with art? There are questions we still don't know or can't anticipate that will dictate how we continue to build.

1 Bar Raval by PARTISANS.
Background: Side view of the Turbine Hall and venues

7 JUNE

NS: I want to circle back to this idea of banishing the term 'museum'. Why do you think the idea of the museum is no longer useful in the twenty-first century?

AJ: So we're joking about penetration and the container getting filled, but one of the earliest theoretical projects I worked on was in response to a competition announced in Italy several years ago where the biggest power generating company in the country created this huge prize. The theme for the first one focused on art and energy. So I thought, we're in an energy crisis, but we're also in an art crisis. There's too much art. There's an embarrassment of riches. How do you archive an embarrassment of riches? What happens to the traditional sarcophagus for art?

CR: Which is known as the museum…

AJ: Which is known as the museum. So what I proposed was to install these condom-like sheets on the doors of the museums and have them inflate, like the building was full and you could no longer enter because there was too much art, and you could no longer process or prioritize the information. It was all about excess and the double-edged sword of people appreciating art these days. Art has become this luxury commodity that you can buy into at any level. So when we were working on the Hearn, I was excited by this idea of using it as a platform, but also started to think that maybe it could become a fluid stage for something that's continuously evolving. And why isn't that the future manifestation of the art institution? Art institutions today are in some ways calcified manifestations of someone's philanthropic will. They reflect a particular moment in time and that moment's way of dealing with the embarrassment of riches.

NS: But does that mean we necessarily lose the term altogether?

AJ: Isn't it a problem with language in the end? The people practising architecture are criticizing the use, purpose and function of these places, but isn't that in conflict with the public's idea of what these museums or repositories or containers do? We're criticizing the very possibility of these things as a sustainable model, and yet at the same time people are very much willing to consume them in their traditional definition.

CR: I think we all need the term 'museum' because we know it, but then we're stymied or intimidated by it at the same time. The name 'museum' is both appealing, because we need to feel like we've done something great and we've exposed ourselves to culture in some higher sense, but it's also the thing that keeps it from being more effective in general.

AJ: I was reflecting on Jörn's notion of a 'Culture Cave' and I had this whacky idea. The standard operating practice for new museums across the world is to find the donor and hold the design competition, or sometimes vice versa. But wouldn't it be interesting if, for example, your potential institution is in Helsinki and the Hearn is just sitting empty here in Toronto. Why not say, what are you trying to do in Helsinki? Why Helsinki? Why doesn't Helsinki come to the Hearn and try out the idea first? The space is big enough for anything. It can be the museum of museums.

NS: So you're imagining the Hearn as a beta space…?

AJ: Yeah, you could put multiple institutions into the place at any given moment in time. If you're actually trying to do something different, try it out before you build something permanent!

CR: And what is the Guggenheim doing in Helsinki anyway? It's a sort of militarization or colonization…

1 Rome Museum competition proposal by Alex Josephson
2&3 Renderings of the Culture Shed by Diller Scofidio + Renfro
Background: Hearn study with Ferris wheel entrance

STRATEGIES AND IMPACT—How to Start Moving

AJ: It's imperialism. It's serious penetration.

CR: And not in a good way, not in a good way.... It's date rape!

AJ: Date rape!

CR: There are several things happening in the world that illustrate what you just said. One of them is a development in London on the recent Olympic grounds, which, for lack of a better word, I'm going to call a culture mall. Across from Zaha's Aquatics Centre, there's going to be a big multi-use building that will become a collector for international institutions, including the V&A and the Smithsonian, who will go there and be tenants.

NS: The greatest hits.

CR: The greatest hits, exactly. Whereas our idea for the Culture Shed is kind of the reverse. One of the original concepts for the Shed—you can even hear it in the name—was to create a newly-made found space. That was our challenge to ourselves. How do you make something that's akin to the Park Avenue Armory, but has all the bells and whistles of the most technologically advanced presentation space available? And the idea with tenancy was for it to be an open-frame system where groups or institutions from across the world, like, say, the Louvre, could come and set up camp for a given period of time and hang out their shingle.

NS: A pop-up Louvre! The Shed will offer a versatile space that allows you to erase or blur disciplinary boundaries. Is this the new normal for the twenty-first-century design of arts and culture spaces? We prize these ideas of flexibility, transformability and multi-use, but do we also perhaps risk losing specificity or something else when we privilege these values?

AJ: I think the risk is that when you build something that's supposedly flexible, but you put something in it that's so successful it ends up remaining there in that specific form, you've turned your back on the theory and practice of what your idea represented. That's why I find what happened with The Blur Building so incredible—you stayed true to your idea.

CR: It's so fascinating what you said, that success can lead to death, because why would someone want to kill something that's successful? With Blur, it was wonderfully successful, but that's precisely because it had a shelf life and everybody knew it. There was so much energy around the idea of its temporality that changing its mode of reception would have killed the actual content it was delivering. But in terms of building spaces dedicated to the arts of now—whether it's the twenty-first or twenty-second century—you just don't know how or where things are going to go. The Shed was built to be both idiosyncratic and neutral, and completely flexible. There's a director, a board, a donor, and the mandate of the facility is completely fungible. But one of the main drivers of the design was to make a space that could help fund itself by being rentable. There hasn't been a museum that's been built from the get-go as a museum and as a space available to the commercial culture industry. Now, whether or not you can make a space that can be all things to all people, that remains to be seen. And I'm not going to say we've solved the problem. However, we've kicked the can down the road, at the very least, but I think also changed its course by dealing with the elephant in the room: financial performance.

1&2 Renderings of The Broad by Diller Scofidio + Renfro
3 Design model of the Hearn created during the festival by PARTISANS and students from OCAD University
4 Study for the Hearn by PARTISANS
Background: Elevation of the Hearn with the Hearn Theatre

AJ: Every museum these days is trying to cover their costs by renting themselves out to the highest bidders for weddings and parties! The funny thing is, a party with

300 or 400 or 500 people, huffing and puffing because they're dancing and drinking and creating heat—the systems in the building can't deal with the overload!

CR: There are Monets with sweat beads on them…

AJ: I kid you not; I just saw this in Paris at the Palais de Tokyo. It got really rowdy in there and the walls were basically dripping.

NS: Alex, you've described the Hearn as the "anti-Bilbao". What does that mean?

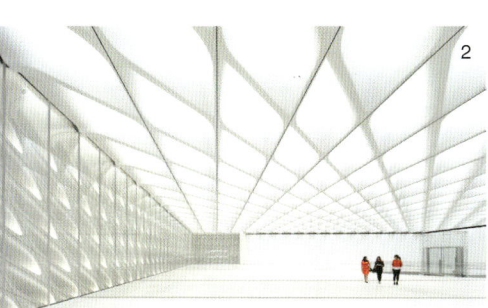

AJ: On a literal and practical level, it is the anti-Bilbao. It is readily available. It has incredible possibility in terms of space. Making it work was a $16 per square foot proposition. And by the way, that included everything—all the production and all the programming. Off the top of my head, I think Bilbao cost something more like $3,000 per square foot, and that's not including the art! But from a programmatic perspective, Bilbao is calcified. It's a place with specific exhibitions. For instance, the Richard Serra sculptures there will never move. They cannot move. If they do, they can't be there anymore. In a way, the whole point in the Hearn was that there was no loyalty to a specific program. It could be anything to anyone at any time so long as it was a good idea. This idea of producing just the framework versus the shell was very interesting. It's actually the opposite of what most architects do today because what they're interested in is a manifestation of their brand that can then beget other projects.

CR: That you can publish online and photograph.

AJ: And what's fascinating about the Hearn is that it did photograph very well, but the vocabulary for people to consume it didn't and doesn't really exist. It wasn't overly choreographed. It was more about programming in time than in space. So it is the anti-Bilbao because the architecture of Bilbao is so easily consumed, whereas the proposition of the Hearn was not. And yet at the same time, it was so accessible and free to the public.

CR: I think there's a kind of lie built into Bilbao. It seems like it's trying to convince everyone through its fluid forms and dynamic shape-making that it's alive and changeable, when in fact it's exactly the opposite. It's almost an act of war or military operation. It's propaganda.

AJ: It's brand propaganda. It's two brands, Guggenheim's and Gehry's, and they come together to conquer the world. The American model is *the* art model. It's like military bases!

CR: It's colonization and idea corruption. It's trying to convince people that it's about freethinking and all of these kinds of things you think museums should be about, but yet it's dictatorial and exclusive.

NS: What should we demand of museums and cultural institutions in the twenty-first century? What are the values we want them to espouse?

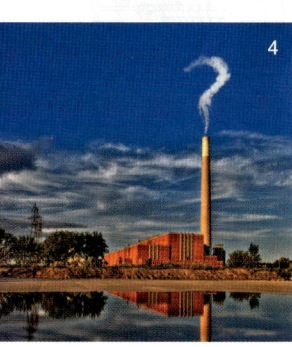

AJ: I feel they shouldn't be allowed to keep things in storage. The Art Gallery of Ontario, like the Met, hoards art. You shouldn't be allowed to build a museum that keeps art away from people for more than a certain period of time.

CR: We're in an age of curation. Ten years ago, there was no such thing as a major in curation, and now they're all over the world of higher education. I teach in one. We have the internet to thank or blame for this age of curation. We also have the expansion of art into every nook and cranny of our lives,

particularly if we live in cities. And we need curation because there's so much stuff, and that's one of the things that museums still must do; they must package things. While I do think you're right that there shouldn't be so much storage—one should be able to access everything—there's just too much of it. I imagine there are enough multi-million-dollar paintings that every resident of America could be given one. Think about what that could do!

NS: Diller Scofidio + Renfro's "veil-and-vault" design for the Broad museum in LA tackled storage as part of the architectural vision.

CR: We turned the storage into part of the experience, but it's curated. I think it's going to happen more and more, the opening up of archives. It does relate to the accessibility of everything on the internet, which is also about storage. We can store so much more stuff now and we all demand access to it all the time. But what I lament—and this might be about museums or it might be about our cultural condition right now—is the loss of expertise. I think there's a myth about our liberation in the information age, that it's going to open us up, make us smarter, more tolerant, less bigoted. In fact, it's almost doing the exact opposite. Search engines, information storage and commerce have unwittingly colluded to give us that which we already know, those people we already like, and that which we've already purchased. Our horizons have been narrowed. So museums have the opportunity to tackle this, in real time and space, by showing us art we aren't familiar with among people we may not already know. And guess what? The art's not for sale! Museums are the antidote to the internet. Let's hope they develop a jamming app that will disable people's smartphones to work while they're in them. We could probably make some money off of that...

AJ: With the internet and digitization, there's this implicit idea that we're just extensions of mechanical frameworks. And we aren't. We really aren't. We're not just complex machines that absorb whatever interface is in front of us.

CR: All of those algorithms that are ostensibly geared toward efficiency are exactly the opposite patterning of what should be happening in our cultural spaces. Our cultural spaces should be anti-efficiency machines. They should be places to get lost in.

NS: Alex, if you could do the Hearn all over again, what would you do differently? And if you had an unlimited budget, what would you imagine for the future of the Hearn?

AJ: We were really proud of the project. I don't think we would have done anything all that materially different except maybe to have made the building even more vertically accessible throughout. It would have been amazing to have turned it into a kind of jungle gym for adults. But alas, there was only so far the safety and building inspectors were willing to go. We might have also built more bars and food spaces. But if we were presented with a larger mandate and budget and could really dream big, we would turn the Hearn into the largest continuous incubator for cultural experimentation in the world. That would mean upgrading the shell of the building so that its entire interior could be occupied year-round by a rotating roster of different cultural organizations—not unlike the idea for the Shed. But the Hearn is just so enormous. It could be, as I said earlier, a museum of museums wherein the very act of cultural display, from performing arts to anthropology to sports to fine art, could all happen in a single volume of enclosed space. That is precisely the kind of delirious space that the world really needs. It captures the essence of life tomorrow and has the potential to be as mutable as the pace of civilization.

Background: Elevation of the Hearn Theatre

STRATEGIES AND IMPACT—How to Start Moving

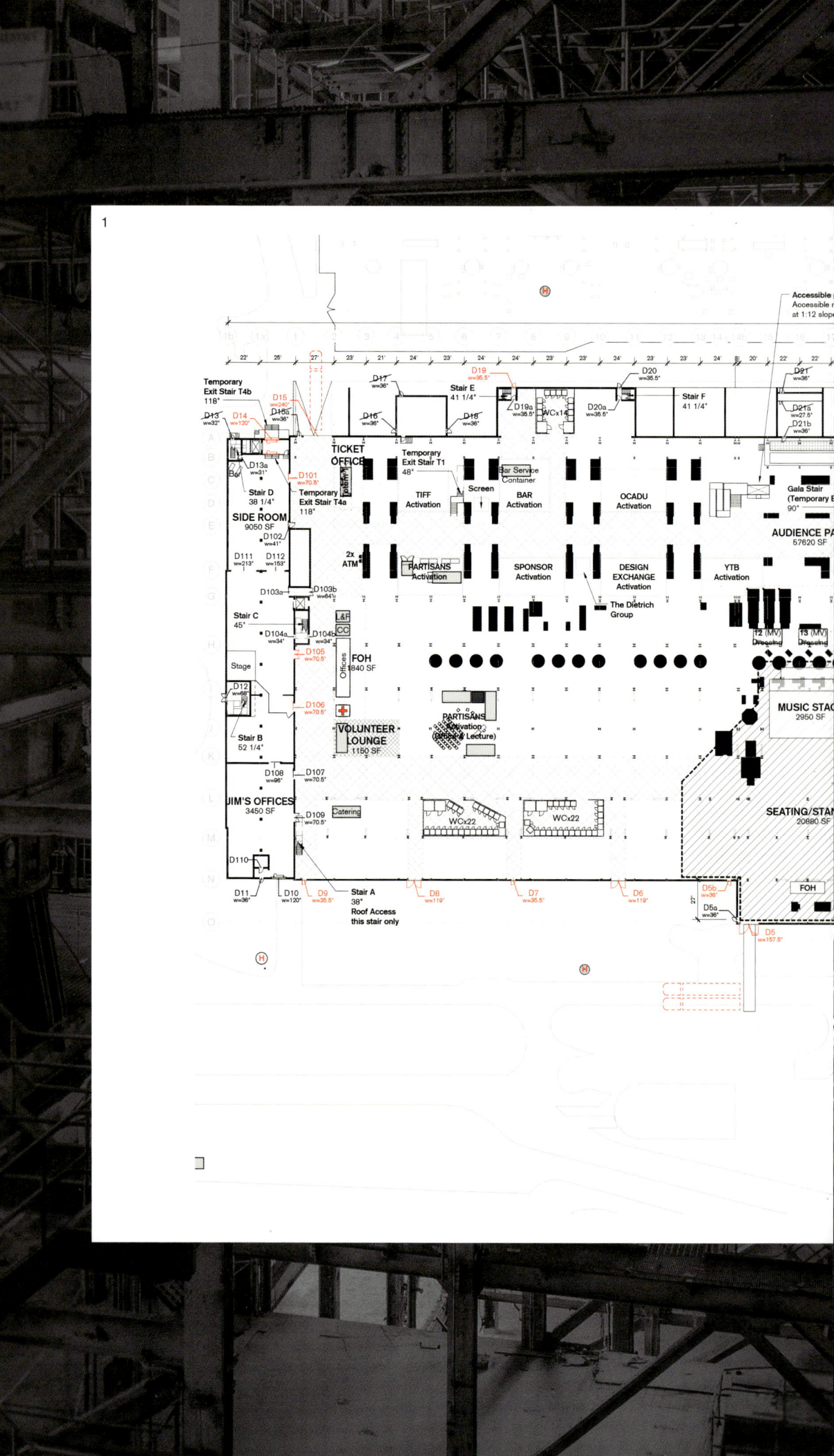

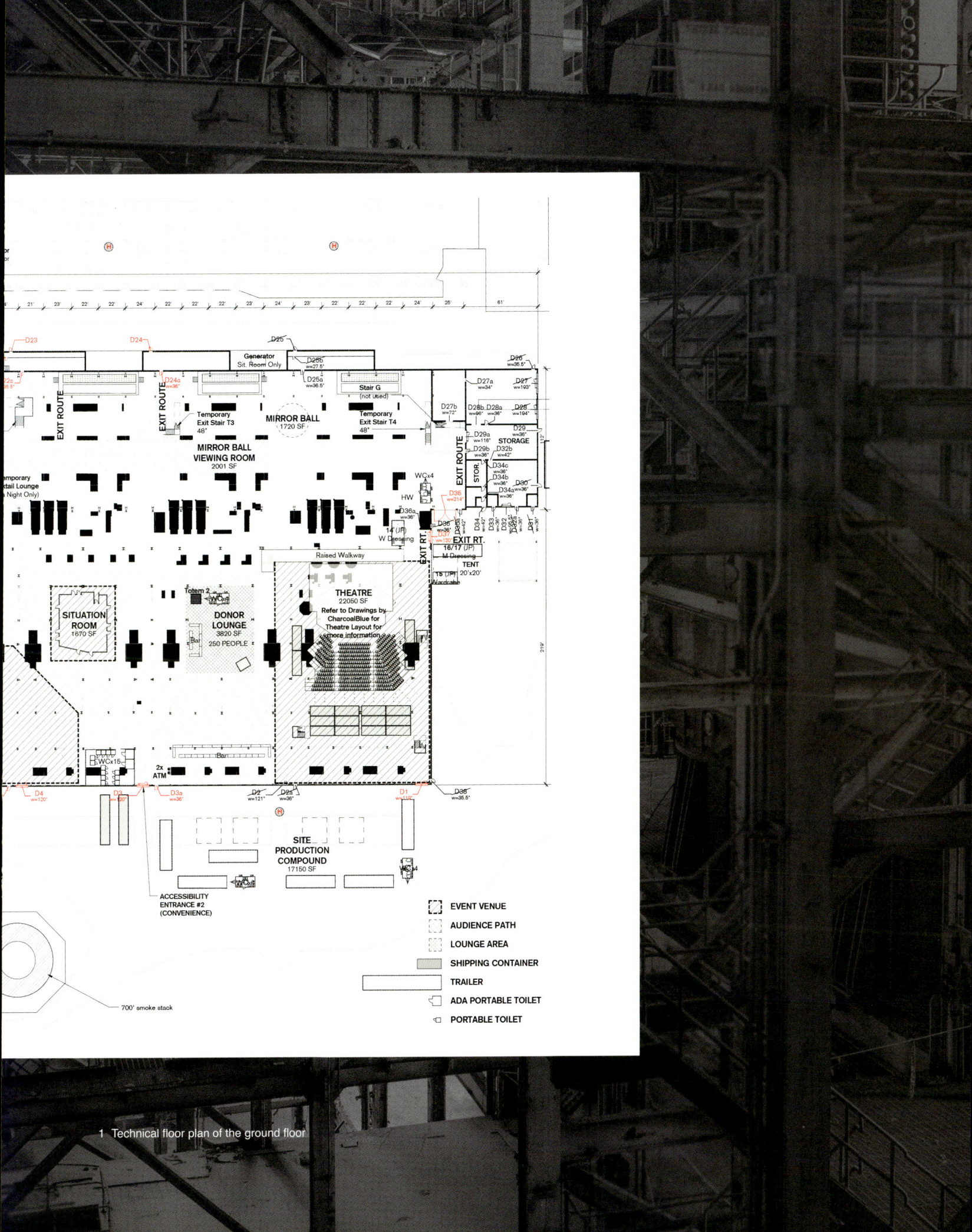

1 Technical floor plan of the ground floor

Why do Temporary Theatres Work?
Jerad Schomer and Clemeth Abercrombie, of Charcoalblue

Temporary theatre has been around in the West at least since the Middle Ages, when pageant wagons took the medieval mystery plays out of European churches and into the town squares and countryside. It has had many heydays and has evolved numerous times: the pageant wagon gave way to the strolling Spanish players; the closing of theatres in seventeenth-century England pushed performance underground into improvised, clandestine spaces; the twentieth-century festival and circus tents became environmental theatre, became site-specific, became pop-up.

Whatever you call it, a temporary theatre has intrigue because of its temporal nature: it won't last long and you don't want to miss it. It has ambition, because it inevitably involves more effort than putting on a show in a purpose-built performance space—at a minimum, you usually have to bring in seats. It has surprise because no one has ever seen a show in it before—audiences don't even get to guess where performers will enter from.

There are several basic questions that must be answered at the beginning of the design process for any temporary performance space:

— Is an enclosure required? Shelter? Ventilation? Heat?
— What exists that we might re-use?
— How will the audience see and hear the performers?
— What materials can be used to create a performance environment in a place not built for it?
— Will the temporary space respond to the surroundings or try to separate from them?
— How much time is available to build it and take it back apart?
— How will we limit the impact of our choice to build a temporary venue, rather than using an existing one, on the environment?
— Importantly: what is the budget?

But really it starts with the program: what will be performed in this temporary space?

There are different expectations from artists and audience alike depending on what is being presented. For a theatre performance, the text can help determine how the theatre form develops. If it is spectacle-driven, a presentational theatre form such as end stage might be more appropriate. If the show is focused on the intimacy of conversation, the shape might edge towards an encircling format to allow more audience proximity to the performers.

For musical and spoken word performance, the design of the space can aid the audience to hear and understand the performers as much as good scenic and lighting design can tell the audience where to look. The auditory experience of a non-theatrical space should inform design choices. The siting of a temporary venue within a larger space can play a role by relying on existing materials and surfaces to carve out a sonic space within a larger room. Materials and surfaces can also be added, which provide audible cues to mimic the proportion and acoustic experience in a purpose-built theatre, without denying the power of the larger space.

The most successful projects become a dialogue between the programming, the site, the production design and the audience format, with each influencing the other. Ideally the show is being designed specifically to fit the site and shape of the temporary space being constructed. Too often, the producers of festivals and temporary theatre rely on existing productions, a rented tent and squared-off modular seating risers to create an audience experience. Hang a couple loudspeakers and you've got all the ingredients for a generic arts festival. With a bit of creativity, and not necessarily more money, more memorable happenings can be created.

1 A depiction of a traditional medieval pageant wagon by Robert Chambers, 1864
2 The Crystal Palace in London during The Great Exhibition in 1851
Background (opposite): Floor plan for Music Stage seating

1 *Twelve Ophelias*, produced by Woodshed Collective at McCarren Park Pool, Brooklyn, NY, 2008
2 Papyrus of the Abydos Passion Play in Egypt, first staged 5,000 years ago and performed in the open
Background (opposite): Elevation of the Turbine Hall with mirror ball

In 2008, there was a production of Caridad Svich's *Twelve Ophelias* performed by the Woodshed Collective in the then-derelict McCarren Park Pool in Brooklyn. The site was an outdoor Works Progress Administration-era Olympic-size swimming pool—the largest pool in New York. To engender intimacy, an immersive (pun unintended) setting was created, with three to four separate scenic settings placed amongst a seated audience on packing blankets and improvised chairs in the centre of the drained pool. The performers moved amongst audience members from scene to scene such that intimate moments were created by proximity and larger, epic visuals were created by using the distance and scale possible in an empty swimming pool with the open sky above. The design of the play both responded to and influenced the use of the pool as a space.

Neighbourhood people who could see into the pool from the balconies of their newly built condos came to see what the fuss was about. Non-theatre people came. It got attention. Crowds started coming early, bringing baskets and bottles of wine to sit on a concrete slab and have a picnic dinner, then watch the show. What started as an audience of a couple dozen friends at the beginning of the run bloomed to hundreds of strangers by the end, with no marketing to speak of. But was it the show that drew them?

It was the setting. It was the adventure. Yes, it was free, and there was beer for sale, but have you ever seen a theatre piece performed in an abandoned pool? Classical music in a railway station? Opera in an armoury? How about industrial noise music in a coal-fired power station? This juxtaposition can provide something new to a performance; it could become a new form, which is perhaps greater than the sum of its parts.

It is no coincidence that the most memorable examples of this type of event are fleeting. They tend to happen in transitional areas and former industrial, or otherwise abandoned, sites. In fact, these experiences and productions can help drive neighbourhood transition. Think of St Ann's Warehouse staging TR Warszawa's *Macbeth* in an abandoned tobacco warehouse under the Brooklyn Bridge. This production cemented the desire for that particular site to be redeveloped for arts use. Ten years later, it is now St Ann's permanent home, and Dumbo has become one of the hottest neighbourhoods in New York City. McCarren Park Pool is also now redeveloped and is a functional swimming pool again for the first time since 1984. It sits at the nexus of two areas on the front edge of the continuous cultural migration across the East River: Greenpoint and Williamsburg. Theatre and music produced in an abandoned pool helped draw people to the area, and they've stayed.

But this story is larger than the gentrification of certain Brooklyn neighbourhoods. The Ruhrtriennale has, since 2002, been creating temporary performance venues for music, theatre, opera and dance in former industrial sites in northern Germany. Some of the sites it uses have now been declared UNESCO World Heritage Sites, preserving long unused modern ruins and bringing them to life. Companies like Punchdrunk in the UK, and Woodshed and Third Rail Projects in New York, have been luring audiences to abandoned factory buildings, disused offices and train tunnels for nearly two decades. Often these sites are available as a result of coming development, either just prior to demolition to make way for something new or to help spark interest in a rehabilitation. The art helps draw interest to the site in much the same way as the unique site draws audiences to the art.

The transformation of the Hearn Generating Station is a similar story. The interest in the industrial area around the Hearn has been growing—it is a huge parcel of lakefront land within biking distance of some of Toronto's most enviable properties. At the centre sits the Hearn, an enormous, derelict coal-fired power plant on the shore of Lake Ontario. Art can once again be a catalyst for the reclamation of under-used, desirable public land by drawing people to an adventurous and unfamiliar site right under their noses.

Likewise, the programming of the Luminato Festival yearned for a connection across a multitude of performances—something to draw them together and add emphasis to the whole. In the summer of 2016, the Luminato Festival inhabited the Hearn for a 17-day-long multidisciplinary arts festival. The framework was a multi-venue performing arts centre without any walls, with productions programmed across time to avoid disruption. This was an innovative approach for any arts festival, one which is more ambitious in many ways than any previous example of a temporary venue—to create an institutional

1 Orchestra-level seating plan for the Hearn Theatre. Designer Charcoalblue
2 Plan drawing of Bayreuth Festspielhaus, conceived by Gottfried Semper as a temporary building
Background (opposite): 3D interior rendering of the Hearn for sound analysis

framework of cross-pollination between audiences by forcing them to collide in a single, open volume. There would be a sizeable formal theatre, a large-scale music venue, an immersive theatre, multiple art galleries, a restaurant, a music club, a beer garden, campground, lobby spaces, restrooms, lounges and a giant mirror ball.

The design of the venues was uniquely crafted to fit in the larger Hearn space. It both responded to and influenced the use of the larger space. They could be transported and built somewhere else, but it wouldn't make much sense. This bespoke character made for a singular experience for the audience, and one which drove conversation around Toronto during the festival. "Have you been to the Hearn Theatre yet? You'd better go see it before it's all over."

Beyond the question of the adventurous and momentary audience experience, designers and planners of temporary spaces do still need to provide quality design which references the training audiences have had through years of attending performances in purpose-built music and theatre venues. To be unique is not enough, and the temporary nature of the venue is no excuse for a sacrifice in sightlines or visibility, auditory clarity or audience comfort.

To be successful, a temporary venue must invest a great deal of time and energy into the quality of design. This seems expensive, but while it's difficult to quantify the adventure factor of a temporary venue, there are ways to economize without huge sacrifice.

Modular, reusable materials can be used and stored for future reconfiguration by producers without resorting to the readily available kit of parts in the typical event rental market. Even a small amount of customization of these elements can provide a wide variety of venue configurations that can respond to various sites. Sites themselves can be chosen that inform and complement the programming, rather than fighting against it. Venues and producers who host temporary performance setups are frequently seeing the benefit of engaging design teams early and commissioning new work which is fully suited to their site. Their investment in some stock elements becomes a toolkit, which design teams can choose to use or not, as befits their production.

Some might ask whether the expenditure of energy and consumable resources for the creation of a temporary event is an environmentally sound choice when purpose-built venues already exist with chairs, a stage and existing lighting positions—particularly if they happen to see the enormous dumpsters being carted out after it's all over. But if we take a step back and hold 'permanent' buildings to the same light, we see that many buildings fail to meet their long-term goal of supporting and interacting with art in a way which is truly beloved by the community. Take the famed David Geffen Hall at Lincoln Center for example—a concert hall which was newly opened in 1962 as Philharmonic Hall (later Avery Fisher Hall), underwent a major renovation just 14 years later in 1976 to address acoustical problems, was renovated again in 1992 for the same purpose and is currently in the process of yet another complete renovation. We see a building which is permanent but requires regular feeding and maintenance—consuming resources which could have been dedicated to the support of a more temporally relevant home, perhaps one which served a current need and artistic vision, rather than a home for music which some believe is more tolerated than loved.

As the cycle of technology quickens and the demands placed on our collective attention increase, the struggle to remain relevant becomes more difficult. In response, our desire to adapt the spaces in which we already perform will likely become more frequent. If we treat the 'temporary' combination of art and space as a viable alternative to the theatre building—one built to last a few weeks or even a few years rather than 50—the pressure to serve an unknown vision of the future is released. If you think you can future-proof your building against artistic ambition, you're wrong. In a temporary environment, resources and energy can be focused on the task at hand; allowing the designers to cull away the safety net of unnecessary elements, or to find that existing structure or landscape which presents the ideal symbiosis for the performance currently envisioned. If we compare the energy spent inhabiting or adapting spaces and building more ethereal installations over the course of 15 years (a plausible life cycle between renovations to a theatre building) to the energy spent on constructing a brick-and-mortar theatre, then the environmental question becomes more difficult to answer.

1 Installing condenser units inside the concrete structures that would become the Luminato Festival's Turbine Hall.

Inspired by the atmosphere of discovery possible in found venues, and perhaps by the questions above, new producing organizations are cropping up worldwide, whose sole purpose is to provide a blank canvas for the creation of temporary auditoriums and other art installations. Projects such as the Shed in New York and the Factory in Manchester take inspiration from the Ruhrtriennale and the Park Avenue Armory. They intend to provide the excitement of a newly configured temporary venue, within a purpose-built shell, with all the technological capability and immense space to fully achieve designers' visions. Time will tell whether these new spaces can produce the magic of a temporary theatre in a found space.

As the long history of temporary performance continues to wind and turn, it is clear that its magic remains as vibrant today as it was before there was any alternative. This fact helps validate the art of combining performance and space as a fruitful ground for creativity. When an audience and performer's environment is completely intertwined with the story that is being told, there is an opportunity for artists to move beyond mere temporary performance into a new art form, one which draws previously unrealized connections between architecture, performance and experience.

Charcoalblue on the Hearn: "A Challenging Site"

The ambition of the Hearn's programming went a step beyond more conventional flexible venues, which typically focus on a single piece of art at a time and dedicate the entire venue to that piece, or, like the Schaubühne in Berlin, allow for multiple pieces of simultaneous programming by closing off sections of the larger venue both visually and acoustically. At the Hearn, the very genesis of the site's design concept was a multi-arts institution with no physical separation whatsoever, where audiences arriving for an evening performance on the Music Stage might see and hear a portion of a matinee performance in the theatre while lingering in an open sculpture gallery. In a way, this was a framework for a new kind of cultural institution; Lincoln Center meets the New Museum and Berghain, but without any walls.

A mostly level concrete-slab floor was punctuated with gravel trenches and mounded piles of broken cement. A forest of steel columns and girders provided a staccato rhythm to the space, which made its completely open volume of 650,000 cubic metres feel even more immense. On one side of the building, an open hall nearly twice the size of Tate Modern's Turbine Hall was dominated by hulking concrete furnace plinths. On the other side, there were four large, open bays in the steelwork of the building, which were the only places where performances on the envisioned scale could occur free of steelwork obstruction.

For the theatre, the best choice was the bay closest to the exterior wall: it would aid in the feeling of acoustic enclosure essential to creating the naturalistic sonic character desired by the National Theatre of Scotland. For the music venue, the large bay opposite the theatre would do nicely. It was in the middle of the space, appropriate for the size of audience expected, and expansive enough to accommodate Rufus Wainwright, the Toronto Symphony Orchestra and the band Sunn O)))—part of the Unsound Festival.

The open bays between these two major venues could accommodate the immersive theatre and a large, open lobby and lounge space. The audiences for each performance would be encouraged to cross-pollinate while walking by and experiencing the open atmosphere of other venues. This was an essential component of Luminato's concept for the site.

Shipping containers were used as an essential building block for the temporary theatre (and incorporated into the site as a whole). An end-stage theatre form with encircling seated balcony boxes was fashioned from customized high-cube containers—a modular device that almost seemed too perfect for this purpose. When stacked, they created a sense of visual enclosure without completely walling off the rest of the venue. It was an industrially themed Georgian theatre, without walls. The corrugated panels of the shipping containers, some of which had been removed to open the balcony boxes, were used as reflective acoustic surfaces, mimicking the hard exterior wall of the building on one side while helping block long echoes from the other side.

Brave New Cultural World
Karen Brooks Hopkins

Major cultural institutions, such as performing arts centres and museums, often reflect the character and dynamism of the particular locations they call home. Large multidisciplinary festivals that feature a variety of works and art forms over a designated time period often do the same, sometimes with even more intensity, because they facilitate a wide range of activities packed into a compressed calendar.

The good news is that cultural centres and presentation formats of all kinds are gaining momentum globally, which hopefully over time will give the entire field enhanced respect for the unique role it plays in building the economies and identities of communities.

In the twentieth century, North American cities often built large cultural centres at the behest of local leaders and elected officials who saw them as status symbols for their jurisdictions. Most of these centres adhered to a similar design and layout no matter where they were located.

Huge edifices constructed mainly of marble, surrounding large fountains on public plazas and housing mainly classical art forms (symphony orchestras, opera and ballet companies) and touring Broadway shows, were the norm. Many of these entities were built defensively, separated from nearby streets and sitting atop parking lots, which allowed audience members to enter and leave without any interaction with the neighbourhood above. Audiences were for the most part older, white and financially prosperous.

As the first decade of the twenty-first century evolved, the concept of public participation in the arts started to change and the idea of creative placemaking began to inform new construction, as well as the adaptive reuse of old buildings to house collections and present theatrical events. Cultural districts formed organically around the world and many of the twentieth-century centres were forced to raise and spend billions of dollars to reinvent themselves for the next generation.

The cultural districts—like the one I helped develop in Brooklyn, where I served as President of the Brooklyn Academy of Music (BAM) from 1999 to 2015—had a different vibe and geography to their twentieth-century predecessors. The Brooklyn Cultural District is anchored by BAM's large, historic, multi-theatre buildings, but also welcomes a variety of smaller organizations as its neighbours. These entities are very diverse in size, disciplinary offerings (visual arts, performing arts, literary arts etc) and ethnicity. They are pulled together by a common streetscape and lighting plan, and sometimes work together on joint programs. Optimally, districts such as this offer many different entry points for all different kinds of people. In essence, the Brooklyn Cultural District was designed to emulate the energy of a twenty-first-century New York with a mix of organizations and a churn of activities on the ground augmented by restaurants and other audience amenities. Apartments, including large amounts of affordable housing and space for local businesses, are located on the floors above the cultural space, and in turn they generate new audiences for arts events.

1 Outdoor fountain, Marcus Center for the Performing Arts, Milwaukee, Wisconsin
2 Outdoor fountain, Lincoln Center, NY
3 Master plan of the West Kowloon Cultural District, Hong Kong, by Foster + Partners
4 Plan for a traditional Luo Homestead in Kenya

10 JUNE

Another excellent example of a highly successful cultural rehab project is AS220, which actually opened in the 1990s but exemplifies the spirit of the twenty-first-century cultural district. Located in Providence, Rhode Island, a city that lost nearly 100,000 of its 250,000 residents after the Second World War, AS220 is an artist-run organization that occupies 100,000 square feet of renovated space on Empire Street in the Downtown area. Its programs and facilities include space for exhibits, performances, classes, media arts, youth programs, studios, a print shop, other labs and open creative space.

Finally, another star in the world of cultural revitalization is artist Theaster Gates working on the South Side of Chicago. Since 2006, Gates has purchased and renovated dozens of abandoned or dilapidated structures, including a bank, a Catholic elementary school and a series of housing entities. The reimagined spaces include cinemas, cafes, studios and a bookstore. Over time, Gates, a force of nature, has stimulated in excess of $42 million of outside investment in the neighbourhood—notwithstanding his own projects. Beyond these dynamic concepts, other new ideas and strategies in cultural regeneration are coming to the forefront every day!

Both the twenty-first-century districts and the twentieth-century centres offer substantial potential for collaboration between nearby resident groups for joint programs, educational services and community outreach. In addition, both models provide opportunities for local businesses to sponsor events and have their executives serve on boards. The cultural district concept targets both new and existing residents as potential members and subscribers. The ultimate goal is to involve everyone (residents, local business owners, developers etc) in the life of the district, but, as we have often observed, as neighbourhoods change they can encourage gentrification. New development sometimes displaces existing tenants and chain stores push out local businesses, destroying the authenticity that defined these districts at their inception.

The tenth anniversary edition of Toronto's Luminato Festival, which took place entirely within the walls and adjacent outdoor arena of the decommissioned Hearn Generating Station, appears to be another iteration and wholly new approach to the creation of a cultural community. The Hearn, a massive, hulking structure located in a largely empty industrial area, represents the perfect alignment of past and present in terms of architecture and experience, activating an abandoned part of the city. The Hearn provided a thrilling, easily navigable way for audiences to participate in multiple events in various venues, including restaurants, clubs and interactive performance spaces, all in one or two days. The Hearn, in a sense, was an entire district contained in one gigantic building. This concept brings audience members together, both as neighbours and as a kind of cultural relay team. The Hearn 'generated' a bond between audience, artists, and venue in a manner that was completely original and that felt 'hand in glove'.

The secret sauce in a setting such as this is to simply leave it in its natural, deteriorated state. Obviously the venue needs to be safe, clean and technically sophisticated, but any major cosmetic changes alter the gritty adventurousness of the endeavour for all participants. The Hearn evoked both the venue's history and future simultaneously, adding to its specialness. Of course, any venue—old or new—is only as good as its programs, and Luminato delivered compelling individual productions across a variety of disciplines.

The concept of a single-venue festival also has limitations. Theatre and concert events must occur sequentially rather than all at once and, for a 'city-wide' festival, this set-up imposes a restriction in that all activities are confined to one location alone. But programmers of truly city-wide festivals have their challenges as well, striving to establish an identity and a centre when events take place over a wide geographic swath. The Hearn model both served as a centre and offered a variety of venues.

While each approach to broad-based artistic presentation has both advantages and problems, there is no question that the time has arrived for the cultural field to take ownership of its well-deserved place, defining the personality and economy of its communities.

Departures from the White Cube
Kitty Scott

Normally, the decommissioned Hearn Generating Station, located to the east of downtown Toronto on the shore of Lake Ontario, is asleep. However, during summer 2016 the Hearn woke up; the massive, imposing brown-brick and cement hulk and its surrounding post-industrial landscape were chosen as the location for an iconic iteration of Luminato, the Toronto arts festival.

Artistic director Jörn Weisbrodt's idea of transforming the Hearn into a dynamic, large-scale, mixed-use venue for Luminato opened up a completely new way of understanding how the city could present the diversity of today's creativity. It was as if a great new institution—housing multiple stages, galleries and a series of environments in which to experience contemporary boundary-crossing experiences, as well as a restaurant—'popped up' for ten days and changed everything.

While this event presented a new model for the performing and visual arts in Toronto, the relationship between this type of building, the post-industrial conditions of the city and contemporary art practice is key to understanding a major change in the conception of new museums throughout Europe and North America. All manner of obsolete buildings—factories, warehouses, hospitals—have metamorphosed into art galleries. The resulting exhibition spaces range from the highly finished, which are virtually indistinguishable from purpose-built museums, to those with an 'unfinished' or raw aesthetic. In their current and most generic form, these large spaces house rooms with white walls, floors made of concrete or wood (sometimes polished or varnished) and ceilings consisting of combinations of skylights and lighting fixtures. The pared-down interiors often 'lie', giving the appearance of the absence, rather than the presence, of an architect: they are made to look as if they have not been designed. The buildings themselves are generally considered to be anonymous and are often located, like the Hearn, in what were once marginal 'elsewheres'.

In its development over the past decades, this category of exhibition space has presented contemporary artists with an option outside the prevailing conventions of the art museum. It was broadly pioneered by a range of artists, particularly those working in the artist-run galleries of the 1960s, and later by dealers and private collectors. But Tate's decision in the early 1990s to convert an obsolete structure, the Bankside Power Station, into the new location for its museum of modern and contemporary art proved that the use of buildings with previous histories could become a model for large-scale cultural institutions.

An abundance of private and public conversions provides precedents for this type of move. In Los Angeles in 1983, architect Frank Gehry turned what was once a police car warehouse into the Temporary Contemporary at MOCA. The spacious De Pont museum, located in a former wool-spinning mill and designed by Benthem Crouwel Architects, opened in Tilburg in the Netherlands in 1992. Belgian collectors Anton and Annick Herbert display their highly regarded private collection of contemporary art, including work by Gerhard Richter, Dan Graham and Giovanni Anselmo, under the fluorescent lights of a modified industrial complex. The now defunct Hallen für Neue Kunst in Schaffhausen, which once housed the collection of Urs and Christel Raussmüller, is frequently cited as an ideal model, with a raw industrial setting highly sympathetic to the minimal, conceptual and Arte Povera work that had been displayed within. Richard Gluckman, known for his conversions on behalf of commercial and private galleries in New York, transformed a Pittsburgh warehouse into the Andy Warhol Museum in 1994. Finally, artist Robert Irwin and the architects of OpenOffice collaborated to rehabilitate a Nabisco box-printing factory on the Hudson River into Dia:Beacon in 2003.

How, then, did these outdated, old-fashioned, sometimes even derelict buildings come to be recognized as appropriate settings for modern and contemporary art? The answer seems to lie in a combination of the long European tradition of building reuse and the

postwar American trend for artists to occupy former industrial spaces. In New York, as early as the 1950s, being an artist was synonymous with having a studio in an industrial building in the districts of SoHo or Tribeca. Artists such as Robert Rauschenberg, Mark Rothko and Agnes Martin were attracted to large, cheap downtown spaces with big windows and skylights. Eventually art dealers and other businesses followed. By 1962, Andy Warhol had moved into a midtown studio nicknamed 'The Factory', and in 1968 Donald Judd bought 101 Spring Street, a factory building in SoHo that he converted into spaces for eating, working and sleeping. It was here that Judd conceived the idea of large permanent installations; 101 Spring Street became the basis for his later experiments in Marfa, Texas.

In Europe, though, there is another history: that of recycling buildings, transforming them from private to public spaces. Such changes were, especially in France, linked to the democratization of culture and were emblematic of the Enlightenment. The Louvre, of course, was once a palace. The British Museum was once housed in Montagu House, a former private residence. These different histories, the European and the American, first intersect with respect to contemporary art practice in spaces such as the Villa Menafoglio Litta Panza, in Varese, Italy, where the Italian collector Giuseppe Panza converted its former stables to house his collection. Panza did not hire an architect; instead, he and the artists involved made sure the walls were well-finished and painted white and the floors restored. During the late 1960s and early 1970s, Panza was one of a very few individuals collecting sculptures, paintings and installations by minimal and conceptual artists, from Judd and Dan Flavin to James Turrell and Bruce Nauman. For the most part, works by these artists required a specific type of space: a simple, minimal white room. It was crucial that the spectator view and experience the work in its environment. Meaning hinged on the complex interrelationship of these three inseparable elements.

There exists a cavalier use of the word 'neutral' in discussions of museum and gallery spaces. Not surprisingly, the neutrality of the converted industrial space is regularly cited as a rationalization for why artists, dealers, collectors and gallery professionals are drawn to it. Yet, as artist Richard Serra and others have emphatically stated, "there is no neutral site". It appears from a study implemented by Tate during the period before the Bankside came into being that many contemporary artists prefer spaces with an obvious previous history to those of the purpose-built museum. The brief for Tate's competition to select an architect for the development of Bankside stated that one of artists' preferences was for "daylit conversions of existing buildings, where architectural intervention [is] minimal". Judd is exemplary in this respect: in the high, wide-open rangeland of Marfa, he established, with the help of the Dia Art Foundation, an influential complex for living, working and permanently displaying his and other artists' work. Disenchanted with the museum world of New York, he bought an old military base—barracks, airplane hangars, artillery sheds—

1 Workshop for *Overture* for *KA MOUNTAIN and GUARDenia Terrace* in Robert Wilson's loft on 147 Spring Street, SoHo, NY
2 Chinati Foundation, Marfa, Texas

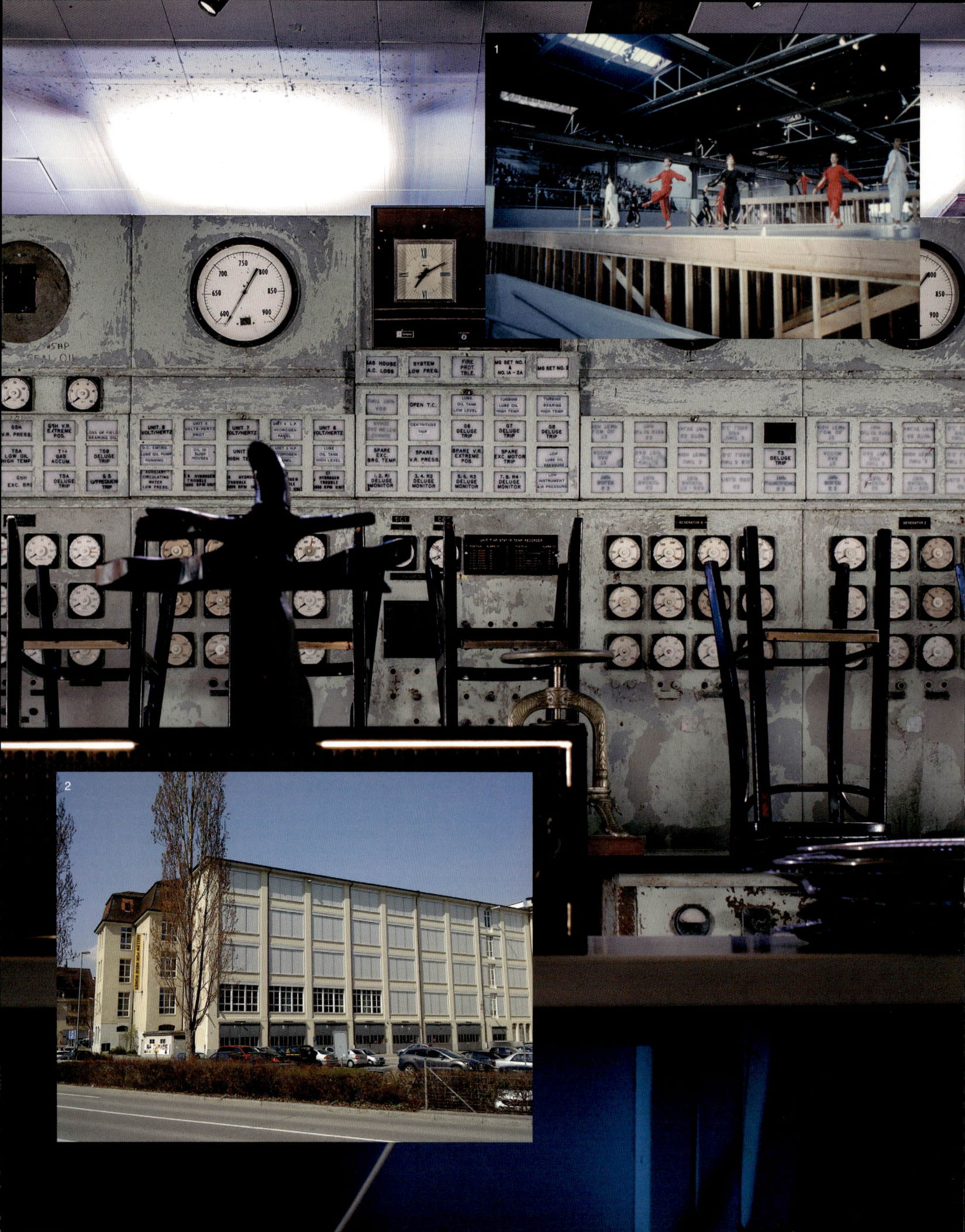

and in the early 1970s began the process of converting some of it into vast exhibition spaces appropriate for permanent, large-scale installations of his minimalist art. This group of buildings and outdoor installations, now called the Chinati Foundation/La Fundación Chinati, is one of the largest unchanging collections of contemporary art in the world.

In the late 1960s, Germain Bazin, a past curator at the Louvre, wrote that new museum buildings were an exception in Europe and that one of the advantages of a recycled building was that it "affords an opportunity of installing works of art in an authentic period setting". While Bazin was referring to eighteenth-century palazzi, his words might still be applied to Bankside, since a precise "period setting" for much, though by no means all, contemporary art is an industrial one. Many works, even those made by artists who have what is known as a 'post-studio' practice, continue to be made in industrial spaces, whether they are produced in studios or by commercial fabricators. These are sometimes first exhibited in commercial or artist-initiated galleries, which are often in ex-industrial settings.

At this time, converted industrial space is very much part of the way we see contemporary art. This once remote 'other' space has been appropriated and institutionalized. Much of the contemporary beauty of Marfa lies precisely in its dry desert landscape and great distance from any official museum or large city. Although the Hearn is quite close to the bright, new city of Toronto, it is faraway in terms of its appearance; it is more a ruin, a relic or a fossil of our repressed industrial past. The flat, exposed landscape surrounding the building—composed of low brush, trees, gravel and tarmac—emphasizes its degraded and worn character. What further distinguishes the recent iteration of the Hearn from other industrial conversions is the approach to the site. Whereas most conversions result in permanent venues made up of distinct purpose-built spaces dedicated to various art forms, seeking, like the traditional museum, to create an autonomous space, Weisbrodt's approach to the Hearn was open and fluid. Rather than an architecture that created a definitive boundary or frame around the work, he looked to shape a place where art forms would cross over and be in continuous dialogue.

If art from the last 20 years or so has frequently found its home in the sort of renovated spaces enumerated above, more recent work is seeking a different kind of environment. On a site near the Hearn, within a forgotten field of concrete rubble, weeds and gravel, artist Pierre Huyghe contributed to Luminato by placing a statue of a reclining woman, an unremarkable object but for the beehive that entirely obscures its head. *Untilled (Liegender Frauenakt)*, 2012, daringly opened up the artwork to interaction, not just with the visiting public but with a whole ecosystem: the bee colony pollinated surrounding flora and extended the work beyond an anthropocentric definition of art.

As contemporary science recognizes that animals possess more and more of the capabilities formerly thought of as uniquely human, and as technology produces machines ever more capable of mimicking human thought and actions, we find ourselves questioning the boundaries between "live things and inanimate things, made and not made"—to quote Huyghe's description of his materials for *Untilled (Liegender Frauenakt)*. This headless sculpture with its cloud of swarming bees is both an uncanny index of our shifting cultural landscape and an assertion of the remarkable beauty to be found in our new, strange world.

1 The Temporary Contemporary, Los Angeles, with *Available Light* performance by Lucinda Childs with a set by Frank Gehry
2 Hallen für Neue Kunst, Schaffhausen, Switzerland

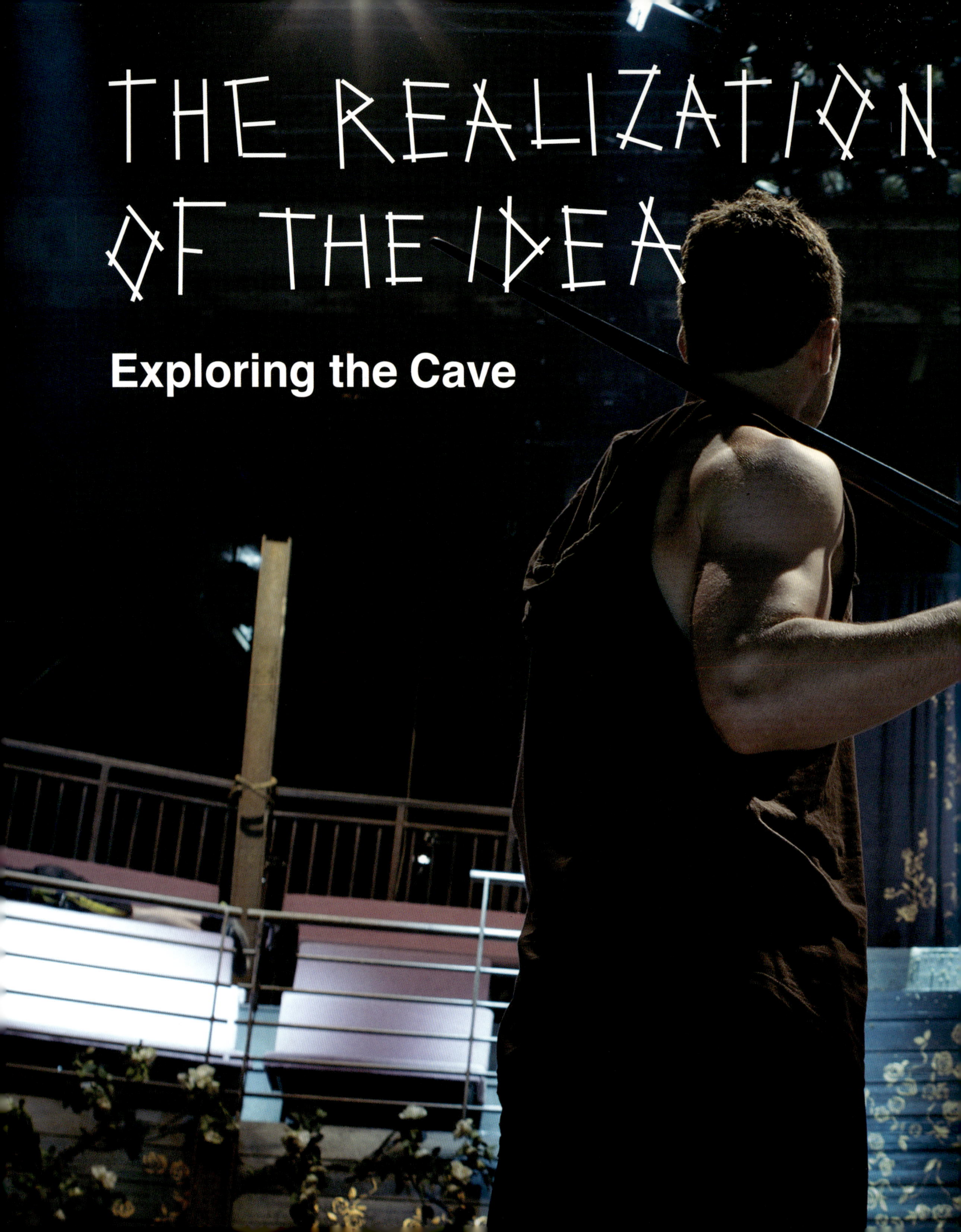

THE REALIZATION OF THE IDEA

Exploring the Cave

1 Cris Derkson performing during *Iftar at the Hearn*
2 Guests at *Iftar at the Hearn*
3 Volunteers handing out programs to festival audience members.
4 Visitors to the Hearn

Gathering Citizens
Adrienne Clarkson

As for me, I loved the Hearn Generating Station from the first time I stepped inside it. I felt that I was inside a Piranesi etching, with the endless staircases and fantastic turns into a ceiling that never seemed to end—the darkness, the light, the shafts of dust were enormously appealing. It was as Marguerite Yourcenar wrote of Piranesi's 'imaginary prisons' that they represent the "negation of time, incoherence of space, suggested levitation, intoxication of the impossible, reconciled or transcended". In other words, they have the same quality of either dreams or nightmares. I was not at the Hearn the first time Luminato presented something there. I heard about it: that there was mud on the floor, there were sequins and strobe lights everywhere, and the electronic music resounded perfectly. I learned what it was to go into this labyrinth with its tricky perspectives and its crowding of huge spaces, which seems to be built on things as Yourcenar says "of calculations which we know to be exact and which bare on proportions which we know to be false".

I had to wait a year until I decided that I would go every single day to the Hearn, no matter what was happening, because it had become for me the destination of destinations. Situated where it is, actually below Toronto and out in the lake somewhere in that vague area called the Port Lands, it is in a no man's land, not only geographically but emotionally. It is a space that somebody who has lived in Toronto for 60 years still could not imagine really existed. And yet, I have to remember that when I first arrived in Toronto to go to university, the Hearn had only been built a few years previously and was fully functioning. And what kind of function! Burning all that coal in order to give extra energy so that people could make as much toast as they wanted in the morning and plug electric kettles in for their Nescafé, or watch the evening news before they went to bed. What could be more important to modern life than this peak effort!?

Driving out through the wilderness and wasteland into an area where Pier Paolo Pasolini could have been murdered (I have seen the place where he was murdered outside Rome and it looks exactly like the lands around the Hearn) gave me the feeling that I was gaining access to a vision which was hellish but somehow compelling. It is a space beyond our known territory. It is a space to be created and recreated.

During the life of Luminato, the Institute for Canadian Citizenship, of which John Ralston Saul and I are co-chairs and co-founders, always had a citizenship ceremony attracting huge crowds to the Luminato hub. I didn't know what it would be like this year, but I thought it would be very interesting to welcome new citizens into this context of a no man's land which could become everybody's land. I know there were people who had doubts about it because it looked somewhat sleazy, and whatever opinions Canadians have of themselves, sleazy is not one of the adjectives they wish to apply to themselves. I knew it was going to happen between a *biergarten* and an Airstream trailer situated on acres of accidental grass and casual rubble. I'm always willing to suspend judgment until I see what happens.

The Institute for Canadian Citizenship has as its mission to give new Canadians, from the day they swear their oath to Canada to become citizens, a feeling they can get hold of what this country is about, plug into its culture and its excitement and start contributing by participating, volunteering and voting. I always thought of Luminato as the ideal partner for this, because Luminato itself is so determined to give voice to all aspects of human creation. Terence, the Roman playwright who began his life as a slave from North Africa, said something which has become my motto: "I am human; nothing human is alien to me." I take this very seriously because I think to live in the kind of Canada which we have created and to which I have devoted my personal and public life, we have to look at human beings in all their aspects, and respect and regard each other in all our diversity.

We welcome everybody in the world to this country and we have been doing so for the past four or five decades with the greatest success. We weren't always like this;

we rejected and despised many in the past—Chinese, Japanese, Jews, Italians and Ukrainians. On the other hand, we were accepting vast numbers of immigrants from the end of the nineteenth century on. This collision of action and ideals actually worked out very well for us because we emerged from it as a country that is as welcoming and open as any in the world today. It has been to our benefit; we have prospered under it. Canadians aren't perfect people but we have learned from our mistakes, stumbling through moral thickets of darkness and thorns in order to arrive at a relatively well-lit, clear space—in fact, much like the clearing in which the Hearn finds itself. Not beautiful, but expansive and open. A space where anything can, and does, happen.

It is important for us to understand that in order for us to have any civilized and democratic society we have to trust each other. The artistic message of Luminato has always been that we will trust a festival like this with its boldness and its willingness to risk. It appeals to the young and courageous because it is like them, and to the old and conservative because they should know. It's helped us to build trust, and by moving into this building, which is exciting but by no means dilapidated (just look at how good the pointing is on the brickwork!), we understand that this building isn't about to fall down, even though it is immense and unused. And, in a way, it's a symbol of the fact that we have that trust in each other in very solid brick. Brick is THE building material of Toronto, and has been ever since devastating fires in the nineteenth century, culminating in 1904, forced through building codes to make brick the dominant aesthetic of this lakeside city.

When trust has disappeared from the public sphere, rot and breakdown set in. I take the Hearn to symbolize something that has not been broken down, even though it has been disused. And this idea of trust makes us feel that we can trust each other and listen to each other even when things are said, sung and envisioned for us that we would never have dreamed of for ourselves. But I like the Hearn, for the fact that it was giving us some level of wariness, which we as citizens must never lose. Even when we trust each other we should always be wary that something can change, in a moment, in a blinking of an eye. This kind of necessary distrust is wonderful for creative artists because it means that they have to prove themselves as worthy of being watched, listened to and dreamed with.

A place like the Hearn is not a purpose-built pleasure palace. It is not part of that 'if you build it, they will come' urban dream. It is intensely gritty and difficult and symbolizes a kind of indomitable hope. That huge smokestack! Those six-storey walls without a break! Those vast openings into a yawning Turbine Hall, which made you feel as though you were in an Egyptian tomb, walking freely under the Gardiner Expressway or part of a subterranean city where only colossi could live! In a way, this very much represented to me the way one feels coming to a new country, especially like I did—as a refugee, as a person with no place, a human being with no belongings. It seems to me that this place can play a fundamental role in our image of ourselves. It's in wonderful condition, really, apart from the fact that there is no domestic floor. But nothing falls down on your head and it is protected from the rain and elements. It is also a welcoming environment because it gives shelter that does not impose itself any more than it must to stay standing. This is what a festival that is in a city like ours needs.

Toronto is a city of five million people, with 52 per cent of its population not born in Canada. In this city, you don't have to talk very much about what it means to be uprooted and to be thrown somewhere else. In the majority of people's psyches, they either had the experience themselves or are only one generation removed from having the feeling of being taken away from where they were born to be situated in an utterly different environment. The kind of immigration that we have been having over the last 50 years comes from places so different to Canada that virtually everybody who comes here has to make a huge adjustment. Before 1960, our immigration was mainly from Europe and basically Caucasian, and we could pretend to ourselves that we were just getting more and more people 'like us'. That's no longer the case and we all recognize it. At any one of our citizenship ceremonies, where 49 people are getting their citizenship, they come from an average of 26 different countries. Over 80 per cent of the people who first come here as landed immigrants decide to take up Canadian citizenship. They do this not because they will be among people like them, but because they are willing to participate in what we all feel unconsciously is one of the great experiments in the

1–3 Nai Syriant Children's Choir performing during *Iftar at the Hearn*

13 JUNE

14 JUNE

1 First Nations hoop dancer Nimkii Osawamick performing with Cris Derkson and Jesse Baird during *Iftar at the Hearn*
2 Ojibwe Elder Duke Redbird welcoming Syrian newcomers to Toronto during *Iftar at the Hearn*

world: a society where people come from somewhere else and create something strong, democratic and truly interesting.

When I look back at the ten years of Luminato that I have enjoyed, I think of some of the highlights; I remember Salā Lemi Ponifasio's *Stones in Her Mouth*, which was an interpretation of the earth and its movements seen through Maori and South Pacific influences, put on by New Zealanders, Samoans and other people from the South Pacific region. It is no stranger and no less familiar than having Tanya Tagaq, the Inuit throatsinger, collaborate on music with the Kronos Quartet. Very tellingly, they took colours to be their guide and their collaboration had a life of its own, in which northern sounds became created on the violin in the situation of openness and mutual excitement.

Luminato has never been just about bringing the best, most interesting things to a city like Toronto: it has also always been about putting things together which would never have been put together. Just like our kind of citizenship. Just like our kind of country. Like hearing Joni Mitchell talk about Emily Carr (who knew!) and saying how she had been so influenced by the feeling of the spirit within the images of trees and rocks in Carr's paintings. How she felt that Carr and her tight, terse prose were able to help her with the processing of her own musical work. Seeing Marina Abramović in Robert Wilson's *The Life and Death of Marina Abramović* exhorts us to understand what beginnings and endings could be. And then, through the artists who have come back a number of times over the festival's ten-year history (Laurie Anderson and Kid Koala, to name just two) we are given familiarity and a sense of security.

I was asked by a lot of people who knew I was going to the Hearn every day if I felt safe there. I can honestly say that it never occurred to me to ask the question, and I think that's the answer. Sometimes I have felt a little unsafe at the corner of Queen and John on late Saturday nights even with other people, but I never felt unsafe at the Hearn. Perhaps that is also an analogy for the kind of country that Canada is, with its great sense of protectiveness. Because it is so large, so diverse in its landscape, so huge in its expanse, so challenging in its climate. This is what the Hearn symbolized to me and what I felt about it.

As a peaking plant, taking care of people's needs for toast or for television, it could perform its function for a brief period when we could use fossil fuels that way. Now, it doesn't do that and it can't do it. But it could perform another function for us, as a city, as a country. It symbolizes something that can no longer be done and doesn't need to be done, thank goodness. It is really about us and how we are as citizens in a large, covered space together.

One night, when I was there singing with Choir! Choir! Choir! as we rehearsed to sing "Hallelujah" with Rufus Wainwright, I felt part of a group of 1,500 people who didn't know each other and who were divided only by their vocal ranges: high, middle and low. I moved during rehearsals (we rehearsed three or four times very intensely for an hour) from high to mid, and each time I was with a different group of people who jostled and sang. It's one of the few times in my life when I have been relatively happy in a crowd and not distressed by not having my own personal space. When the moment came for Rufus to join us, we were all prepared in our own way. I don't think we could have gotten any better, and I don't think we would have gotten any worse, even if we'd sung it ten times with him. It all came together in the most wonderful way: full of life, generosity and a kind of radiant peace. I knew nobody in any of the groups that I joined in the rehearsals or the performance. I have rarely enjoyed myself as much as during those two hours. Perhaps it was that the night before I had spent a number of hours listening to Unsound—the full light show and the music which had found its perfect home. You couldn't get me into any club playing that type of music—I wouldn't be able to really hear it. It's not a matter of my ears, but I think it's not suited to being played in clubs; it's suited to being played at the Hearn, and all 5,000 people at the Hearn felt that. And that's what we are: living in Canada as the citizens of a country in which we can contribute everything that we are, and where we have a level of neutral trust and generosity towards each other. Perhaps the Hearn is only a symbol, but in any case it's one that is worth working on. It is a symbol that has a real meaning for us as Canadians.

Toronto Needs the Hearn to Remind It of Itself
Shawn Micallef

Toronto is a city of illusions.

We call our electricity 'hydro', a most pleasant euphemism that belies where our power actually comes from. In the province of Ontario there's a great mythology around electricity production that goes back a century to when politician Adam Beck advocated for a publicly owned electrical grid fed by hydroelectricity, generated by the water-driven turbines at Niagara Falls and other Ontario waterways. Today the generating stations at the falls are named after Beck and the founding mythology is still strong, even though only under a quarter of the province's power comes from hydro, the rest generated in updated versions of the Hearn Generating Station. Nuclear accounts for over half of Ontario's power generation, with gas, wind and, until recently, coal fuelling the rest. Yet the idea of hydro endures.

The landscape in Toronto is also untrustworthy. It's hard to know if the ground we're standing on is 'original', manipulated or even wholly created by humans: the city is full of buried creeks; the waterfront edge has been extended out into the lake for over a century; and there are grass-covered hills with ski lifts on them that used to be garbage dumps. The line between real and unreal is so blurry it doesn't matter anymore, as long as the ground is firm.

In typical Toronto fashion, the Port Lands district the Hearn was built on is also artificial, made from the rubble created by the growing city; recycling the city itself for even more city. Toronto is a place that has always been growing fast. Too fast for some, not fast enough for others. All cities reach a point where they choose to boldly go forward or fall behind. Toronto has had chaotic politics of late; the subways and streetcars are jammed, and the roads are often gridlocked. This is a long moment to think big or succumb to our success. Cities that don't have these problems and opportunities—and there are many that don't—wish they did. It's the burden of growth and prosperity that great cities carry.

The Hearn is a good place to think about all of that.

In the future, the city's infrastructure is going to be smaller, more invisible and microchip-sized, but more powerful than ever before. The Hearn represents a kind of visible, analogue power and infrastructure that was so raw it ran on chunks of coal dug up from the earth. Running a city has always required herculean efforts to keep it going, even if we can't see it happening.

The Portlands Energy Centre, a relatively new 550-megawatt natural gas electrical generating station next door to the Hearn, kicks into operation when there's a need for more power to make our air conditioners, laptops and phones work. You can see it and the Hearn from the city's near east end, both of them sitting there across the turning basin, the magnificent artificial body of water created for the St Lawrence Seaway. The Port Lands were once the Ashbridge's Bay marsh, the biggest wetland on Lake Ontario and the delta of the Don River that drained a massive watershed. But, beginning in the 1880s, the marsh was gradually filled in, first with livestock waste and refuse from the nearby Gooderham and Worts distillery, and later with cleaner fill. The mouth of the Don was contained, put into a canal-like channel, and rerouted into the harbour. All of this happened just a few kilometres from downtown Toronto.

In anticipation of the creation of the St Lawrence Seaway that would allow ocean-going vessels passage into the Great Lakes, the Toronto Harbour Commission created the Port Lands for shipping traffic that ultimately never came, as it was easier to unload goods in Montreal or even Halifax. The vast project also created land for factories and other manufacturing concerns but deindustrialization in the late twentieth century saw many of these disappear. Toronto is left with a massive tract of fallow urban landscape, a place where failed Olympic bids have been pinned and new communities dreamed of. The turning basin, where the massive ships would rotate in order to exit the port, is Toronto's great inland lake that might one day be part of something magnificent, the jewel of whatever this post-industrial part of town turns into.

1 Richard L Hearn Generating Station brochure produced by Ontario Hydro when the station opened in 1951

152 Into the Culture Cave

1 Turbine under construction at the Hearn, May 1951

Yet as we live more electronic and ephemeral lives, and as the Port Lands becomes a much less industrial place as plans to renaturalize the Don and create housing materialize, maybe we should still be able to see where some of the raw power that keeps our intimate and essential devices running comes from, to remind us it isn't all magic, that it's still a herculean thing. Though dramatically cleaner and more efficient than other types of fossil fuel plants, the Portlands Energy Centre encountered considerable resistance when planned a decade ago, revealing the great urban conundrum of a need for great amounts of power, but an unwillingness to see or be near where it comes from. The Hearn is from a dirtier time and is a testament to how quickly new technology makes big, not-so-old things obsolete, but both generating stations together demonstrate our never ending consumption of power.

The new plant next door to the Hearn is petite in comparison, and it doesn't have the cinematic and romantic appeal of the Hearn, a monument to Toronto's growth and to the foresight of planning for the future with gusto, building the kind of infrastructure needed to keep the city going. Just as the Hearn was built while its decommissioning was being planned, the creation of the Port Lands was an economic crapshoot, hoping Seaway traffic would bring the city more riches. Yet the city kept growing despite that setback: Toronto is a provisional city and always has been, pivoting and lurching to accommodate new directions and new people. The city is perpetually nervous about its growth: are there 'too many condos', are there 'too many people', it's so 'congested'. The complaints are endless; the fear a reaction to an unknown future.

Since the Second World War, Toronto has seen almost non-stop explosive growth, save for a handful of major recessions here and there, devouring what was once prime farmland less than a dozen kilometres from downtown into a thick urban city, all in living memory. Urbanity is moving closer to the Port Lands all the time, of late converting the formerly industrial West Don Lands into residential and commercial areas, expanding the city ever further.

Next will be these Port Lands. Think again of the turning basin and the long shipping canal that connects it to the harbour: in a few decades residential and commercial buildings will ring it if Toronto isn't afflicted with some economic calamity. The post-industrial scrubland around the Hearn won't be there forever. The film studios and concrete plants there now may stay for some time, but they'll more than likely move somewhere else with more open space to suit their needs.

South of the Port Lands is the Leslie Street Spit, another artificial chunk of land, Toronto's own Dubai-like peninsula extending into the water, but instead of a quick industrial-to-urban transformation, it's a place of slow-growth nature. Even as it still grows—every day of the week sees more trucks unloading more rubble from growing Toronto—it has become a natural habitat for birds and wildlife due to the efforts of the Toronto and Region Conservation Authority that oversees both its growth and naturalization. "Please Brake for Snakes", read the signs on the road to the tip of the Spit, a remarkable kind of plea not far from the downtown of the fourth biggest municipality in North America.

This wild refuge will be next to the most urbane of places when the Port Lands are finished, continuing the town-and-country mix Toronto has with the vast ravine system that meanders its way through nearly every neighbourhood in the city and suburb. The development means space for new people, the people who keep coming to Toronto, as they always have; if we don't keep building, it will become both unaffordable and boring, a place only for the rich and their pursuits. It has to be done right though and kept intentionally affordable.

There needs to be a little roughness left over too. That's what is so magnificent about the area now: it's one of the last unmanicured, feral and artificially organic (if such a thing is possible) parts of Toronto left. Spare a thought too for the small boat clubs between the Hearn and Cherry Beach that provide affordable lake access to people who can't afford a yacht and berth of their own at one of the expensive clubs around town. The Port Lands already provide so much.

The only constant in this city is that it's always changing but occasionally we build something that might, that could, that should endure. The Hearn is one of those things. There are others around the city, some more historic than others, but this temple of

provisional modernity is the biggest of all. The Hearn is a magnificent building in its own right, designed with elegance and grandeur, especially next to the metal shed that is the Portlands Energy Centre. Yet it's doubly important because the Hearn is part of a fleeting industrial landscape in Toronto that is almost gone and forgotten, a reminder of the kind of city this was until recently. Reminders of demonstratively working class Toronto connect with Toronto's current, very much hidden, working class—today tucked away in suburban industrial parks or employed in the service industry where the visual representation of work is much different to that in industrial days. The Hearn, simply by existing, tells Toronto's story as much as the CN Tower, City Hall and the downtown skyline do.

For inspiration to be bold and confident as it heads into the future, Toronto should look to the Hearn. It was temporary but built solid and monumental. If Pink Floyd were from Toronto they would tether their giant pigs to this building and put it on album covers. The urban thinker Jane Jacobs—who made Toronto her home for 40 years because, in part, all the change was exciting to her—said new ideas need old buildings. For three years Luminato inhabited this coarsest of places and brought it to life in a short period of time—nearly overnight in urban revitalization terms—turning this forgotten relic into a place that everybody was talking about, one that got people to move out of their usual geography and go somewhere new for culture and experience.

The Hearn is new but also old now, waiting for its next life. We need it, but right now it needs all of us. Look around it and remember the massive space inside that Luminato filled with performers, giant disco balls and immersive installations. Walk the invented land it sits on, all of it a notion that became reality because people wanted it to happen a century ago, people who believed in the future of this city and willed this entire landscape into being.

Toronto is forever trying to catch up to the city it is becoming. Its infrastructure, its built form, always lags behind the spirit and economy of the place. The Hearn was an attempt to catch up on the infrastructure side, but if opened to the public permanently it could become a place where the city catches up to the culture that its people have created. Luminato was a brief expression of that culture, and people came by the thousands.

The Hearn needs you to make some noise about it now. Tell people it matters to you, that you want it kept public and that you demand it become something extraordinary. Tell people what you want it to be; what you want it, and the land around it, to evolve into.

Don't worry about it being the right idea or the best idea, it just needs the energy of your ideas, your affection and your excitement, to make sure it stays part of the city's future that we can all share.

You're thinking about this old building at the beginning of its new life.

1 Sketch by Jack Diamond of the Side Room at the Hearn

THE REALIZATION OF THE IDEA—Exploring the Cave

Here Before the Hearn
Falen Johnson

The land the Hearn Generating Station stands on has been cared for by many different people. Some, but not all of these people, came from the Wendat, the Anishinaabe, the Haudenosaunee and most recently and specifically the Mississauga Nations. These nations of people all had unique and different customs, languages, traditions and relationships with one another, and these relationships between nations were consistently changing and shifting over the thousands of years they hunted, fished, trapped and traded in the area.

The common bond these people share now is displacement. European settlement forced the original people out of the area of Toronto. Some have now returned, but the life that once was has certainly changed.

It can be hard to think of the land we stand on before we stood on it. The sounds of the city deafen our footsteps on the ground. It is easy to forget where our feet land.

The history of Toronto—and not just here, of everywhere—can be difficult to grasp. Monuments of stone and metal are erected to state that 'we were here'. The original people passing through this area and living here didn't create monuments like this. Indigenous monuments are waterways and forests; they are the land and the places we bury our ancestors.

When we look at Old City Hall in downtown Toronto we see almost 120 years of the city, of life, of civilization. But when we look at the Don River which runs through Toronto, many people don't see a monument. We don't see what once was an essential resource, a source of economy and life; we see a destroyed river.

Discussion about the history of Toronto (and of Canada) tends to drift towards a sterilized version of post-contact. We are just beginning to acknowledge the foundation of this country in many ways. And it is hard. Admission of what happened here can be difficult, but in order to move forward it is necessary.

But let's talk about here as specifically as we can. Toronto is here. Toronto is old. Older than the word. It has been called many things by many people. It has been called a meeting or gathering place, and a place of plenty. The current title of this space, Toronto (or *tkaronto* as it was called by the Mohawk people), translates to 'where the trees stand in the water'.

So, why did so many people pass through here? What makes this space so special? Why here?

Toronto, like many large cities in the world, is not an arbitrary space. People come and stay in spaces like these because they serve multiple purposes. Indigenous people first came to Toronto for a very deliberate reason: the water. Water is essential to the development of this place. During the last ice age over 12,000 years ago, melting glaciers formed a giant lake which would eventually recede to form what is commonly known as the Great Lakes.

Both Indigenous and non-Indigenous peoples saw the importance of the area that is now Toronto. John Graves Simcoe, a British settler who has been spoken of as the founder of Toronto, set up a fort in the area because of the land's proximity to water.

Waterways in Toronto, including lakes, rivers and streams, all travel from the north and empty into Lake Ontario. This afforded the people efficient travel, as well as a lot of fish. Transport means trade, and trade means forts, and forts mean economy. Cities like New York, St Petersburg, Hamburg, Boston and New Orleans were all built in similarly marshy areas. This is no mistake.

Numerous waterways run through Toronto: the Don River, Taylor Creek and the Humber River are the major ones, but there are smaller waterways as well. All of these bodies of water were essential to life in the city. Most of these waterways were diverted underground because they had become polluted or they were deemed inconvenient for urban development. The water still runs; it is now just unseen as it drains underground into sewers and storm drainage systems.

The area surrounding the Hearn was once marsh, as was most of the waterfront area of Toronto. When Toronto's subway was built in the 1940s, the earth that was excavated to create the tunnels was repurposed to fill the waterfront of the city.

It has been said that when the Mississaugas of New Credit took part in the Toronto Purchase between 1787 and 1805 they negotiated the right to retain use of the waterways for fishing. This could be—and has been—interpreted to mean that the land created by filling in the waterfront was Mississauga land, and the water that was diverted underground was Mississauga water.

It is also important to note the significance of the Toronto Islands when we speak about Toronto's waterfront. The Toronto Islands were used by the Mississaugas as a birthing place for women who would travel by canoe to the island to labour. Many of the plants that grow on the islands are considered sacred to the Mississauga people. It has been said that when the Mississauga negotiated the Toronto Purchase they never gave over the islands, as that space was considered too sacred to surrender.

The Mississauga people settled the land dispute in 2010 for a sum of $145 million, most of which is being held in trust, which is quite a deal for Canada when you consider the value of the city of Toronto. The Mississaugas now reside next to the Six Nations of the Grand River.

The Hearn is situated between two major, and thus historically relevant, water spaces: the Don River to the west and Ashbridge's Bay to the east. These spaces provided hunting and fishing grounds for the people who would have lived there. Ashbridge's Bay was filled in over the years to make way for industrial development, and the Don River was heavily polluted by industry and settlement.

It is impossible to speak about the Haudenosaunee relationship to water without addressing the story of the Peacemaker, one of the oldest and most important stories of the Haudenosaunee people, which speaks to the origins of how the Six Nations Confederacy came to be. The Peacemaker was born in the thirteenth or fourteenth century and worked to unify the then warring Six Nations.[1] He travelled from Tyendinaga across Lake Ontario to upstate New York to visit with chiefs and leaders in each community, bringing them teachings that would help to bring peace to each of the Six Nations. Lake Ontario is sometimes referred to as the 'holy lands' of the Haudenosaunee people.

No stone or metal monuments signify the original people of this land, not in the same way Canada commemorates wars, feats of architecture or transportation milestones. Monuments for Indigenous people are the waterways and the land. If we could begin to see the value of these elements as well as the history of these spaces with the same value that is placed on parliament buildings or Old City Hall, perhaps we could see the history of here, this place we call Toronto.

---

1 Mohawk, Oneida, Onondaga, Cayuga, Seneca and Tuscarora comprise the Six Nation Confederacy of the Haudenosaunee.

1

A History of the Hearn Generating Station
Nicole Hurtubise

The RL Hearn Generating Station opened on 26 October 1951. Named after Richard Lancaster Hearn, Ontario Hydro Commission General Manager and Chief Engineer, it was Canada's first and largest steam generating station. From 1951 to 1983, the Hearn produced steam generated electricity for Ontario Hydro's southern network—first burning coal before eventually shifting to natural gas in the late 1960s, and returning to a mix of coal and natural gas by the late 1970s. Situated along the shore of Lake Ontario in Toronto's Port Lands with a footprint of 27,573 square metres (equivalent to three and half international soccer fields or 17 professional hockey rinks), the Hearn is a monument to twentieth-century industrial ideals; a shiny, streamlined dream of electric futures fuelled by seemingly unlimited natural resources, which from the day its doors opened was destined to be replaced by newer and more efficient systems already in development.

The Hearn operated as a peaking facility, providing electricity to Toronto's power grid at peak times throughout the day. In the morning when the city switched on its kettles, coffee makers and toasters, and in the evening when stoves, ovens and televisions turned on, the demand for electricity increased and peaking stations like the Hearn came alive.

Initially housing two steam turbines, each one capable of generating 100 megawatts of electricity, the Hearn increased in size and capacity as the need for power increased, eventually expanding to house four larger turbines with 200 megawatts of capacity. Each turbine connected to a system which generated steam through massive boilers drawing water from Lake Ontario. The steam from the boilers propelled the turbine engines, generating electricity that then travelled out into the transformer yard on its way to the Ontario Hydro power network.

Electricity itself has become a ubiquitous presence in our daily lives, yet few of us have ever had the experience of seeing this process in action. Although a seemingly straightforward process, the scale and force of the Hearn's operations are evident through the sheer size of the infrastructure contained within the building itself. At the core of this process are the massive boilers which produced the steam to run the turbines. Within the plant these were located in what was known as the Boiler Bay.

Running 300 metres across and up to 55 metres high, the Boiler Bay was once the beating heart of the Hearn. At the peak of its operation it housed eight enormous boilers suspended from the rooftop, rising from 50 to 53 metres in height. The boilers produced steam from water drawn from Lake Ontario, by burning vast amounts of pulverized coal.

Coal was managed in what was called the Coal Bay, located south of the boilers. The Hearn's internal coal bunkers were able to store up to 1,000 tonnes of coal (equivalent to the weight of 200 full-sized pickup trucks), distributed through a system of conveyors and hoppers into pulverizing mills, where the coal was crushed by giant hollow steel balls into fine powder to be blown into the boilers, which created steam to propel the turbines.

These turbines were housed above the Turbine Bay, resting upon eight enormous concrete pads. Steam produced by the boilers moved through these giant turbine engines generating an electrical current that was then transmitted through generator transformers housed in the Power Bay, and eventually out to the yard and into the local power grid. The area below the Turbine Bay also contained the intricate machinery that ultimately transformed the steam back into water and fed it back into the boilers to begin the entire process all over again.

Within the plant there were also several control rooms. These were the command centres for the various stages of electricity production. The central control room,

1 Close up of boiler tube erection, 1950
2 Unit one in operation, 1952
3 Units one to four in operation, undated
4 Condensate booster pumps, 1951
5 Building exterior in progress, 1951
6 Heater drip pumps, 1951

No.A-5857 - Condensate booster pumps. - Dec./51

No.9790 - Shows completion of brick wall on the power house and administration building, and weather protection for boiler house. - Jan.23/51

A-1768 - Heater drip pumps - Aug.20/51

where the restaurant Le Pavillon was located during the Luminato Festival, directed the process in response to the demands of the power grid. The call for increased output would be received over the phone; the controller would increase the output, turning up the heat to the units required until the load was met. The operators in the central control room also oversaw and maintained the status of the equipment, pressure, output and heat. The upper control room, which was not accessible during the Luminato Festival, oversaw the tricky business of converting the voltage of the power generated into the correct voltage for transmission into the grid.

After the steam turned the turbines, generating a current, and once the steam returned to vapour to run the boilers, there was still the business of releasing the dust and smoke created by the coal that drove these processes. Each generating unit originally connected to a single smokestack 61 metres high. As the capacity of the plant grew, a new chimney sprouted with the addition of each new turbine unit. Eventually eight chimneys lined the northern end of the building. Accordingly, eight chimneys also discharged vast quantities of dust, ash and smoke out across the city, causing significant concerns about the impact of the low-lying emissions to the air quality of the nearby areas of Toronto.

In response to these concerns, in 1971 all eight chimneys were replaced by a single smokestack which towered over the city at 235 metres high. Erected before the CN Tower, the Hearn smokestack was at that time the tallest structure in Toronto. This new smokestack successfully reduced ground level concentrations of sulphur dioxide emissions from the plant by over 90 per cent through its capacity to keep dangerous gases far from ground level until they were able to dissipate into the atmosphere. This effort, combined with a transition to burning natural gas in place of coal, significantly reduced the immediate environmental impact of the Hearn. Most obviously it reduced the ground-level impact of the emissions. However, it was not a viable long-term solution as the emissions were not so much reduced as just pushed higher into the atmosphere. Knowing what we know now about emissions and their environmental impact, we are able to identify and perhaps even understand the good intentions behind this solution, but also to perceive through our contemporary lens a certain disregard for, or lack of knowledge about, the long-term impacts of coal emissions and dust expelled into the atmosphere.

From the late 1950s and well into the 1980s, nuclear power plants were being explored as more efficient sources of power generation. In 1962, the first prototype nuclear power plant, known as Nuclear Power Demonstration, was erected in Rolphton, Ontario. Four more nuclear power plants were built in Ontario between 1968 and 1992. In addition to the growth of nuclear power, the industry continued to explore and refine the process of steam-generated electricity using natural gas, with an eye to improving efficiency and reducing emissions. At present there are five steam-generated power plants in operation in Ontario. One of the most recent is the Portlands Energy Centre built in 2003 next to the present shell of the Hearn in the very spot where massive piles of coal waited to be transported into the plant.

The Portlands Energy Centre, although working from the same principles as the Hearn, is a very different kind of power plant. It is significantly smaller than the Hearn, with a footprint of 13,000 metres. It produces 550 megawatts from two natural gas powered turbines and also operates as a peaking plant in much the same way as the Hearn once did. In contrast to the Hearn's eight turbines, which generated 1,200 megawatts, the Portlands Energy Centre demonstrates the growing efficiency in power generation that over time made the Hearn, and plants of its size and capacity, obsolete.

As coal became less prevalent, the price of natural gas rose and new technologies for power generation became more efficient, it became evident that plants like the Hearn were no longer cost effective or sustainable. By the end of the 1970s five of the Hearn's eight turbine generating units were shut down. The final three operating units ran on a combination of coal and natural gas until they were finally decommissioned in 1983. From that point it continued to operate some of the generators as synchronous condensers to improve power quality in Toronto and the electrical control room and switchyard continued to operate until 1995.

At its peak the Hearn was capable of producing 1,200 megawatts of electricity. This means that when all eight units were operating at their full capacity the Hearn was sending a steady flow of 1,200,000 kilowatts of electricity out into the grid. This is enough electrify to power approximately 1,000,000 toasters, 1,200,000 kettles or 20 million 60-watt lightbulbs.

Additionally, the Hearn, when operating at full capacity, consumed more than 40 tonnes of coal per hour and used 108,000 gallons of
cooling water per minute. That comes to nearly 3,000 tonnes (2,721,000 kilograms) of coal per day, as well as more than three million gallons of water (equivalent to four and a half Olympic swimming pools of water) every five minutes. Over the course of a year, the Hearn would use over one million tonnes of coal. This exceeds the average annual output of the Grand Lake mines in Nova Scotia during the 1950s and 1960s.

Hindsight now affords us a privileged view of the twentieth-century dream of unlimited resources.

We now know that natural resources are finite and the impact we have on the air, land and water is indelible. This power plant—which, by the time it was built, was already in the process of being phased out and replaced with nuclear power and new thermal efficiencies—is a testament to twentieth-century ambition, as well as to its limitations.

Postscript

In 2002 the Hearn was leased to Studios of America for the purpose of transforming it into a giant sound stage for film and television. Although this vision has not yet been realized, over the years the Hearn has become a popular location for film and television shoots, appearing in numerous well-known films and TV series, including *Orphan Black*, *Suicide Squad*, *Robocop* and *Pacific Rim*. The building continued to be closed to the public until Luminato's 2016 festival, which has inspired the imaginations of citizens, city builders and dreamers to envision a range of new possibilities for the site.

1 Richard L Hearn turning on the Hearn Generating Station in 1951

17 JUNE

Don't Look Back | Back Look Don't
Clyde Wagner

At the entrance to the Hearn Generating Station, on the main wall just before you walked in the doors, was printed in large type "Don't Look Back". And yet here we are making a book about the Hearn—the ultimate self-reflexive journey, the turn around and review. So, let's go back. Let's go back to the start and ask 'why?'.

Did it start on 5 October with a 7.53 pm email from Jörn asking to meet? Maybe.

Did it start when the festival first set foot in the Hearn for its gala in 2014? Possibly.

Or did it start the year the festival was born? Probably.

In the first few months of starting the festival ten years ago, the incomparable David Pecaut brought into the office an article written by Robertson Davies in the *Peterborough Examiner* in 1952. Quoting Tyrone Guthrie, Davies wrote that a festival "may be an expression of what is finest in the life and aspiration of a country", and went on to say: "In the world of art Canada has no prestige whatever… we must gain it by showing the world that we can do something which cannot be duplicated elsewhere."

When I do look back I realize that the festival itself had always been in peak form when it took on the projects that married it with other civic, local or national initiatives. For example the installation by KPMB Architects and Michael Levine, *Light Play*, in Yonge-Dundas Square in 2008 helped the public envision Toronto's answer to Times Square as more than just a paved paradise in the most dense urban environment, but rather as a place for fun and entertainment in a family friendly and safe space. Also, in 2009 when the partnership with the City of Toronto, Harbourfront Centre and Cirque du Soleil closed the waterfront of the city to cars and created a pedestrian walkway for a long weekend free to the public, almost a million people came to celebrate. This was definitely the beginning.

So when Jörn peeked around the corner on 6 October and proposed that we put everything into the Hearn, the whole festival, and create a pop-up performing arts centre, it just made sense. It made sense as an answer to the City of Toronto's request for proposals that had been disseminated weeks before, asking for ideas on what to do with the five 'catalytic' sites, of which the Hearn was one. It made sense that the festival would do more than write another wordy strategic management document about the effect of arts and culture on public spaces, about the potential that the creative industries have to change people's minds and ignite their imaginations; we could do more than that. It made sense to build a living, breathing 17-day proposal in answer to the question of the future of this historic space and, in so doing to permanently change how the public would see the Hearn.

The perception would change because instead of just reading about a concert in the immense volume of the long main hallway, they could actually come and hear one by Rufus Wainwright or the Toronto Symphony Orchestra or Yes Yes Y'all, Dudebox and Skratch Bastid. Instead of looking at a drawing or diagram of a theatre carefully set on the page, they could actually come and see the performers striding the vast stage built specifically for the National Theatre of Scotland's *The James Plays*. And instead of dreaming of the delicacies that could be served by one of Canada's best chefs in an imaginary restaurant looking out across the bay to Toronto's downtown skyline, they could actually sit at the real table and gorge themselves with delight (if they reserved in advance).

The Hearn was exactly what it was meant to be, a catalyst and a proposal. It was a real 'do tank' (thank you David).

And so, through the efforts of an amazing team of people, some brilliant designers (Charcoalblue/PARTISANS) and our stalwart partners (Solotech/LRI), the festival created for 17 days a real temporary performing arts centre in the Hearn and, in so doing, accomplished something we only achieved once or twice before in our ten years of programming. We made an expression of Toronto's aspirations to be a global city and we did something that couldn't easily be recreated elsewhere. Only Toronto has the Hearn. Thank you Jörn for coming up with the idea.

Without a team nothing big happens. I don't know if I was able to say thank you enough

Background: Complete production schedule

168   Into the Culture Cave

1 The morning production meeting

From: Jörn Weisbrodt
Sent: Monday, October 5, 2015
To: Clyde Wagner
Subject: Re: An idea

Great! Let's do that! J

From: Clyde Wagner
Sent: Monday, October 5, 2015 8:32:50 PM
To: Jorn Weisbrodt
Subject: Re: An idea

Yes of course! I am supposed to meet to my team. Thank you. Below is my best attempt to gather them all close and give them credit. If I have missed someone I apologize; it wasn't on purpose. Here are the real people who made it happen:

Alexandra West, Alison Uttley, Anthony Sargent, April Moon, Ashley Ballantyne, Cam McKinnon, Caroline Hollway, Chiara Lacey, Clyde Wagner, Coman Poon, Daniel He, Denyse Karn, Donna Dwyer, Erin Michel, Jeff Paterson, Jen Stein, Jennifer Perras, Jeremy Forsyth, Jörn Weisbrodt, Julie Belzing, Kafi Gibson, Ksenia Sabouloua, Leah Schoenmakers, Leonardo Oliveira, Lindsay Paquette, Lindsey Williams, Lise Sorokopud, Liz MacInnis, Marcia McNabb, Martha Haldenby, Matthew Irving, Matthew King, Matthew Lederman, Matthew Moore, Michelle Doon, Michelle Gormek, Naomi Campbell, Natasha Udovic, Nicole Culp, Nicole Hurtubise, Peter Eaton, Rebecca Fallis, Sarah Jarvis, Saskia Rinkoff, Sean Richards, Seowon Bang, Shannon Linde, Shawn Hernden, Stephen Barber, Stephanie Tonietto, Sue Konynenburg, Swapnaa Tamhane, Tania Alvarez, Tanya Hart, Tenny Nigoghossian, Tim Whalley, Tyler Shaw, Veronica Barton, Winston Tang, Bob Mitchell, Derek Andrews, Janet Sellery, Phil Hornung, Sean Hooper, Rich Hagan, Duncan MacMillan, Scott McLaughlin, Frank Cianni, John Lacina, Sam Stuart, Ben Malone, Andrew Brown, Derek Brown, James Feenstra, Tony Brand, Mark Singelis, Louise Simpson, Telford Wilson, Ryan Racine, Greg Evans, Kevin Chan, Max Kinsella, Kaitlyn MacMillan, Cory Austin, Adrian Sterling, Mario Monastero, Vanessa Vai, Andy Byers, Jackson Wraight, Yolanda Do, Evan Thompson, Cary Kataoka, Louise Reilly, Rebecca Campbell, Robert Kennedy, Mike Chrobok, Stéphane Vézina, Daniel Kroft, Andrew Lockwood, Adam Achacon, Aaron Alford, Ahmed Ali, Alexander Allotta, Ryan Alovisi, Thomas Andre, Joseph Aresenault, Christina Bagnato, Jordan Baker, Jesse Barnes, Noel Baron, Joel Battle, Joel Beauchamp, Joel Belerique, Mike Benadik, Mairen Benson, Robin Benson, David Blasman, Evgeny Boutvilovsky, Mike Bowers Knorr, Dan Bradshaw, Jon Brooks, Tempest Buie Pope, Grant Burns, Dan Carriero, Hosan Chang, Richard Chevier, Shannon Henry Cogan, Shara Colabewala, Lucinda Collyer, Emmanuel Cortez, Anthony Crittenden, Sean Currell, Jake David Eddy, Bakari Diawara, Thomasz Dobrowolski, Craig Donaldson, Quincey Donavan, Lauren Dowell, Andrew Dunn, Joseph Dunn, Jacob Duqette, Liam Ellis, Pete Filipou, Yehuda Fisher, Kelly Folley, Gareth Freeman, Paul Gallagher, Tramaine Gardiner, Sean Gilhuly, Natalie Goik, Eric Greene, Nick Greenland, Kurt Grieves, Andrew Grigsby, John Grigsby, Mary Gullion, Nicole Guogen, Brianne Gwartz, Veronica Hernandez, Daniel Herridge, Jason Herzig, Rachel Hsu, Monique Huron, Gary Hutchinson, Terence Jaques, Mike Jenkins, Derek Johns, Ian Kelly, Sima Kuday, Dan LaFraugh, Sarah Lalonde, Alex Lappano, David Lau, Stefan Lavoi, Lisa Lee, Carolyn Li, Max Lieberman, Peter Ma, Andrew Macleod, Upinder Madahar, David Madgett, Alex Mak, Rashma Manjra, Bruce McCallum, Samantha McCamon, Craig McClement, Jonathan McCormack, Amy McEnaney, Mary McGee, Sean McKimmon, Dwayne McLeod, Karen McMichael, James Mele, Mikhael Melnikoff, Julian Milne, Sharon Minor, Lloyd Mitchell, Dan Monaco, Craig Munro, Nam Nguyen, Mark Nielsen, Steve Nurse, John O'Flaherty, Steven Oppedisano, Robin Orilik, Jojo Osei, Justin Osmond, Nicholas Petican, Andrew Petrie, David Pineda, Dante Pizzirusso, Tom Polci, Laura Polischuchiuk, Sergio Quiljiano, Karl Ranosky, Zack Rattray, Chris Ritchie, Ted Rumleskie, Tai Sa, Brendan Salmon, Tamar Sargent, Michael W Sheridan, Mason Sissons, Caitlin Stafford, Chris Stansbury, Mitchell Steinberg, Martin Stewart, Tyler Stewart, Brandon Sullivan, Roy Thompson, Kevin Thornton, Neil Thornton, Corey Tidd, Jules Tindungan, Raymond Tso, Barenger Turner, Rory Turner, David Vanderpool, Jason Veronaeu, Robert Wagner, Rory Whelan, Anisah Whines, Gary Whitney, Nicole Wile, Ray Williams, Paul Witko, Cassius Wray

before then.

Clyde Wagner
Executive Producer
t. 416 368 3100 ext 224
c. 416 525 2212
f. 416 368 4010
e. cwagner@luminato.com

180 Shaw Street, Suite 301,
Toronto, ON, M6J 2W5
luminatofestival.com

June 19–28, 2015

From: Jorn Weisbrodt
Sent: October 5, 2015 7:53 PM
To: Clyde Wagner
Subject: An idea

Dear Clyde,
Do you have time tomorrow after the morning meeting about the strategic direction to talk about an idea that I had?
Best, Jorn

Privy to Everything
Atom Egoyan

It was a building I knew from the outside.

I had passed it several times over the four decades I had been living in Toronto, its monumental smokestack something I would see at the end of a road on the way to a park.

The park itself was made of reclaimed land, concrete and dirt from a Toronto that was disappearing in one place so a new Toronto could be built from the giant holes and spaces cleared for new buildings and new lives.

The Hearn Generating Station was built on land that had been reclaimed from a place where no land existed before.

The land this building stands on emerged from the waters of Lake Ontario.

It was built from earth that had been unspoiled by the claims of people who had lived there for centuries; the ancient tribes of the Huron people.

The soil that the Hearn now stands on is infused, and perhaps even polluted, by its migrated history. It stands on land that had been moved from a space full of history and has now been transported to a place where a new history could begin.

The tenth anniversary of the Luminato Festival has become a part of this new history.

For many years this building was discarded. It was an empty shell. It had been built as a source to generate power and was now powerless. It was waiting to be rediscovered and reconsidered.

Much of my time has been spent in cultural spaces. I have rehearsed operas in converted brick warehouses, shot films in cavernous studios, listened to music in splendid theatres, seen art in beautifully designed galleries. In most of these situations, the program of each experience was governed by the expectation of the activity created inside.

The Hearn, on the other hand, was a revolutionary space. It created its own distinct program and invited a completely new physical manifestation of cultural activity.

Upon entering the Hearn in June 2016, I was overwhelmed by a sense of vast openness. Full of creative zones (concert spaces, theatres, galleries) that were all connected to each other with no walls. Sounds and sights overlapped. A monumental mirror ball—remembered from its previous incarnation at a civic park at a previous edition of

1 A reproduction of a Wendat house

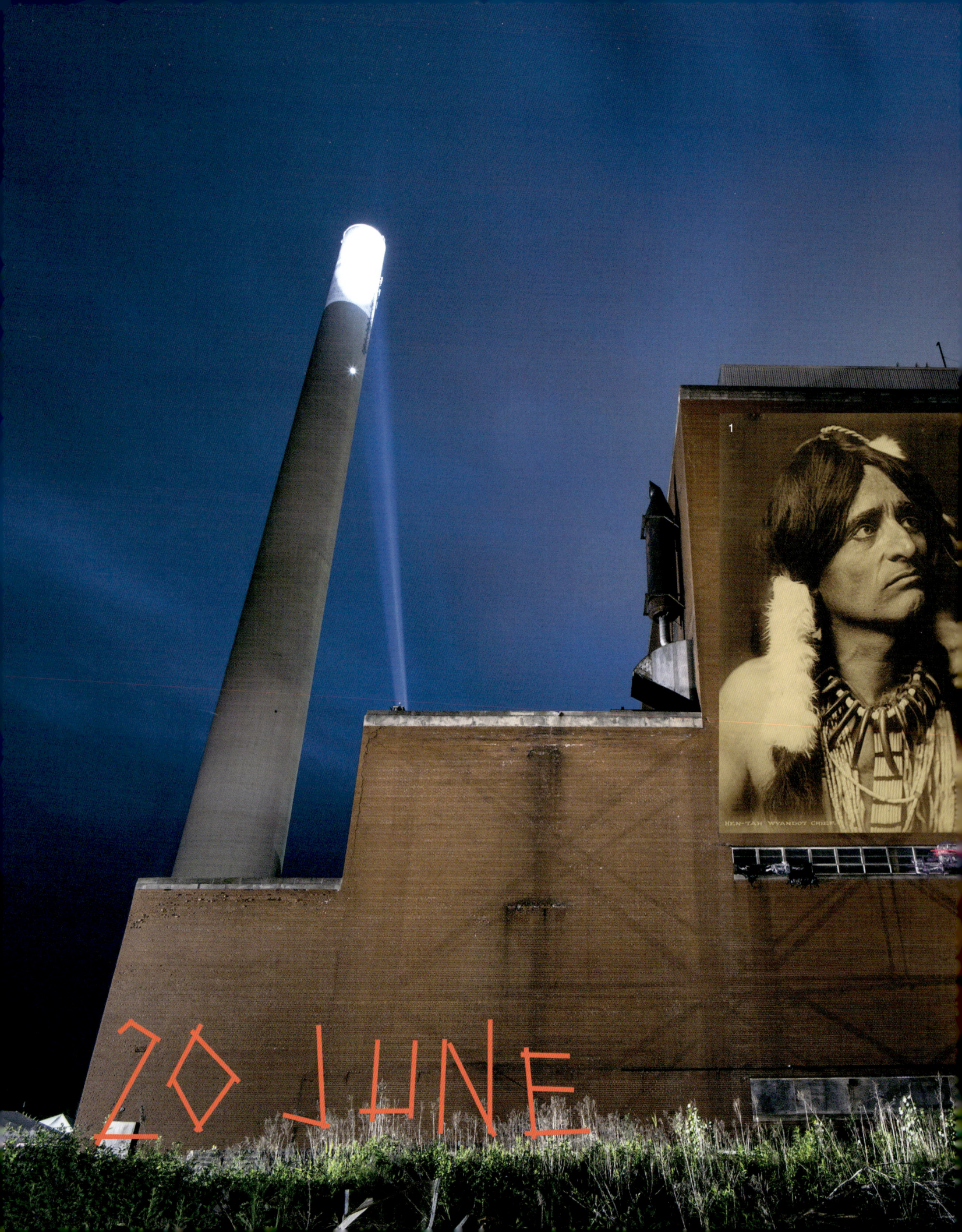

1. Hen-Tah, a Wyandot chief by George Bancroft Cornish, 1909

Luminato—now hung in this cavernous space. Fragments of reflected light bounced off the brick walls.

The Hearn was built to supply energy. The energy sent from this building dissipated into hundreds of thousands of homes and factories. Now, years after it had been decommissioned, energy was concentrated within its walls. Thousands of people made the pilgrimage to the Hearn to experience this new source of creative power.

This creative energy was available and open to everyone who entered the building. The extraordinary transformation from a hidden source of power—a place not available to the public who used its energy—was revealed with a force and generosity that took Toronto by surprise. No one expected that such a new public space could be so suddenly and miraculously revealed. The nature of this gift was monumental and even overwhelming.

It was a revolutionary creative space where access was omnipresent. Sounds from various shows and performances seeped into each other with little attention to traditional acoustic design. Everyone attending the Hearn during Luminato's tenth anniversary was privy to everything that was happening inside.

The experience was both intensely private and explosively public. No experience of negotiating the Hearn could be remotely similar to anyone else's, yet anyone could witness the individual transformative experiences of their fellow participants. All of the 'audience' became performers in the collective aspiration of this new cultural proposal.

The effect was exhilarating and full of wonder. We were allowed into a massive playroom where our imaginations were ignited in amazing ways. We became collective voyeurs of everything happening inside, watching not only the exhibitions and shows but also the faces of the audience as they navigated their way through this unique journey of discovery.

Everyone entering the Hearn felt that they wanted this to last forever. The feeling of revelation was so powerful that it seemed to warrant permanent fixture on the landscape of the city. Something so powerful and unique should never be allowed to go away.

Yet it came to an end after 17 days. The building is still there, as are the memories of what is ignited as one might approach that magnificent and lonely tower at the end of a road.

The land it stands on and the memories it claims are both mutable and enduring.

The Twenty-First-Century Concert Hall
Mat Schulz

One nascent future for the concert hall is taking shape: a condition created by technology in which we sit alone in virtual/physical space.

Artists, curators and tech companies are making the first awkward moves toward such virtual environments, with immersive installations involving image and sound accessed by putting on a headset. In the future, people will look back upon these experiments and feel like we do now when watching early Lumière Brothers' films or the video game *Pong*. Even the most advanced visions will seem clunky and naive, but full of the possibility to come.

Like space travel, virtual reality has us in thrall with the idea of what could be. What would an advanced virtual concert hall look and feel like? How would we relate to and interact with its performers? Would we lose the communal sense of sitting with others, or would we experience it differently?

One form of the twenty-first-century virtual concert hall in which all of us can sit right now is the multiplex cinema. Not the synchronized HD-movie-theatre transmission of opera at the Met screened around the world—though that is one version. Rather the big-budget blockbuster, where sound and music combine to wrap around you in a way that verges upon virtual reality. Is this a concert? No. But for many people it's the closest they get: cinema where a state-of-the-art sound system plays a crucial role.

Regarding movie theatres and sound systems, I'm reminded of *Cinema for the Ear*, presented during Unsound New York 2011. The program was comprised of 5.1 surround-sound works in a dark cinema environment, without a visual component, flipping the usual experience of sitting in a cinema, causing our senses to recalibrate. Sound, usually in the background, rose to the fore.

The twenty-first-century hall could be a traditional concert hall—a place created for the purpose of performing classical music, for example, or a theatre. Think of Lincoln Center's Alice Tully Hall in New York. What would it mean to have drone metal band Sunn O))) play there, bathing the audience in the extreme physicality of their sound? Or Venezuelan electronic producer Arca accompanied by the visual work of artist Jesse Kanda— whose images of surreal, alien bodies prompted Instagram to delete Arca's account. Such hallowed cultural spaces can, and should, be unlocked or cracked open to reach completely different audiences, and remain crucial nodes in contemporary live music culture. The twenty-first-century concert hall cannot be static. It has to shift. It has to bend.

Through Unsound, I've thought a lot about the way that architecture intersects with sound and performance. I don't just mean in acoustic terms, though that's part of it— how sound reverberates in a fifteenth-century gothic church or a synagogue in Krakow. I've thought about video projections—if, for example, they will damage priceless Polish paintings hung in a nineteenth-century gallery on the city's main square. Or what to do if safety regulations prohibit a smoke machine from being used in a philharmonic hall. How to tell an artist they cannot turn off the EXIT signs beside the stage in an 830-seat, communist-era cinema.

These are some of the venues we have used, which dictate in acoustic and practical terms what is possible.

But more fascinating is the question of how sitting in a space for a show affects the way you perceive the building and feel there. The people who constructed that gothic church in Krakow, for example, thought about how music and sound worked in the space, in the form of organs and the human voice. When an Unsound artist performs there, they connect directly with the building's history. What is different, of course, are the sounds presented— in 2010, Canadian experimental musician Tim Hecker placed microphones in the ancient pipes of the church organ and altered their sounds, part of an ambient show that veered into noise music, so it sounded unlike anything medieval ears could have imagined. But, if many in a contemporary audience heard only the power of architecture, I don't doubt

Unsound Toronto

that a medieval audience would have heard God in Hecker's sound; possibly it would have frightened them, evoking the apocalypse.

I believe such a show also respects the place, revealing the power its architects wished to convey; how the listener interprets that power is, as always, up to them, but I can imagine an open-minded twenty-first-century priest becoming lost in wonder as he listens.

That is not to say everyone feels that way. In fact, after six years of putting on shows in Krakow churches, in 2015 a right-wing blogger accused our artists and festival of promoting Satanism. This absurd claim resulted in four shows having to be relocated. It indicated the strength of cultural barriers that still exist in regard to opening such spaces via sound, even if the aim is to make them more alive, more relevant and more open.

Reanimating abandoned buildings is safer territory, as nobody lays claim to such spaces via cultural and religious rituals.

The history of such spaces in relation to club music is long. Promoters first produced illegal raves in the UK in the 1980s, creating feelings of community, optimism and physical communion. Via the use of lasers, lights, music, drugs and architecture, perceptions of reality were altered. Time stretched or shrank. Participants existed in an autonomous zone.

The rush that many felt upon entering the Hearn for the first time during Unsound Toronto at the Luminato Festival in 2015, and again in 2016, echoed how people must have felt entering those raves. The audience was thrilled to see wires, puddles and barricades—a roughness that is the opposite of the slick club and the everyday. The venue also referenced other spaces: for example, the cathedral-like expanse of Berlin's Berghain, the most famous club in the world created in a post-industrial space, or Unsound's use of the abandoned communist-era Hotel Forum in Krakow. As with those other venues, the Hearn itself became the main headliner.

Inside, concert and club music collapsed in upon one another, blurring, revealing the ways genres infect. The 83-year-old modular synth pioneer Morton Subotnick, for example, found himself on a program that also included techno DJs such as Helena Hauff and Lena Willikens. Noise music bled into ambient into techno.

One of the things I like to do during a club night in an unusual venue is to stand outside and listen. The music sounds distant and blurry, evoking the work of recent artists who have reprocessed rave music to fill it with nostalgia. It references the past and the future. These venues also blur with spaces online where some of the most fascinating music is currently located—especially in terms of club sounds—where genres from different parts of the world collide, from Chicago's footwork to Rihanna's pop, to folk traditions such as *candombe* and *kuduro*. In a context where Jon Hassell's *Fourth World* no longer has meaning, individuals and collectives in Mexico, Uruguay and Lisbon rub up against Berlin, New York, Johannesburg, London, Chicago, Tokyo, Warsaw and Toronto.

I wrote this short essay in the midst of political roiling, upheaval and uncertainty, and one thing is clear: the twenty-first-century concert hall must also break down walls in other ways. It must be a place of inclusion, its spaces filled with artists of different genders, skin colours and cultures. Its audience must be one that rejects narrow definitions of identity and is globalized as well as local. Thus, most importantly, the twenty-first-century concert hall must also be a place of protest that involves more than notions of architecture. This protest will manifest itself in ways we cannot yet imagine, but is part of a long tradition of culture, from which some of our most lasting art forms have come. So yes, by all means we should explore future forms of performance in terms of headsets, implants and online connectivity, but the twenty-first-century concert hall must always also remain defiantly human, full of empathy and the desire to take real risks.

Audiences and performances at Unsound Toronto. (Centre) Attila Csihar, lead singer of Sunn O)))

The Coating Project
The Dietrich Group

Inside the cavernous Hearn Generating Station on a cold spring day, 13 dancers peel off their winter jackets, toques and gloves, exposing a thin coating of orange unitard or no covering at all. So began the day for DA Hoskins' arts coalition, The Dietrich Group, and their creation was *The Coating Project*: part documentary, part narrative fantasy, part visual poem.

The Coating Project is an idea Hoskins had been gestating for years. Initially it was conceived as a photographic documentary project for a now defunct alternative performance/gallery space in Kensington Market, notorious in the indie theatre and queer community, called VideoFag. Hoskins wished to explore liberty and sexuality by infusing the room with a collection of naked bodies and inviting a small group of photographers with very little direction to capture spontaneous forms and images from both inside and outside the ground-floor space. In addition, a videographer recording the entire process would provide the raw material with which to create short-form art content to be presented online as a culmination of the project. The project never came to fruition at VideoFag, despite interest from curators William Ellis and Governor General's Award-winning playwright Jordan Tannahill, but instead mutated and resurfaced for the Luminato Festival.

Hoskins turned Jörn Weisbrodt on to the idea of relating the rawness of bodies to the rawness of this unique space. The vast scale, crumbling walls and exposed, twisted, rusted rebar of the Hearn presented a mythic opportunity rarely found in Toronto, one more reminiscent of historic cities such as Berlin or Paris. The shooting team was a small crew of long-time collaborators: Nico Stagias and Robert Kingsbury as directors of photography, and Katherina Limo and Javier Castellanos as photographers. The opportunity to let loose and freely document dance artists exploring the epic space became, for Hoskins, a recipe for capturing the classic beauty of bodies and architecture, referencing biblical and Greek imagery. As Michael Crabb wrote in the *Toronto Star*:

> The naked body is observed in tight shots for its sheer sculptural splendour. Other sequences, such as those shot in the former Hearn locker room, crackle with erotic potential.

Hoskins grew up a gay teenager in North Bay, Ontario, in a dual religious household of Catholic and Mormon faith. He felt the full societal weight of repression. His older brother, also gay, escaped North Bay at the age of 15 for Toronto. Hoskins stuck it out, managing to cope with a small circle of supportive friends and, most importantly, by discovering the arts. At a high school teacher's recommendation, he saw a touring production of Les Ballets Jazz de Montréal. Seated at the front of the theatre, he could see into the wings as the dancers changed from one costume to the next, bearing witness to all sorts of physical liberties. To Hoskins this was more than just a dance, but a movement. It was political. A statement on the embodied liberty and free expression of the physical self:

> My work thrives on a sense of immediacy in constant response to my surroundings. With *The Coating Project*, I implemented a series of images with historical associations that engage liturgical and iconic archetypes. We occupied the Hearn Generating Plant in a play of barriers—inundating and exploring to create a re-emergence of past into present—the rejuvenation of a decaying landscape. At the heart of the shoot was a physiological excavation. A fountain of images—captured—that offer the viewer a puzzle. A collective mass of souls— vibrant remnants of a desiccated space filled with warm bodies.

Hoskins' performance works have been littered with nakedness. He sees it as a way of engaging individuals in a realm of physical freedom while offering an immediate sensuality.

2

1 (Left to right) Will Ellis, Robert Kingsbury, Jennifer Dahl, Vanessa Jane Kimmons, Mariana Medellin-Meinke, Corrado Cerruto, Tyler Gledhill
2 (Left to right) Mariana Medellin-Meinke, Will Ellis, Justin De Luna, Vanessa Jane Kimmons, Corrado Cerruto, Jennifer Dahl
3 Will Ellis, Danielle Baskerville

1 (Left to right) Robert Kingsbury,
   Kaitlin Standeven, Christopher Valentini,
   Jennifer Dahl, Brodie Stevenson
2 Damian Norman, Robert Kingsbury

1 Vanessa Jane Kimmons, Jennifer Dahl.
2 (Left to right) Justin de Luna, Vanessa Jane Kimmons, Will Ellis, Corrado Cerruto
3 The audience watching *The Coating Project* in a covered bay in the Turbine Hall

Dancers in his work often reflect on the empowerment of being so exposed, noting that once they are past the initial hesitation, it is often extremely liberating. There is no room in being shy—there is a certain force to the moment. Hoskins suggests that nudity can be perceived as another costume: one of liberation.

The grand decay of a building designed to create energy collides with the lithe liveness of naked bodies at play, in repose, in motion, in games of both childhood exploration and very adult narration. The Turbine Hall, that epic repetition of cement archways that served as the Luminato Festival's entrance, was designed for pure function. The structure's monumental beauty, however, startles and invigorates the senses when enlivened with the dancers' explorations. Since it was decommissioned, the Hearn has been captured many times over by photographers and urban explorers who pursue what is 'affectionately' known as 'Ruin Porn'. The Dietrich Group takes this tradition of guerrilla photography and weaves it into *The Coating Project*.

With the evolving future of the Hearn in limbo, *The Coating Project* becomes a timely statement on the force of change afoot in Toronto—a decaying industrial past colliding with an immediate future of vibrant cultural and visual change. From the back of the building, the glass walls of condo towers reflect a new era for Toronto. Our massive industrial history serving as host for a dynamic cultural city—an utterly exceptional moment to be captured by the creative. This is why Hoskins, when approached by Luminato, pursued the creation of something new instead of importing from The Dietrich Group repertoire. *The Coating Project* was born as a fusion of dance, documentary and historical fantasy completely unique to both Luminato and The Dietrich Group.

Most people won't have the opportunity to navigate the corners, hallways, staircases and confined and expansive rooms that give a poetic satisfaction by revealing the romance and secrets of an industrial building, even those lucky enough to have wandered through the safety-approved selected spaces during the run of the festival. One hopes the city will honour the possibilities offered by the Hearn, but Toronto's track record for demolishing places of history is well documented. A good thing The Dietrich Group pounced on the opportunity to capture it through their own lens.

THE REALIZATION OF THE IDEA—Exploring the Cave

WHAT IS "CHOIR! CHOIR! CHOIR!"?

WE ASKED NOBU A WHOLE BUNCH OF QUESTIONS TO UNDERSTAND! :)

-NU-

-DA!-

Q1: WHEN DID YOU HAVE THE IDEA TO START 'C!C!C!', NOBU?
A1: OVER THE YEARS OUR FRIENDS HAVE OFTEN GOTTEN TOGETHER TO SING. FOR AWHILE I CALLED MYSELF "MR. NOBU AND HIS CHOIR OF A THOUSAND VOICES." IT'S LESS LONELY TO SING WITH THOUSANDS.

Q2: HOW DID IT BEGIN?
A2: MY FRIEND AMANDA ASKED TO ASSEMBLE A CHOIR FOR A SURPRISE PARTY. SHE BROUGHT DAVEED TO PLAY GUITAR. AT THAT POINT I KNEW HIM FROM AROUND BUT WE DIDN'T HANG OUT. THE PARTY-PERFORMANCE WENT REALLY WELL. A COUPLE YEARS LATER DAVEED ASKED ME (FOR THE UMPTEENTH TIME) WHEN WE WERE GOING TO HAVE ANOTHER EVENT. SO, WE DID! WE INVITED FRIENDS TO SING, CALLED OUR FIRST FB EVENT "CHOIR! CHOIR! CHOIR!", THE NAME STUCK, AND THE REST IS HISTORY.

Q3: WHAT HAPPENS AT A CHOIR! CHOIR! CHOIR! EVENT?
A3: EVERY ONE OF OUR SESSIONS HAS A GOAL: TO TEACH A GROUP OF PEOPLE (SOMETIMES 200, SOMETIMES 2000) AN ORIGINAL VOCAL ARRANGEMENT OF A POP SONG AND—AFTER AN HOUR AND HALF OF PRACTICE—RECORD IT. MEANWHILE, STRANGERS BECOME FRIENDS, AND RANDOM PEOPLE SHARE THEIR LIVES WITH US.

Q4: HAS IT EVER *NOT* WORKED?
A4: IN YEAR ONE WE ATTEMPTED TO SING THE POINTER SISTERS' *I'M SO EXCITED*. IT WASN'T THE BEST. BUT IN GENERAL OUR BATTING AVERAGE HAS BEEN REALLY HIGH.

Q5: WHY DID YOU CHOOSE *HALLELUJAH* FOR THE EVENT AT THE HEARN?
A5: HALLELUJAH IS A BEAUTIFUL, MOVING SONG, BELOVED AROUND THE WORLD, BUT ESPECIALLY IN CANADA. RUFUS WAINWRIGHT IS AN EXCEPTIONAL TALENT, AND THE HEARN IS AN EPIC, MYSTERIOUS SPACE. 1500 PEOPLE COMING TOGETHER TO SING THAT SONG IN *THAT* SPACE WAS A BEAUTIFUL DREAM.

Q6: WERE YOU OVERWHELMED?
A6: WE FELT PRESSURE, BUT WE HAD TO WORK SO FAST TO TEACH THE PARTS TO 1500 SINGERS THAT WE HAD NO *TIME* TO BE OVERWHELMED. IT WAS PROBABLY THE FASTEST C!C!C! SESSION OF ALL TIME!

Q7: LEONARD COHEN ONCE CALLED FOR A MORATORIUM ON "HALLELUJAH." DO YOU THINK HE WOULD LIKE YOUR VERSION?
A7: WE FIRST COVERED *HALLELUJAH* IN 2013 AND A CHOIR MEMBER CONNECTED TO LEONARD COHEN SENT IT TO HIM. HE EMAILED BACK AND SAID THAT WE HAD "BREATHED NEW LIFE" INTO IT! IF HE LIKED THAT VERSION, WE HOPE HE WOULD'VE LOVED THE ONE WE DID AT LUMINATO!

Q8: WHAT IS THE NEXT *DREAM* FOR CHOIR! CHOIR! CHOIR!?
A8: WE WANT TO CONTINUE COLLABORATING WITH ARTISTS—YOUNG AND OLD—AND PERFORMING IN UNUSUAL SPACES AROUND THE WORLD. WE ALSO WANT TO BRING A C!C!C! SHOW TO *BROADWAY*. THAT FEELS IMPOSSIBLE, BUT EVERYTHING WE'VE DONE SO FAR FELT LIKE A PIPEDREAM AT ONE POINT. WE'LL SEE.

Q9: WHAT DO YOU HOPE PEOPLE TAKE AWAY FROM THE EXPERIENCE OF 'CHOIR! CHOIR! CHOIR!'
A9: EARLY ON, AN OLD FRIEND WHO WAS GOING THROUGH A TERRIBLE TIME, TOLD ME HE HAD TRIED THERAPY, EXERCISE, AND MEDITATION BUT CHOIR! WAS THE ONLY THING THAT MADE HIM FEEL BETTER. WE'VE RECEIVED VERY EMOTIONAL LETTERS FROM PEOPLE WHO HAVE LOST LOVED ONES AND REDISCOVERED THEIR VOICE AND COMMUNITY AT OUR SESSIONS. WE'VE GOTTEN A LOT OF SUPPORT FROM MUSICIANS WE'VE COVERED. WE'RE NOT IRONIC ABOUT WHAT WE'RE DOING, AND PEOPLE FEEL THAT. I JUST THINK IT MAKES PEOPLE FEEL REALLY GOOD.

WHAT IS "CHOIR! CHOIR! CHOIR!"?

WE ALSO ASKED DAVEED A WHOLE BUNCH OF QUESTIONS...

Q1: WHEN DID YOU HAVE THE IDEA TO START 'C!C!C!', DAVEED?

A1: IT WAS THE FIRST TIME I STEPPED INTO A PÊNA, IN ARGENTINA. A PÊNA IS AN AFTER-HOURS BAR WHERE PEOPLE FROM ALL WALKS OF LIFE COME TOGETHER TO SING FOLK SONGS. IT WAS SO BEAUTIFUL TO SEE AND HEAR.

Q2: HOW DID IT BEGIN?

A2: IT BEGAN AT A FRIEND'S REAL ESTATE OFFICE, BELIEVE IT OR NOT. 20 OF US GATHERED IN THE MIDDLE OF THE BIGGEST SNOWSTORM OF THE YEAR AND SANG THE BEATLES' NOWHERE MAN. IT WASN'T GREAT-SOUNDING, BUT THE VIBE WAS RIGHT, AND WE KNEW WE HAD SOMETHING.

Q3: WHAT HAPPENS AT A 'C!C!C!' EVENT?

A3: A C!C!C! EVENT IS QUITE SIMPLY NOBU AND I ON STAGE, A ROOM FULL OF PEOPLE WHO ARE UP FOR ANYTHING, AND WE GO FROM THERE. THE NIGHT INVOLVES A LOT OF MUSIC AND COMEDY, BUT IT'S REALLY ABOUT SETTING THE MOOD THAT BRINGS PEOPLE TOGETHER TO CREATE SOMETHING BEAUTIFUL.

Q4: HAS IT EVER *NOT* WORKED?

A4: AS FAR AS PICKING SONGS, I'D SAY WE'VE GOTTEN PRETTY GOOD AT IT. WE HAVE A PRETTY GOOD BATTING AVERAGE, SO TO SPEAK. WE ALSO KNOW HOW TO REVEL IN THOSE MOMENTS WHERE SOMETHING IS CLEARLY *NOT* WORKING, AND WE CREATE A VIBE AROUND THAT. IT'S ALL PART OF THE CHALLENGE OF MAKING EACH NIGHT SPECIAL IN ITS OWN WAY.

Q5: WHY DID YOU CHOOSE *HALLELUJAH* FOR THE EVENT AT *THE HEARN*?

A5: THERE IS SOMETHING BEAUTIFUL ABOUT THIS SONG. IT MAKES PEOPLE THINK AND FEEL. IT'S REFLECTIVE AND SAD, YET BEAUTIFUL AND HOPEFUL. IT'S GOT IT ALL. OF COURSE, THE OPPORTUNITY TO CREATE WITH RUFUS WAINWRIGHT MADE THE FIT EVEN MORE POWERFUL.

Q6: WERE YOU OVERWHELMED?

A6: THE EVENT WAS RATHER STRESSFUL AS WE WERE UNDER SERIOUS TIME CONSTRAINTS. I WOULD SAY, HOWEVER, THAT I WAS ALSO KEENLY AWARE THAT THE ATTENDEES WERE EXPERIENCING SOMETHING MAGICAL THEY WILL NEVER FORGET. THAT IS OVERWHELMING TO THINK ABOUT.

Q7: LEONARD COHEN ONCE CALLED FOR A MORATORIUM ON 'HALLELUJAH'. DO YOU THINK HE WOULD'VE LIKED YOUR VERSION?

A7: TRUTHFULLY, THAT SONG BELONGS TO THE PEOPLE NOW. THEY WILL DECIDE WHEN AND WHERE IT'S PERFORMED. I CAN'T IMAGINE LEONARD COHEN WOULDN'T HAVE BEEN MOVED BY WHAT WE DID, BUT YOU NEVER KNOW. I AM QUITE PROUD THAT WE CREATED WHAT IS, IN MY ESTIMATION, THE MOST EPIC VERSION OF THE MOST EPIC SONG OF ALL TIME.

Q8: WHAT IS THE NEXT DREAM FOR CHOIR! CHOIR! CHOIR!

A8: THERE ARE SO MANY THINGS WE HAVE YET TO DO. IF I HAVE ONE THING I WOULD LIKE TO DO, I WOULD SAY IT WOULD BE TO DO A C!C!C! EVENT IN JERUSALEM WITH BOTH ISRAELIS AND PALESTINIANS SINGING JOHN LENNON'S 'IMAGINE' ALONG WITH HIS VIDEO IMAGE ON LEAD VOCALS. IF I MANAGE TO MAKE THAT HAPPEN I WILL OFFICIALLY RETIRE.

Q9: WHAT DO YOU HOPE PEOPLE TAKE AWAY FROM THE EXPERIENCE OF CHOIR! CHOIR! CHOIR!?

A9: WE HAVE RECEIVED COUNTLESS EMAILS, CARDS AND WELL-WISHES FROM PEOPLE WHO HAVE BEEN AFFECTED BY C!C!C! IT'S UNBELIEVABLE, REALLY. IT'S ONE OF THE STRONGEST MOTIVATORS TO KEEP WORKING SO HARD AT WHAT WE DO. WE REALIZED AT SOME POINT THAT IF C!C!C! CHANGED OUR LIVES AS MUCH AS IT DID, IT MUST HAVE AFFECTED SO MANY OTHERS.

HALLELUJAH by Leonard Cohen

Now, I've heard there was a secret chord
That David played, and it pleased the Lord
But you don't really care for music, do you?
It goes like this: the fourth, the fifth
The minor fall, the major lift
The baffled king composing Hallelujah

Hallelujah (x4)

Your faith was strong but you needed proof
You saw her bathing on the roof
Her beauty and the moonlight overthrew ya
She tied you to a kitchen chair
She broke your throne, and she cut your hair
And from your lips she drew the Hallelujah

Hallelujah (x4)

You say I took the name in vain
I don't even know the name
But if I did, well really, what's it to ya?
There's a blaze of light in every word
It doesn't matter which you heard
The holy or the broken Hallelujah

Hallelujah (x4)

I did my best, it wasn't much
I couldn't feel so I tried to touch
I've told the truth, I didn't come to fool you
And even though it went all wrong
I'll stand before the Lord of Song
With nothing on my tongue but Hallelujah

Hallelujah (x18)

pp 194–195, 198–200: Illustrations by Steve Manale

A Canadian Dream
Rufus Wainwright

Having been brought up in Canada, I am naturally imbued with a certain amount of prudence and disbelief.

Often at odds with my more brash American side, the cautious Canadian side has served as a kind of anchor for me over the years through my surreal showbiz wanderings, both in helping to concentrate on what matters professionally and, just as importantly, being yanked up on occasion in order to socially navigate to safer waters when an evening gets choppy.

Both my sister Martha and I can attest that, no matter what the glorious victories are—Juno awards, Grammy nominations, strings of sold-out Carnegie Hall shows—once home in Montreal, surrounded by the family, a kind of encrusted order sets in, and in no uncertain terms unequivocally it is assumed that there are NO STARS in the McGarrigle family.

In fact, one of the big reasons my mom and aunt (the incredible McGarrigle sisters) didn't tour that much was that someone, at some point, had to mow the lawn up north.

I am proud to have been brought up around this quality (arguably, who needs it more then me?) and definitely credit both my personal and professional success in a large part to that good old no-nonsense Canadian cold read of every situation. But, I also must admit that at times this national presence can become a negative force, and that is why, to a large extent, I married a German.

Nobody dreams like a German.

1. Rufus Wainwright performing *Rufus Does Judy* at Carnegie Hall in 2006
2. Rufus Wainwright performing *Rufus Does Judy Again* at the Hearn
3. Rehearsals for *Rufus Does Judy Again*

1 Poster for Carnegie Hall performance, 2006
2 Show curtain for *Rufus Does Judy Again* at the Hearn
3 Martha Wainwright in *Rufus Does Judy Again* at the Hearn
4 Rufus Wainwright and China Forbes at the Hearn
5 Poster for *Rufus Does Judy Again* at the Hearn

I must make a confession: When my beloved husband Jörn began his epic journey of transforming the Hearn into the centrepiece of the 2016 Luminato Festival, sadly, my guard immediately sprang up and I was totally miffed and seized with apprehension. How would people get there? Would it be safe? What if no one showed up? My rigid northern spine buckled and the prospect of looming disaster filled my heart with dread.

It wasn't that I didn't get the concept or understand the grand gesture. It's not that us Canadians DON'T dream; in fact, for about six months out of the year that's about all we do!

It was just those slabs of dilapidated cement about 300 feet up in the air... they made me pretty nervous.

Anyway, now I would like to cut to several months later near the back end of the festival when my Judy Garland tribute shows, Rufus Rufus Rufus Does Judy Judy Judy Again Again Again, were in full swing during the final weekend of Luminato and I was enjoying it as much as Carnegie Hall.

Rarely in my life have I so misread a situation. During the wind down of the glorious 2016 Luminato festival, following weeks of cutting edge theatre, music, dance, art and FANTASTIC food (here I insert a 'thank you' to Fred Morin from Le Pavillon for spurring several weeks of workouts)—I will now always remember, instead of the paralyzing fear, energetically running around on stage with a 30-piece orchestra seated behind me, them in black and myself attired in sparkling red sequins singing "clang, clang, clang went the trolley", all of us looking out at the glorious dream my husband had the vision, audacity and passion to create.

Thank you Toronto for believing in Jörn before I did.

1, 2, 4 *Rufus Does Judy Again* at the Hearn
3 *Rufus Does Judy* at Carnegie Hall in 2006

Snails and Chablis in Odd Places
Fred Morin

Conflicted traditionalists at heart, it was hard to think of anything else other than the classic French restaurants of the type that settled in every metropolis through the last century, complete with fresh flowers, crisp linens, spirits and fares straight from the dog-eared pages of our Escoffier or the stretched VHS tapes of Julia Child.

The space in the control room, not without reminding us of Homer Simpson's workplace, would seem a better fit on a Kraftwerk album cover than as the home of this fleeting 'grand restaurant français', but that's the fun.

The iridescent glow of the dials, the institutional 'Paris' green and the grand doors provided shelter then from the infernal rumble of the spinning turbines, as they do now from the performances and the dust.

The herculean work of placing such a restaurant in this space is not unlike pulling a ship over a mountain. Such an endeavour illustrates the perfect dynamic between me and John Bil. John pulled the ship over the mountain, David Dundas hauled it along. Titanesque work soon forgotten as we put on our evening attires.

We opened the restaurant as if there were no end in sight, as if it were always there and always would be.

Everyone was confused: the inspectors, the chefs, the waiters, the art and food world and the public. But once you walked in and sat down there was no need for a complex synopsis to understand what was going on. The room was beautiful, the dishes delicious, the oysters iced and briny and the white wines crisp and bottomless. Every corner of the room was taken over by diners, antiques and flowers. No need for convoluted explanations: it worked.

I cannot thank the people who helped us enough: suppliers, winemakers, colleagues of the industry. It was a delightful kind of hippie cooperation.

 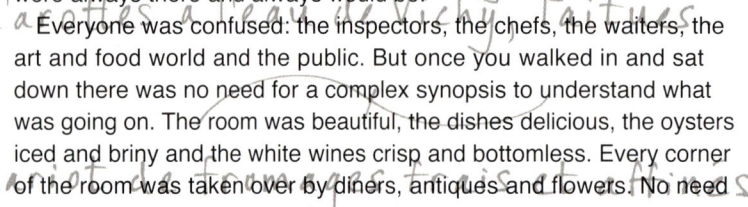 
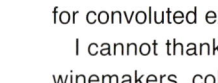 
 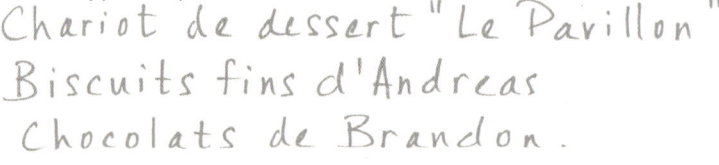

June 11-26, Hearn Control Room

Le Pavillon

Seated dinners

A la Carte Wines, Oysters, & Meats

Frederic Morin (Joe Beef)
John Bil (Honest Weight)

Booking through luminato.com
Seating is very limited

24 JUNE

1 Le Pavillon advert

LE PAVILLON MARTHA WAINWRIGHT MIX
Orfeo et Euridice, Act II: Dance of the Furies—Pierre Monteux and Rome Opera Orchestra
Je serai douce—Barbara
Canção Verdes Anos—Kronos Quartet
Satie: Je te veux, valse chantée—Mady Mesplé and Aldo Ciccolini
Pleasant Street—Tim Buckley
Hier encore—Charles Aznavour
Movie music 1—Van Dyke Parks
Je bois—Boris Vian
Eglantine—Barbara
The Dying Swan, "Romance poétique", RO 76 Op 100—Philip Martin
Manhã de Carnaval (Eurydice)—Elizeth Cardoso and Luiz Bonfá
Movie music 2—Van Dyke Parks
Szomoru Vasarnap (Gloomy Sunday)—Kronos Quartet
La valse à mille temps—Jacques Brel
Look into my eyes—Martha Wainwright
Quand Vous Mourez de Nos Amours (Live)—Rufus Wainwright
The Model—Kraftwerk
Ordinaire—Robert Charlebois
Les vieux pianos—Claude Léveillée
Tu m'aimes-tu—Richard Desjardins
Mon Pays—Claude Leveille
Dis, Quand Reviendras-Tu?—Martha Wainwright

LE PAVILLON RUFUS WAINWRIGHT MIX
Les nuits d'une demoiselle—Colette Renard
Je suis snob—Boris Vian
Amour sans amour—Serge Gainsbourg
Vingt ans—Léo Ferré
Message personnel—Françoise Hardy
Le chasseur—Michel Delpech
La groupie du pianist—Michel Berger
69 année érotique—Jane Birkin & Serge Gainsbourg
Les adieux d' un sexe symbol—Diane Dufresne
Comme ils disent—Charles Aznavour
Fais moi mal Johnny—Jeanne Moreau & Boris Vian
La valse à mille temps—Jacques Brel
Les vacances au bord de la mer—Michel Jonasz
Macadam—Bagarre
La nuit je mens—Alain Bashung
Antitaxi—La Femme
Crocodile—Adrien Gallo
Dis, quand reviendras-tu?—Barbara
L'aigle noir—Barbara
Nantes—Barbara
Tu ne te souviendras pas—Barbara
New York USA—Serge Gainsbourg
Mambo Miam Miam—Serge Gainsbourg
Sous le soleil exactement—Serge Gainsbourg
Je suis venu te dire que je m'en vais—Serge Gainsbourg
Milord—Edith Piaf
C'est toujours la même histoire—Edith Piaf
Les trois cloches—Edith Piaf

1 Le Pavillon design sketch by Fred Morin

Trove: A View of Toronto in 50 of its Treasures
A City as a Gallery of Art
Jörn Weisbrodt

This project started out with a very simple question: what are the 50 most important objects, works of art, maybe even ideas, in Toronto, and how can we bring them to the public? What lies within the walls of museums, behind doors of collectors and within institutions that only those who know they are there seek out? What if we took all of these treasures—which only a fraction of Torontonians know about—and used the city of Toronto as one huge, gigantic art gallery, creating an exhibition in the open, for everyone to see, for everyone to be proud of?

Trove: A View of Toronto in 50 of its Treasures was conceived for the tenth anniversary of the Luminato Festival and was directly linked to the idea of the 'Culture Cave' and its sketch-like expression at the Hearn Generating Station. The Culture Cave brings all the arts and forms of human activity under one shelter without any dividing walls. *Trove* equally reflects these values of openness and accessibility but in a completely decentralized version. It establishes the cityscape itself as a gallery for art, diluting any notion of keeping and showing art within walls—even the one womb-like wall of the cave itself. It would be almost impossible to see the entire body of 50 works in a day in the city, adding to the notion of openness, of endlessness. In the mezzanine gallery of the Hearn, all the images could be seen together; it was the only location where this was possible.

It celebrated what makes Toronto great and what makes it special. It surprised those who saw the images on a street corner, on the side of a building, on a digital billboard, in a shop window or in the Hearn, and made them wonder why they didn't know that these treasures—which make up the rich tapestry that defines who and what the city and the people who live in it are—were in Toronto. We looked wide and deep, we wrote to hundreds of people and museums and asked them for ideas. We had to make choices and reduce—not everything made the final cut of 50 treasures. The selection was not definitive or objective: it was highly personal and subjective. We did not want to come up with objective criteria, like monetary value, which would have excluded so many things, but applied more instinctive values—like what we would save in an earthquake—which, pieced together, would paint a picture and tell a story of this city.

No institution would ever put an exhibition like this together. It would probably be impossible as the objects of these images are too diverse, too widespread, some of them too valuable—one of them even needs food and water. But as photographic images in

1 Jackman Gallery on the mezzanine of the Hearn
2 Exhibition talk and tour at the Hearn
3 Visitors to *Trove* at the Hearn.
Background: Map showing the citywide locations of *Trove*.
Overleaf: (top left) Princess Florine and Prince Florimund costumes from *The Sleeping Beauty*, 1972. Worn by Karen Kain and Rudolf Nureyev, National Ballet Of Canada.
(top right) Electric Chair, c 1905.
(bottom left) First map of the North Pole by Gerhard Mercator. Published in 1595.
(bottom right) Kara Walker, *10 Years Massacre (and its Retelling) #1–3*, 2009

1. *Trove* Pandas from the Toronto Zoo at Daniels Spectrum in Toronto
2. Taking down the *Trove* exhibition at the Hearn

Background (opposite): *Trove* flyer

the public space, it becomes possible to bring all of these together in one exhibition. The idea was to free ourselves from the institutional walls, to be on the outside of the institutions and buildings that house our possessions and not inside. The art came to the public rather than the public to the art.

Scott McFarland composed the images. He photographed the physical objects and works of art in their places of origin. He collaborated with the Toronto-based architecture firm PARTISANS, who also worked on the digital design of an art gallery inside the Hearn. Then Scott placed the objects inside 3D renderings of the fictional Hearn Gallery. In order to create a photo-realistic image, Scott also took pictures inside the Hearn Generating Station that he incorporated into the 3D renderings by PARTISANS. The final images are like exhibition shots of Toronto's 50 treasures in a future Hearn Gallery.

Of course, choosing the Hearn, the location of the 2016 Luminato Festival, as the site for this virtual future gallery was a very conscious decision. *Trove* made a proposal for what a future art gallery could look like inside the Hearn. It utilizes only a small portion of the space, the upper level of the former Turbine Hall, as it supported the Culture Cave idea of institutional multidisciplinarity without walls. In that very same space at the Hearn, for which PARTISANS designed the fictional gallery, all 50 images could be seen together for the duration of the festival. Past, present and potential future were fused together. The rest of them were scattered throughout hundreds of locations across the city. PARTISANS' virtual gallery design inside the Hearn created about 14 distinct galleries. The objects were curated like a real exhibition among these 14 galleries. The way they were grouped together in these galleries was more in the spirit of a *Wunderkammer* (the encyclopedic collections of the European Renaissance, long before museums became more and more specialized repositories for historical objects), where objects and works of art were not distinguished by their provenance, category or discipline. We explicitly did not want to divide up the objects into any categories. We also did not want to divide them up by how they might historically be placed within different departments in an institution. We wanted to create free associations, counterpoints, surprise combinations that invite the audience to associate and develop their own narrative. It was like a mirror to the city of Toronto that is at a point of metamorphosis, that is branching out in new ways, becoming more diverse and leaving the single-narrative historical track descending from the British Empire. Scott's images give a glimpse into these curatorial decisions, as most images not only contain the main object but also the secondary objects in the background—as they would if the shots were taken in a real gallery.

Yes Yes Y'all @ Luminato
Sammy Rawal

Formed in 2009 in Toronto by myself and four friends as a reaction to the local queer scene in the city, Yes Yes Y'all has become an institution within the city. Having never felt a strong connection to the Church Street gay scene and recognizing a lack of inclusion and space for queer people of colour, Yes Yes Y'all was a way to shake things up a little. Following in the footsteps of local cultural icons such as Will Munro and DJ Blackcat, we assembled as a crew to throw a free hip-hop/dancehall party for our friends. What started as a cute 150-person event at a now defunct backpackers' hostel has evolved into something much bigger and more important over the course of seven years. Understanding the cultural importance of what we were trying to do, our mandate has always been to provide space for queer people of colour, while trying to bridge communities within a city and scene that, up until then, had seemingly only catered to a white demographic. We started to charge a nominal door price that allowed us to keep things accessible and affordable to all, but also to start aligning ourselves with local charities and contributing to their social causes. It quickly became apparent that the monthly party was attracting more than just our queer family: every third Friday of the month saw more people coming out to the inclusive party. From this spawned the subversive tagline "a straight-friendly jam", which we often used in our promotion. People started talking. Line-ups into the party started getting longer. The hype around Yes Yes Y'all started to build. Suddenly, blogs and media outlets halfway across the world were hitting us up because word had spread. We quickly outgrew the original venue and scrambled to find a space that could accommodate the 700-plus people coming out to our party every month. These were all good problems to have and we were riding a high….

Fast forward to 12 June 2016. While most were, perhaps, in bed sleeping soundly in the comfort and safety of their own home, 49 members of our family were shot and killed in the deadliest mass shooting in American history, and 53 others were injured. We may not have known them personally, but they were our family. Pulse nightclub in Orlando was a safe place for LGBT people of colour. Being very similar in respect to patronage, demographic and music format to Yes Yes Y'all, the horror that took place there really hit close to home. It rattled us to the core. Over the course of seven years, we had become comfortable in this local scene that was growing at an exponential rate and had forgotten about the dangers that still existed for LGBT folks outside this bubble we existed in. A man had casually walked into this place of love and celebration and attempted to destroy it with hatred in his heart and assault rifles in his hands.

What made things more complex and troublesome for me was the fact that the shooter was a Muslim man. As a Muslim man myself, I found it (and still do) incompressible how someone from a similar background and belief system could be ruled by such disgusting hatred. This was not the Islam I knew: Islam's foundation is rooted in peace. As media outlets caught wind of the story, the narrative shifted and became all about Islamic extremism. How could someone so seemingly similar be so incredibly different from me? I was left feeling confused, angry, hurt and afraid… afraid that something similar could happen at Yes Yes Y'all… afraid that I could face the wrath of growing Islamophobia, not only outside our scene but within it. We knew we had to react and do something in light of these tragic events, and we had five days to figure it out before the much-hyped Luminato x Yes Yes Y'all x Dudebox party at the Hearn the following weekend.

Along with Dudebox (a party within Toronto that has donated tens of thousands of profits to local charities), we decided to adapt our donation idea. Originally we had intended to donate partial proceeds of the party to the Regent Park School of Music. However, it became of utmost importance to us to also donate money to the Pulse nightclub GoFundMe page that had been created to aid the victims of the mass shooting and their families. Knowing that many people were still trying to process the trauma of what went down in Orlando the weekend before and could be easily triggered, we found volunteers trained in active listening to walk around the party at the Hearn providing support to anyone who might have needed it.

Over 3,000 people started to trickle into the Hearn on Friday, 17 June 2016. Backstage, we waited in anticipation and didn't really know what to expect. It soon became apparent that love was going to bring everyone together that night as our biggest party to date unfolded in front of us. The vibe inside was undeniably magical… a feeling I hadn't felt since our very first party. Shad, rapper and host of "q" on CBC Radio One, graciously agreed to lead a moment of silence at the height of the party. We stood on stage in absolute silence, looking out to the endless sea of people in front of us with their heads lowered as a bright rainbow coloured beating heart was projected behind us on a screen. We, as Yes Yes Y'all, briefly glanced at each other, recognizing the magnitude of what was happening at that moment… a city coming together to not only mourn the tragic events of the week before, but to celebrate, to support and to love one another under the roof of the Hearn.

The Weather's Getting In:
The James Plays in The Hearn
Laurie Sansom

There was a moment when the plan to bring *The James Plays* to the Luminato Festival for their North American premiere was looking precarious. The initial invitation had been warmly accepted. Jörn Weisbrodt had seen the trilogy in 2014 at the National Theatre in London and we were thrilled that the worldwide tour planned for 2016 would end in one of Toronto's finest theatres.

And then we were told it wouldn't. Things had changed. The plan now was for the whole festival to put down camp in a derelict power station. We were supposed to get excited about playing a cavernous, industrial behemoth, with a leaking roof, pillars and cables everywhere and no backstage facilities. And while Luminato were promising to construct a theatre just for us within this health and safety nightmare, they wouldn't be fashioning a hermetically sealed auditorium: the guts of the building were to be on view for all to see. One space would open out into another, sound and light would be as leaky and unpredictable as the rain that might pour through the roof. And we'd be competing with art installations, bars and cafes, families out for the day, clubbing teenagers, a drag dog show, Rufus Wainwright and even Godspeed You! Black Emperor, all essentially jostling for attention in the same space. My technical team was appalled.

I would also have to sell this to my acting company, who by that stage would be at the end of a gruelling year-long tour, often playing six shows in two days before getting on a plane to do it all over again. The least we could promise them were dressing rooms in an actual building, proper toilets and a city centre location. Instead there was talk of dirt floors, hard-hat conditions, and even the whispered possibility of raccoon infestation.

After weeks of to-ing and fro-ing, queries raised, solutions suggested, designs exchanged, Jörn and I were to have a make-or-break conversation. The truth was that, for all the reassurance we'd been given, this still seemed like an almighty risk. Could we responsibly take the shows to the Hearn or would we feel compelled to withdraw from the festival? We'd opened the show two years earlier in a venue with state-of-the-art equipment, velvet curtains and pristine backstage facilities and then settled into a four-month run in the National Theatre's Olivier auditorium on London's South Bank. We were now planning a year-long tour to some of the UK's most well-appointed theatres and international festivals in New Zealand and Australia. So why end this extraordinary adventure in this ill-equipped, badly appointed death trap of broken glass and twisted metal? Would the shows survive? Would the actors survive? But then I thought about how the whole project had started.

When I took up my position as Artistic Director/Chief Executive of the National Theatre of Scotland, the first drafts of Rona Munro's new history cycle about three medieval Scottish kings were already sitting on my desk. That was quite a welcome. Commissioned by my predecessor Vicky Featherstone, they were an extraordinary work of imagination, taking an all but forgotten period of Scottish history and giving it irreverent, vigorous life. But they also asked urgent questions about what kind of nation Scotland wanted to be. As we stood on the cusp of a historic referendum on Scotland's future, it was clear that writing of such immediacy, wit and vitality about the fashioning of a nation could play a central role in celebrating Scotland's past and imagining its future. But, more than that, these were remarkable and universal stories about how we love, how we hate, how we survive, and as I breathlessly turned the pages I felt I was lucky enough to have some of the most brilliantly realized plays to have yet been written this century in my hands.

The National Theatre of Scotland, founded in 2006 as the first national theatre in the world not to have its own theatre, is proud to call itself a "theatre without walls". Its mission is to be truly national, appearing in halls and theatres up and down the country, as well as

1 James III: The True Mirror
2 James I: The Key Will Keep the Lock

in ferries, shopping centres and forests. It already had a reputation for making bold and surprising work, but it had never produced anything on this scale. The trilogy day would last over 11 hours, with a company of 20 actors and 25 crew telling the story from the moment Henry V sends Scotland's king-in-exile, James I, back to Scotland after holding him prisoner for 18 years, to the crowning of James IV following the killing of his father James III. Significant partners would be required, and with the Edinburgh International Festival and the National Theatre of Great Britain as enthused over Rona's scripts as I was, we made an unprecedented partnership that would see us take the plays to the Olivier Theatre in the autumn of 2014 and open at the Edinburgh International Festival earlier that summer. All we had to do now was find a home for them in Edinburgh.

One thing I knew, it mustn't open at the Festival Theatre, a shiny bright temple to both high culture and hit musicals. *The James Plays* were far too down and dirty for that. They broke furiously onto the stage with a war cry on a battlefield in France, featured parliamentary riots, violently lawless games of medieval football, luncheon parties that turned into wrestling matches and dinner parties that ended in rivers of blood. They needed an amphitheatre, or a bear-pit, an environment that allowed one scene to flow into another, where warriors, coronation processions or cloaked assassins could appear from any direction, and rambunctious crowd scenes could melt into intimate chamber scenes. A velvet clad, illusionistic house would kill these plays stone dead. Nothing could be pretend, everything had to be the thing itself—wood had to be wood, metal metal and fire fire. The audience had to smell the sweat, feel the vibrations of the drums and hear the scraping of the swords. And so, after a cursory inspection I dismissed the Festival Theatre, with it's gold brocade curtains and art deco chandeliers.

And so the hunt was on. The producing team and I explored disused theatres, conference centres and sports halls across Edinburgh. Some were wonderfully atmospheric but falling down, some had all mod cons but no atmosphere at all, and some were so far out of town that the audience would be wandering around a deserted business park in between shows. We considered each and dismissed them all: too posh, too small, too far. But the clock was ticking, and the more spaces we saw the more frustrating it became.

One day we were heading back to our offices in Glasgow on the train, trying and failing to convince ourselves that the basketball court we'd just seen might be the answer. I had to concede that we'd seen every available space of any size and the only venue that could practically work was the Festival Theatre. But it still didn't sit right. My instinct told me that a traditional proscenium arch theatre was in danger of sanitizing these plays and turning them into what Rona and I most wanted to avoid: polite, staid period pieces with a whiff of old-school BBC costume drama, often watched on a Sunday afternoon whilst toasting muffins and buttering toast. I just had this feeling that if we presented them to the world in this way their power to thrill, provoke and surprise would be muted and instead they'd be met with polite indifference. But at this late hour, and after trawling around every large room in Edinburgh, the largest proscenium arch theatre in Scotland remained our only option.

I grabbed an envelope and starting drawing. How could we make the ebb and flow of the action wrap around the audience? Could we create a dynamic acting space that encouraged actors to bring their whole selves to the party, and release them from doing that weird British thing of having conversations with each other whilst standing side by side and both looking out front? And could we create a world that matched the honesty, musculature and brutal poetry of Rona's words? I needed to find a way of creating a sense that the story, the set, the nation was being constructed in front of us. My doodle was an attempt to see what would happen if we put some of the audience on the stage. Perhaps the audience could *be* the set, and the playing area could migrate out into the auditorium. This was not a unique idea by any stretch. In recent years the West End revival of *Equus,* starring Daniel Radcliffe, had a steep tier of audience members looking eerily down on the action. More successful perhaps was Jeremy Herrin's production of *This House,* a new play about the party political meltdown in the late 1970s that used pivoting banks of seats to conjure up the House of Commons chamber. If we could get 80 to 100 people up onto the stage, that would be about the right for the size of Scotland's parliament in the fourteenth century, and solve for me a major headache of how to find bodies for parliamentary scenes in both *James I* and *James III*.

The wobbly horse shoe I scribbled on the back of an envelope was a seating bank that enveloped the action, creating entrances and exits from all directions and playing spaces on various levels. My sketch was bad, really very bad, but it allowed me to start visualizing Rona's plays for the first time—which is always a good signal for me that there's something in an idea. Henry V could suddenly appear over the back of the seating bank right next to a startled audience member, a beam of light could pick out a lonely king suspended in a throne room above the action, and the seating bank could become castle battlements, football stands and, yes, a parliament. More than that, we would be watching ourselves watching the plays. We'd be acutely aware that we were sharing an experience, becoming one community over the many hours we watched the action unfold. Designer Jon Bausor picked up this idea and took it to a whole new level. In his hands my crap little doodle became an elegantly brutalist crown of scaffolding and sleepers. In *James I* it was a fortress, a battlefield and a bedchamber. We decided that as James I tried to build the country around a centralized rule of law we should build everything in front of the audience: the throne and the royal bed, the dinner table and the gallows. In the nightmare world of *James II*, the world became charred and broken, shafts of light cut through the space as shards of memory disturbed the young king's sleep. And in *James III*, a much more refined veneer of colour and gilt appeared momentarily, but with a lustre that was wearing as thin as the Scottish people's patience under their capricious king. But for all these shifts in tone and style, what Jon really created was what between the two of us we would refer to as a "Minotaur's pit": something monstrous was always just about to jump out of the shadows and the eyes looking down from all sides made it a gladiatorial arena.

I am delighted to report that the plays were a huge critical and popular success, selling out both the Edinburgh and London runs. I was hugely relieved more than anything else—we'd pulled off the biggest event in Scottish theatrical history, but more than that, Rona's plays had been given an environment in which they could truly be given rude, foot-stomping life—the Festival Theatre became their spiritual home. So why, two years later, would we compromise the productions by plonking them into the huge industrial space of the Hearn?

But thinking back to that doodle on the back of an envelope made me realize what an idiot I'd been in doubting that the productions could thrive in the Hearn. It was in fact the space I'd been dreaming of on those fruitless searches across Edinburgh. It was both the decaying shell of the recent past and an exquisite cathedral of metal, concrete and glass. It reverberated with the energy once generated there, and let in shards of light that waltzed about its surfaces, reflecting off puddles gathering in unexpected places. It had its own brutal glory, its own monsters, its own drama. And it became very clear that we would be working with a team at Luminato who would do everything in their power to make the shows the best they could be. They had employed the very best theatre design consultancy in the world, Charcoalblue, to create a bespoke theatre space that would sit inside the building. They were going to construct it from shipping containers, boxes of the audience looking down on the action from these balconies that had been bolted together. The girders, sleepers and rivets that made up our set continued on into the seating, the lighting rig and the vast eaves above our heads. And this would truly be a "theatre without walls" as there really wasn't a hope in hell of blocking out all ambient light in a disused building three times the size of London's Tate Modern.

In that make or break phone call with Jörn, I had the growing feeling that perhaps *The James Plays* were going to find their most sympathetic home yet. It might have still been a step into the unknown, but the reality was that the Hearn is where the plays found their apotheosis. As soon as I stepped into the space, I knew something astonishing was afoot. The set looked like it had been made to slot right inside, and above the playing area was the most awe inspiring cathedral of space made up of beams, cables and walkways. When the lights under our metal floor went live, it made the metal sky glow, and rather than work harder to hide this sublime space above us, I immediately wanted to throw more light into it. There are moments in *James II* when the King's childhood trauma is triggered and the lights would throb. Perhaps in this space we could light up the cavernous metal

sky above him and make him look even more lost and vulnerable in a world he's struggling to understand. The very first conversation I had with Jörn face-to-face was to ask if we could have a couple of extra lights to take the eye up into this jaw dropping heaven, and so we started the process of letting the world of *The James Plays* graft onto the industrial majesty of the Hearn, exploiting these happy accidents. The sound of children giggling somewhere in the Hearn became a chilling juxtaposition to the torment being inflicted on young James II, and the mechanical whir of the elevator accompanied the rumble of our drawbridge. We had to contend with the world's largest mirror ball, spreading its fabulousness across the entire space, but what better accompaniment for James III's provocative parliamentary entrance in shiny red pants and Cuban heels? The audience who came to *The James Plays* in the Hearn were acutely aware of the liveness of the event and the world that lingered at its edges, and so the plays took on fresh and vital life. And an alert and engaged audience makes for happy actors (that and first-class catering of course). Most of them even came to love the raccoons, or 'tuxedos' as we learnt to call them in case of nearby public ears. They would steal into the props store at night to drink the stage blood, leaving tell-tale paw prints across the floors and tables. Many West End theatres boast of having a theatre cat, but how many can claim to have a theatre raccoon?

Of course, theatre hasn't always been something we did in dark rooms with flock wallpaper and red curtains, with the audience being berated by both management and actors alike for daring to whisper. When did it became an activity reserved for the privileged elite who had acceptable manners and the right clothes? The answer perhaps lies in the many theatre buildings we're now left with, modelled largely on nineteenth-century practices and social structure. They are often beautiful buildings but offer very particular conditions: a focused space with everyone looking in the same direction; a separate stage perfect for creating illusion and hanging exquisite backdrops; protection from the light and sound of the outside world; and, crucially, lots of seats crammed into a small space.

But the world has changed, and with it our audiences. Artists are now moving more fluidly between art forms and the digital world has transformed how we make and receive art whilst the need for culture to challenge global orthodoxies has become even more urgent. Our established temples of culture have struggled to catch up. These often iconic buildings are the products of a time when certain art forms, artists and audiences were considered to be part of an elite, creating a false dichotomy between high and popular art and failing to harness the enormous creative potential of the whole community. In recent years these false and damaging divisions have started to be broken down. Hip-hop has entered commercial musical theatre with the smash hit *Hamilton,* Rufus Wainwright has written for the opera, Jerry Springer has had an opera written about him. Companies such as Rimini Protokoll and Sound & Fury are using technology to expand the possibility of immersive theatre, the all-conquering Harry Potter saga has been extended with the help of some of theatre's boldest innovators, and visual artists such as Steve McQueen and Banksy have moved into the cinema. As the walls between art forms and between actor and spectator are revealed to be permeable or non-existent, new spaces in which to experience the work are required.

For a brief moment this summer, the Hearn showed what could happen when the walls came tumbling down. New flexible buildings aimed at harnessing this new fluidity are already in progress. In the UK, Manchester will soon open The Factory, a home for all art forms that can shift itself into endless spatial permutations. And, in 2019, The Shed is due to open on the Hudson River in New York, devoted to producing new work by artists from across the world in its many flexible spaces. The most successful version of this I've been to is in Havana, where the Fábrica de Arte Cubano has taken over a huge factory space and over the last five years become a huge draw for art lovers, theatre goers and clubbers alike. For 50 pesos (the equivalent of 50 cents) the audience can wander through the building, exploring the contemporary art exhibitions, the cafes and bars or one of the many performance spaces. I watched a young Cuban theatre company perform for an engaged and noisy crowd, wandered in and then out of a concert of experimental Cuban jazz, watched a short film shot in Havana, and then danced into the wee hours to Caribbean electronica. It was an adventure open to all generations, where crowds of locals with a

1 Raccoon footprints
2 Backstage at the Hearn Theatre
3 Raccoon in the Hearn
4 Pink rubber duck
5 Big floor bump
Background: Size comparison between the Hearn and Galleria Vittorio Emanuele II in Milan

THE REALIZATION OF THE IDEA—Exploring the Cave

smattering of tourists enthusiastically prowled its diverse interconnected spaces.

These new ways of presenting work will definitely challenge us as theatre makers. Whilst there will always be a place for work that demands a quiet and focused space, if we want to speak to and of the entire population then it must sometimes lose its formality, and be robust enough to survive and indeed welcome interruption, the unexpected and the accidental. These flexible, reimagined and surprising spaces are pointing the way forward to engaging a broader, more open and more engaged audience.

There is a moment in *James III* that gave me the shivers when played in the Hearn. Lord John, leader of the parliament, frustrated at the king's cavalier approach to ruling the nation, goes to see Queen Margaret to enlist her support and says: "This whole nation is like a house a few of us are trying to hold together with our bare hands. The weather's getting in… the door can't hold its lock… and there's a stormy night coming."

The Hearn was that house, and many people were indeed holding it together; it really was the perfect space for Rona's remarkable vision of a nation building itself, then tearing itself apart, and then trying to piece itself back together. During the closing moments of the final trilogy day, as a young James IV stood on the threshold of his coronation, the heavens opened; rain clattered down on the metal roof and poured down onto a few poor souls high on the onstage seating bank. But it didn't matter. The audience had been crying and laughing with us for 11 hours, and the company were approaching the final moments of a year-long adventure that had changed all our lives forever, and somehow the weather got in at just the right moment. The rain joined the tears of the audience and the actors as a unique event, courtesy of the Hearn, Luminato and the people of Toronto, finally came to an end.

Sadly, I don't now have that hastily done sketch on the back of an envelope. But having been reimagined by the designer and drawn up in meticulous detail for theatres across the world, it has now been transformed again by a tattoo artist, who inked it onto my arm to mark the close of the plays in Toronto. Not only does it mark the end of a three-year project that changed my life, it's also a reminder to both heed those early instincts, and then remain as open as I can to the countless ways in which they might be given shape.

1&2 Laurie Sansom's tattoo of the Hearn Theatre footprint
Background: Technical floor plan of the Hearn Theatre
Opposite: *monumental* by Holy Body Tattoo at the Hearn with Godspeed You! Black Emperor

EPILOGUE

27 JUNE

Yesterday was the Future
Transcript of a speech held at the tenth anniversary gala
of the Luminato Festival in 2016
Jörn Weisbrodt

Twenty years after the tenth-anniversary Luminato Festival opened the doors to this remarkable industrial building I am proud to stand on this stage to open the 'Culture Cave', the largest community and cultural centre in the world. Luminato's tenth anniversary 20 years ago showed Toronto, Canada and the world what a unique place this could be—a gem hidden in what was then just known as the Port Lands, a rough industrial site built on the trash of downtown development. Today, the Hearn Generating Station, a power plant that provided energy to the citizens of Toronto during peak times until 1983, will be renamed the Culture Cave, a cultural and community centre that has no equal in the rest of the world. We want the Culture Cave to be for everyone. A place for the citizens of Toronto, the citizens of Canada and the world.

Canada is the most diverse country in the world. We have our first East Asian, transgender prime minister. 90 per cent of the population have grandparents who were born outside of Canada; half of them came in the last 20 years. Due to the worldwide crisis, we opened our doors and let 30 million immigrants into the country in the last 20 years, with the total population now reaching around 66 million. We are the third largest exporting nation in the world after India and Germany. Our film industry has surpassed the output of Hollywood, with more and more studios moving to Hamilton—having been forced out of Southern California by the water crisis and the growing censorship of our southern neighbour. Art Basel Vancouver is the largest art fair in the world outside the free security zones of the former Western world, the Documenta Venice Biennale PEI has turned the entire province of Prince Edward Island into the biggest celebration of art. The island's economy has completely shifted to supporting artistic creation, and every work exhibited at DocBiennale is made by the people of Prince Edward Island. World EXPO City and our new TED Talk province in the Northern Territories are innovation hubs attracting hundreds of thousands of new immigrants quarterly. Our new education system, based on Indigenous practices, is the best in the world. Our motto of "the entire world in one country for peace, prosperity and

23 JUNE

1 Luminato Gala "Nature versus Industry" at the Hearn, 2015; 2 (Left to right) Tony Gagliano, His Worship John Tory (Mayor of Toronto), Anthony Sargent, The Honourable Kathleen Wynne (Premier of Ontario), Jörn Weisbrodt and Rufus Wainwright during the Luminato Gala "Today is the Future" at the Hearn, 2016; 3 Luminato Gala "Big Bang Bash" at the Hearn, 2014; Background pp 242 & 245: artistic production calendar

1 His Worship John Tory
2 Jörn Weisbrodt's opening-night speech, Hearn Theatre

culture" has paid off. The Culture Cave is the ultimate expression of this motto.

The cave is the simplest shelter known to humankind. All social functions were combined in the cave: from sleeping, eating and protection to congregating, storytelling, music, painting, meditation, ceremony, funerals and dancing. The Culture Cave gives shelter to our minds, our imagination, our hopes, our creativity, our physical endurance, our dreams, our expressions, our thoughts and our experiments. It is a place where no one is excluded, a place that knows no high or low, no departments, no artistic disciplines, no distinction between the body and the soul. It is the largest multi-arts venue in the world that has no walls. Conventional multi-arts centres separate the arts in different spaces—science, sports and entertainment find no place in them. Theatre has its own space, music does, the visual arts do, dance, opera. Here we separate in time, not in space, but everything is under one roof—just like in a cave—everything is contained and open at the same time. The cave is the mother's womb made in stone; it is nature's womb. Much of this thinking was laid out in the very beginning 20 years ago. A book was published a year after the 2016 initiation of the space. Over 30 cultural organizations, club promoters and sports groups in Toronto collaborated during the tenth Luminato Festival, creating an institutional diversity that was new and groundbreaking in the city. Funding for today's institution was not secured yet. But the doors were pushed open, more and more people used it: EXPO2020, the first Triennale outside of Milan, the World X-Games, Glastonbury Canada, TIFF, the World Reads Festival, the Kumbh Mela Toronto, the TSO Symphonic Festival, the World Diversity Forum, the UN 365 conference, the first United Nations of Canada conference, to name a few.

Mayor John Tory, who later became Canada's Prime Minister and made the visionary decision of radically increasing Canada's population by letting in refugees from the war zones of the first Global Civil War, spoke at the opening of the festival. His words, "We have to go down the roads whose ends we don't yet know", were spoken that night for the first time, which later became iconic and changed the psyche of an entire nation. The motto of the evening back then was "Today is the Future", and I am proud to say today, 20 years later, this future was yesterday. Our future today is the Culture Cave.

Thank you very much!

Biographies

Nobu Adilman [18, left]
Nobu Adilman is a Toronto-based artist, journalist, podcaster and interactive web content creator. Adilman is best known for co-founding Choir! Choir! Choir!, a community singing group that has performed at Carnegie Hall and Radio City Music Hall.

Karen Brooks Hopkins [11]
Karen Brooks Hopkins served as President of the Brooklyn Academy of Music from 1999–2015. Hopkins was the chair of the Cultural Institutions Group from 2002–2004, and, most recently, served on Mayor de Blasio's transition committee. Hopkins is currently Senior Fellow in Residence at the Andrew W Mellon Foundation.

Jonathan Castellino [17]
Jonathan Castellino is a photographer based in Toronto, Canada. His main photographic subjects are urban and industrial spaces, within which he explores the intersection of architecture and culture, and of personal meaning and the built environment.

The Rt Hon Adrienne Clarkson [2] [9]
The Rt Hon Adrienne Clarkson is a Hong Kong-born Canadian broadcaster, distinguished public servant and best-selling author, who served as Canada's twenty-sixth Governor General from 1999–2005.

Jack Diamond [16]
AJ "Jack" Diamond is the founding principal of Diamond Schmitt Architects. He is a Royal Architecture Institute of Canada Gold Medallist, a Member of the Order of Ontario and an Officer of the Order of Canada, and his publications include *On Site and Insight*, 2008, and *Sketches from Here and There*, 2010.

Georg Diez [27]
Georg Diez is a writer, cultural critic and columnist for *Der Spiegel* and *Spiegel Online* and the co-founder of the digital long-form platform *60pages.com*. He currently lives in Cambridge, MA, as a Nieman Fellow at Harvard.

Atom Egoyan [4]
Atom Egoyan is one of the most celebrated contemporary filmmakers. His installation *Auroras* was presented for Luminato's inaugural year. His opera production of Feng Yi Ting was performed for the festival in 2013.

Richard Florida [24]
Richard Florida is University Professor and Director of Cities at the Martin Prosperity Institute at the University of Toronto's Rotman School of Management, Global Research Professor at New York University and a Visiting Fellow at Florida International University. He is author of *The Rise of the Creative Class*, 2002. His latest book, *The New Urban Crisis*, was published by Basic Books in April 2017.

Daveed Goldman [18, right]
Daveed Goldman is a singer, songwriter and community creator. He wrote the Jack Layton memorial song "Nothing But Time to Give" and was recognized by the *Globe and Mail* as a Catalyst for co-founding Choir! Choir! Choir!.

DA Hoskins [22]
DA Hoskins' multiple award-winning interdisciplinary platform, The Dietrich Group (TDG), explores, creates and elevates dance through engagement with theatre, film and arts, both nationally and internationally. Launched in 2008, TDG draws from a broad range of artistic disciplines while maintaining a focus on the strength and power of dance in theatre.

Nicole Hurtubise [20]
Nicole Hurtubise is an independent curator and community activator. During the 2016 Luminato Festival, Nicole spearheaded *The Hearn Trail*, exploring the past, present and future of the Hearn Generating Station through a range of walking tours. She also led *Iftar at the Hearn*, an evening of celebration and welcome for Syrian newcomers in Toronto.

Falen Johnson [21]
Falen Johnson is Mohawk and Tuscarora from Six Nations of the Grand River Territory. She is a writer, producer, dramaturge and actor currently living in Toronto.

Alex Josephson [3]
Alex Josephson co-founded PARTISANS in 2012. The only Canadian to have ever received the New York Prize Fellowship from the Van Alen Institute, Josephson was named 2016 Best Emerging Designer by Canada's Design Exchange. He currently lectures at the University of Toronto's Daniels Faculty of Architecture.

Steve Manale [1]
Steve Manale draws storyboards for film and TV, kids comics, band posters, naked people—when he remembers to bring a Sharpie with him—on public bathroom walls. Like, non-stop.

Shawn Micallef [10]
Shawn Micallef is the author of *The Trouble with Brunch: Work, Class and the Pursuit of Leisure*, 2014, *Full Frontal TO*, 2012, and *Stroll: Psychogeographic Walking Tours of Toronto*, 2010. His latest book is *Frontier City: Toronto on the Verge of Greatness*, 2017.

Fred Morin [30, left]
Fred Morin (all in his words) co-owns Joe Beef, Liverpool House and Vin Papillion restaurants in Montreal, and is the co-author of *The Art of Living According to Joe Beef*, 2011. He fathered three offspring that currently prevent him from living a second youth behind the stoves. He also wishes he had gone to college. He divides his time between being fat, becoming slim, being slim and becoming fat.

Sammy Rawal [12]
Sammy Rawal is a Canadian music video/commercial director and photographer, DJ and co-founder of the queer hip-hop/dancehall collective Yes Yes Y'all. He has opened for artists such as A Tribe Called Red, and has performed at venues including The Opera House, Toronto, the Royal Ontario Museum, the Art Gallery of Ontario and Yonge-Dundas Square.

Michael Redhill [23]
Michael Redhill was born in Baltimore, MD, in 1966, but has lived in Toronto most of his life. He has published 16 books in varying genres including five collections of poetry, three plays and seven novels. He still lives in Toronto.

Charles Renfro [15]
Charles Renfro is a Partner at Diller Scofidio + Renfro. Renfro, a graduate of Rice University, holds a Master of Architecture degree from Columbia University, and is currently a professor at the School of Visual Arts in New York. In 2012, he was honoured as a Rice University Distinguished Alumnus, among the youngest alumni to receive the award. In 2014, he was named a National Academy Academician, and in 2015 he received the Texas Medal of the Arts Award.

Laurie Sansom [28]
Until recently, Laurie was the Artistic Director and Chief Executive of the National Theatre of Scotland for whom he directed *The James Plays* trilogy. He has directed for theatres around the UK, including Birmingham Rep, New Vic, West Yorkshire Playhouse and the National Theatre, London.

Mat Schulz [14]
Mat Schulz is the founder and artistic director of Unsound. Based in Krakow, Poland, the festival also travels the world, with editions in New York, London, Toronto (as part of Luminato Festival), Adelaide and many other locations.

Kitty Scott [8] [25]
Kitty Scott is the Carol and Morton Rapp Curator of Modern and Contemporary Art at the Art Gallery of Ontario. Previously she was Director of Visual Arts at The Banff Centre; Chief Curator at the Serpentine Gallery, London; and Curator of Contemporary Art at the National Gallery of Canada.

Jerad Schomer and Clemeth Abercrombie [6]
Jerad Schomer and Clemeth Abercrombie are New York-based theatre designers for Charcoalblue. Jerad is the former technical director of the Park Avenue Armory and also works as a scenery and lighting designer. Clemeth is an acoustician, with collaborations ranging from concert halls around the world to flooding the Park Avenue Armory with Hélène Grimaud and Douglas Gordon in *tears become…streams become…*, 2014.

Nicola Spunt, PhD, Director of Content & Culture, PARTISANS [7]
Nicola is a producer, writer, host and award-winning literary scholar. She founded After School, a speaker series devoted to arts, culture and city-building, has published articles in the *Oxford Literary Review*, the *Henry James Review* and *Hazlitt*, and currently moderates a North America-wide talk series for Soho House called Table Talks.

Bruno Tackels [5]
Bruno Tackels is an essayist and playwright. He has taught aesthetics and the history of contemporary theatre at the University of Rennes 2, the Regional School of Actors of Cannes, and the School of Decorative Arts of Strasbourg and has published three books on Walter Benjamin.

Ian Tattersall [26]
Ian Tattersall is a Curator Emeritus in the Division of Anthropology at the American Museum of Natural History in New York City. His most recent books are *Masters of the Planet: The Search for our Human Origins,* 2012, *The Rickety Cossack and Other Cautionary Tales from Human Evolution*, 2015, and (with Rob DeSalle) *A Natural History of Wine*, 2015.

Clyde Wagner [29]
Clyde Wagner is an internationally accomplished producer. Clyde was also the first producer and general manager for Luminato. Clyde was recently appointed President and CEO of Civic Theatres Toronto.

Rufus Wainwright [13, right] [19, right]
Rufus Wainwright is one of the great male vocalists, composers and songwriters of his generation. He has collaborated with artists ranging from Elton John and David Byrne to Joni Mitchell and Burt Bacharach. The Canadian Opera Company has commissioned Wainwright's second opera, about Roman Emperor Hadrian, to premiere in Toronto in the fall of 2018.

Jörn Weisbrodt [19, left]
Jörn Weisbrodt studied opera directing in Berlin and worked as artistic production director at the Staatsoper Unter den Linden for five years. Between 2006 and 2012 he was the executive director of RW Work Ltd in New York, representing and managing the work of Robert Wilson, and the director of The Watermill Center. From 2012 to 2016 he was artistic director of the Luminato Festival. He is now the artistic advisor to the Music Center in Los Angeles, and is also working with New York Public Radio.

Acknowledgements

Into the Culture Cave
We graciously thank the following donors for making the publication of this book possible: Mohammad and Najla Al Zaibak, Helen Burstyn and her family, Angela and David Feldman of Camrost-Felcorp, Wendy M Cecil, John Donald and Linda Chu, Helene Clarkson and the Max Clarkson Family Foundation, Janice Lewis and Mitchell Cohen, St Joseph Communications, the Haldenby family, Vahan and Susie Kololian, Eleanor McCain, Margaret McCain, Lynda and Jonas Prince, Jay Smith and Laura Rapp, Gretchen and Donald Ross, Phil and Eli Taylor

Luminato Festival 2016
Luminato Festival is deeply grateful to the many people whose vision and generosity made our 2016 festival possible.

SUPPORTERS
We would like to acknowledge and thank all our individual, corporate and foundation supporters for their invaluable contributions.
Supernova Supporters: Anonymous, Lucille Joseph and Urban Joseph OC, Joan and Jerry Lozinski, Jonas and Lynda Prince, Gretchen and Donald Ross, St Joseph Communications, Phil and Eli Taylor
Tenth Anniversary Circle Members: Mohammad and Najla Al Zaibak, John and Leanna Bayliss, Avie Bennett, David W Binet, Ms Susanne Boyce and Dr Brendan Mullen, Helen Burstyn and family, Janice Lewis and Mitchell Cohen, Holly Coll-Black and Rupert Duchesne, Doris and Ed Daughney, Victor and Maureen Dodig, Glenna and George Fierheller, Margaret and Jim Fleck, Kevin and Roger Garland, Goring Family Foundation, James Hinds, Eleanor McCain, Donald and Helen McGillivray, Vanessa and Mark Mulroney, Sandra and Jim Pitblado, La Fondation Sackler/The Sackler Foundation, Anthony Sargent CBE, Sylvia Soyka, Liz Tory, Jörn Weisbrodt and Rufus Wainwright, Robin and David Young
Patron Circle Members: Marina Abramović, Charles and Marilyn Baillie, Rena Bedard and Bill Dillane, Diane Blake and Stephen Smith, Helen Burstyn and family, Wendy M Cecil, Neera and Deepak Chopra, Matteo Corvino and Jérôme Zieseniss, Gail Drummond and Bob Dorrance, Robert and Julia Foster, Anthony and Helen Graham, James and Susan Haldenby, the Hayden Family Foundation, Vahan and Susie Kololian, Roberto and Lucia Martella, Nancy Pencer, Janice Price and Ian Findlay, Colleen Sexsmith, Greg and Kate Sorbara, Elen Steinberg, William Thorsell, Antoinette Tummillo and John Carter, Carol Wilding, Peter Wilkinson (Manulife)
Big Bang Bash Gala: Co-Chairs—Mark and Vanessa Mulroney, Jonas and Lynda Prince; Honorary Co-Chairs—David and Angela Feldman, Tony and Lina Gagliano
Foundation Partners: La Fondation Emmanuelle Gattuso, Hal Jackman Foundation, The Lloyd Carr-Harris Foundation, The McLean Foundation, McLean Smits Family Foundation, The Pottruff Family Foundation, SOCAN Foundation
Corporate Supporters: Aimia, Andrew Richard Designs, LRI Engineering Inc, President's Choice Black Label Collection, Stikeman Elliott LLP, 3M Canada

FUNDERS
We acknowledge gratefully the financial support of the Government of Canada. *Nous reconnaissons avec gratitude l'appui financier du gouvernement du Canada.* We also acknowledge with deep gratitude the support of our founding government partner the Province of Ontario. *Nous reconnaissons aussi avec un profonde gratitude l'appui financier de notre partenaire fondateur, le Province de l'Ontario.*

PARTNERS
We acknowledge gratefully the support of our Government partners the Ontario Cultural Attractions Fund and the Ontario Arts Council and the support of our presenting partners the City of Toronto, CIBC, BMO Financial Group, L'Oréal Canada, OLG and Toronto Port Lands Company. We acknowledge gratefully the support of our official partners: Scotiabank, Van Houtte, Mill Street Brewery, Glacéau Smartwater, Absolut, Slaight Music, Timberland, TD Bank Group, Volvo Cars Canada, Norm Li, Maple Leaf Sports & Entertainment, Campo Viejo, Stoneleigh and Steinway Piano Gallery Toronto. We also acknowledge gratefully the support of our media partners St Joseph Communications and the *Toronto Star*.
Board of Directors: Luminato appreciatively salutes the festival's volunteer board for believing in the vision behind Luminato's tenth anniversary residency in the Hearn Generating Station, and thanks them for their commitment to supporting the realization of that vision.
Luminato Core Staff: We also thank our core management and staff team who worked on Luminato's Tenth Anniversary Festival: Anthony Sargent, CBE CEO; Jörn Weisbrodt, Artistic Director; Clyde Wagner, Executive Producer
Executive and Administration: Marcia McNabb CPA, Winston Tang, Daniel He, Erin Michel, Dave Pennington, Kafi Gibson, Karan Singh
Development: Tenny Nigoghossian, Natasha Udovic, Martha Haldenby, Sarah Jarvis, Tim Whalley, Leah Schoenmakers, Matt Irving, Chiara Lacey, Lindsey Williams, Serina Zheng, Coman Poon
Programming and Production: Naomi Campbell, Nicole Hurtubise, Derek Andrews, Veronica Barton, Denyse Karn, Jennifer Stein, Caroline Hollway, Justina Bohach, Tanya Hart, Swapnaa Tamhane, Jeremy Forsyth, Tyler Shaw, Matthew Lederman, Peter Eaton, Bob Mitchell, Sean Richards, Sue Konynenburg, Stephanie Tonietto, Leonardo Oliveira, Lindsay Paquette, Saskia Rinkoff, Nicole Culp, Cam McKinnon, Matt King
Marketing and Communications: Shawn Hernden, Ashley Ballantyne, Alison Uttley, Stephen Barber, Seowon Bang, Alexandra West, Liz MacInnis, Jennifer Perras, Matt Moore, Thomas Feore, Michelle Gormek, Suzanne Cheriton, Lise Sorokopud, Red Eye Media, The Knot Group

Nicole Hurtubise and Jörn Weisbrodt would additionally like to thank Josephine Ridge, Mauricio Ortiz, Jeremy Forsyth, Swapnaa Tamhane and the OPG Archives for their unique support for this book.

Image Credits

p 17 Courtesy Jack Diamond
pp 24–25 Courtesy AFP/Getty Images
pp 30–31 Courtesy Leiden University; Background: Courtesy PARTISANS
pp 34–35 [1] Courtesy David Leyes; [2] Courtesy Philippe Wojazer/AFP/Getty Images; [3] Allora & Calzadilla, *Raptor's Rapture*, 2012, single channel HD video, colour, sound, 23:30 mins. Copyright Allora & Calzadilla; Courtesy Lisson Gallery; [4] Copyright Michèle Laurent; [5] Courtesy the Bradshaw Foundation; [6&7] Courtesy Jörn Weisbrodt; [8] Courtesy David Leyes; [9] Courtesy Taku Kumabe
pp 38–39 [1] Natalie Jeremijenko, *Tree Logic*, 1999. Photograph by Zoran Orlic; Courtesy MASS MoCA; [2] Copyright I, Kleuske/Wikimedia Commons
pp 40–41 [1] Courtesy the Natural History Museum/Alamy
pp 42–43 [1&2] Courtesy Jörn Weisbrodt; [3] Copyright Scott McFarland; Buckminster Fuller, Project Toronto, 1968; Clara Thomas Archives and Special Collections York University Archives; [4–9] Courtesy Jörn Weisbrodt
pp 48–49 [1–3] Courtesy the Bradshaw Foundation
pp 52–53 [1] Photograph by Hilde Jensen; Copyright University of Tuebingen; [2] Courtesy J Monney/Ministère de la Culture et de la Communication; [3] Photograph by Andreas Praefcke; [4] Photograph by Tim Neale
pp 54–55 [1&2] Courtesy the Bradshaw Foundation
pp 58–59 [1] Courtesy Frank Lennon/Toronto Star/Getty Images; [2&3] Courtesy Jörn Weisbrodt; Background: Courtesy Paul Vaughan
p 63 [1] Photograph by Andreas Praefcke
pp 64–67 Background: Courtesy Paul Vaughan
p 71 [1] Anders Krisár, *Untitled*, 2014–15, acrylic paint on polyester resin, polyurethane, oil paint, board, wood plugs and screws, 115 x 49.5 x 64 cm. Copyright Anders Krisár
pp 72–73 [1] Courtesy Alamy
pp 80–81 [1&2] Courtesy Théâtre du Soleil
pp 82–83 [1–3] Photographs by Marie-Anne Bernard. Courtesy Théâtre du Soleil
pp 88–89 [1] Copyright Jim Linwood/Wikimedia Commons; [2] Copyright CEphoto, Uwe Aranas/Wikimedia Commons; [3] Courtesy Wikimedia Commons; [4] Copyright MykReeve/Wikimedia Commons; [5] Copyright Jakob Montrasio/Flickr; [6] Copyright Hajor/Wikimedia Commons; [7] Copyright Hufton and Crow/Wikimedia Commons
pp 96–97 [1] Copyright Gohnarch/Wikimedia Commons; [2] Courtesy Sasha Waltz & Guests GmbH; [3] Copyright David Berkowitz/Wikimedia Commons; [4] Copyright seier+seier/Wikimedia Commons; [5] Courtesy pixabay; [6] Photograph by Kazuko Oshima; Courtesy the Robert Wilson Archives; [7] Copyright Ungureanu Adrian Danut/Wikimedia Commons; [8] Copyright Nicor/Wikimedia Commons; [9] Courtesy Visual China Group/Getty Images; [10] Courtesy Jörn Weisbrodt; [11] Courtesy Wikimedia Commons; [12] Photograph by Derrick Belcham; [13] Copyright Rainer Lück/Wikimedia Commons
pp 100–101 [1&2] Copyright PARTISANS; Background: Courtesy PARTISANS
pp 102–103 [1&2] Copyright PARTISANS; [3&4] Photographs by Jonathan Friedman. Courtesy PARTISANS; Background: Courtesy PARTISANS
pp 104–105 [1&2] Copyright Cedric Price fonds, Collection Centre Canadien d'Architecture/Canadian Centre for Architecture, Montréal; Background: Courtesy PARTISANS
pp 106–107 [1] Photograph by Beat Widmer; [2&3] Courtesy Diller Scofidio + Renfro
pp 108–109 [1] Photograph by Jonathan Friedman. Courtesy PARTISANS; Background: Courtesy PARTISANS
pp 110–111 [1] Courtesy PARTISANS; [2&3] Courtesy Diller Scofidio + Renfro; Background: Courtesy PARTISANS
pp 112–113 [1&2] Courtesy Diller Scofidio + Renfro; [3&4] Courtesy PARTISANS; Background: Courtesy PARTISANS
p 115 Background: Courtesy PARTISANS
pp 116–117 [1&2] Courtesy PARTISANS and Norm Li
pp 118–119 [1] Courtesy PARTISANS
p 120 Background: Courtesy Charcoalblue

p 121 [1&2] Courtesy Wikimedia Commons
pp 122–123 [1] Courtesy Woodshed Collective; [2] Courtesy Mary Evans Picture Library; Background: Courtesy PARTISANS
p 124 [1] Courtesy Charcoalblue; [2] Courtesy Wikimedia Commons
p 125 Background: Courtesy Charcoalblue
p 126 [1] Courtesy Ontario Power Generation Archives
pp 132–133 [1] Photograph by John December; [2] Copyright Matthew G Bisanz; [3] Copyright Foster + Partners/Dbox; [4] Courtesy John Tyman
pp 136–137 Pierre Huyghe, *Untilled (Liegender Frauenakt)*, 2012, concrete cast on steel armature, bee hive, plastic, wax. Figure: 145 × 45 × 75 cm (57 1/16 × 17 11/16 × 291/2 in). Plinth: 145 × 55 × 30 cm (57 1/16 × 21 5/8 × 11 13/16 in). Art Gallery of Ontario. Purchased with the assistance of the David Yuile and Mary Elizabeth Hodgson Fund, 2013. Copyright Pierre Huyghe
pp 138–139 [1] Photograph by Kazuko Oshima; Courtesy the Robert Wilson Archives; [2] Donald Judd, 100 untitled works in mill aluminum, 1982–1986, 41 x 51 x 72 in. Permanent collection, the Chinati Foundation, Marfa, Texas. Photograph by Douglas Tuck, 2009, Donald Judd Art. Copyright 2016 Judd Foundation/Artists Rights Society (ARS), New York
p 140 [1] Photograph by Tom Vinetz; [2] Copyright Wandervogel/Wikimedia Commons
pp 144–145 [1–4] Courtesy David Leyes
pp 146–147 [1–3] Courtesy David Leyes
p 148 [1&2] Courtesy David Leyes
pp 152–153 [1] Courtesy Ontario Power Generation Archives
p 154 [1] Courtesy Ontario Power Generation Archives
p 157 [1] Courtesy Jack Diamond
pp 160–161 James Gray, *York From Gibraltar Point*, 1828; hand-coloured etching and aquatint with gum Arabic. Overall (max): 35.5 x 59.1 cm (14 x 23 1/4 in). Art Gallery of Ontario. Gift of Dr Harold A Hunter, Toronto, 1989. Image copyright Art Gallery of Ontario, 2016
pp 162–163 [1–6] Courtesy Ontario Power Generation Archives
p 164 Courtesy Ontario Power Generation Archives
p 168 Background: Courtesy Luminato Festival
pp 170–171 Courtesy Jörn Weisbrodt
p 173 Background: Courtesy Luminato Festival
p 175 [1] Copyright Larsovarga. Courtesy Wikimedia Commons
pp 176–177 Photographs by David Leyes and Jörn Weisbrodt
p 178 [1] Courtesy DeGolyer Library
pp 184–185 Photographs by Andrew Williamson and Hector Vasquez
pp 188–193 Photographs by Katherina Limo and Javier Castellanos; Direction by DA Hoskins; Courtesy The Dietrich Group
p 193 [3] Photograph by Mike Moore; Courtesy The Dietrich Group
pp 194–195 Illustration by Steve Manale
pp 196–197 Video stills courtesy Choir! Choir! Choir!
pp 198–199 Illustration by Steve Manale
p 200 Excerpted from *Stranger Music* by Leonard Cohen. Copyright 1993 Leonard Cohen. Reprinted by permission of McClelland & Stewart, a division of Penguin Random House Canada Limited. Illustration by Steve Manale. Photograph by Andrew Williamson
pp 204–205 [1] Photograph by Gus Powell; [2] David Leyes; [3] Jörn Weisbrodt
p 206 [1] Courtesy Rufus Wainwright; [2] Courtesy Luminato Festival; [3&4] Courtesy David Leyes; [5] Courtesy Rufus Wainwright
pp 208–209 [1&2] Courtesy David Leyes; [3] Photograph by Gus Powell; [4] Courtesy David Leyes
p 212 Photographs by David Leyes, Jonathan Castellino, Hector Vasquez, Fred Morin and Jörn Weisbrodt; Background: Courtesy Fred Morin
p 213 [1] Courtesy John Bil and Fred Morin
pp 214–215 Illustration by Fred Morin. Photograph by Mauricio Ortiz
p 217 [1] Illustration by Fred Morin
pp 218–219 Overlay courtesy Luminato Festival
p 220 Background: Map data copyright 2017 Google
p 221 [1&2] Courtesy David Leyes; [3] Courtesy Jörn Weisbrodt
pp 222–223 [top left] Copyright Scott McFarland, Princess Florine and Prince Florimund costumes from *The Sleeping Beauty*, 1972. Worn by Karen Kain and Rudolf Nureyev, National Ballet Of Canada; [top right] Electric Chair, c 1905. Private Collection. Photograph copyright Scott McFarland; [bottom left] Septentrionalium Terrarum descriptio, first map

of the North Pole, by Gerhard Mercator. Published in 1595. Collection of Toronto Public Library. Photograph copyright Scott McFarland; [bottom right] Kara Walker, *10 Years Massacre (and its Retelling) #1-3*, 2009, mixed media, cut paper and acrylic on Gessoed panel. Private Collection. Photograph copyright Scott McFarland

p 224 [1] Giant panda Er Shun and giant panda cubs Jia Panpan and Jia Yueyue. Photograph copyright Scott McFarland; [2] Jörn Weisbrodt

p 225 Background: Courtesy Luminato Festival

pp 228–229 Background: Courtesy Yes Yes Y'all

pp 230–231 Photographs by Yannick Anton and David Leyes

p 233 [1&2] Photographs by Guntar Kravis

pp 234–235 Yannick Grandmont

pp 236–237 [1] Courtesy Michelle Lyons; [2] Courtesy Jonathan Castellino; [3] Courtesy Andrew Kirkby; [4] Courtesy Jörn Weisbrodt; [5] Courtesy Yannick Grandmont; Background: Courtesy Paul Vaughan;

p 238 [1] Tattoo and photo by Richard Blackstar; [2] Photograph by Laurie Sansom; Background: Courtesy Charcoalblue

p 239 Photographs by Yannick Grandmont

pp 242–245 Background: Courtesy Luminato Festival

pp 243–244 Photographs by George Pimental

All full bleed single- or double-page images referenced below are courtesy Jonathan Castellino:

p 1 View from the side into the Turbine Hall
pp 2–3 Upwards view of a Boiler Bay
pp 4–5 Control Room
pp 6–7 Boiler Hall
p 8 Turbine Hall with crane
p 14 Construction of the Hearn Theatre
p 15 Assembly of *1000 Speculations*
pp 18–19 Construction of the Hearn Theatre, seen from the stage into the audience
pp 20–21 Turbine Hall
pp 22–23 *1000 Speculations* by Michel de Broin in the upper Turbine Hall, seen from the mezzanine
p 26 *1000 Speculations* from below
p 27 The Hearn Theatre seating
pp 28–29 Installation of the bar for Le Pavillon in the Control Room
pp 32–33 *Situation Rooms* by Rimini Protokoll under construction in the Boiler Hall
pp 36–37 *1000 Speculations* in the Turbine Hall
pp 38–39 Upside down tree in the Turbine Hall
pp 40–41 Hearn Theatre under construction
pp 44–45 Boiler Hall view towards *Situation Rooms* in Bay 5
pp 46–47 The Music Stage under construction
pp 48–49 Front-of-house trailer
pp 50–51 The upper Turbine Hall
pp 54–55 Installation of the set for *The James Plays* in the Hearn Theatre
pp 56–57 The Hearn Theatre under construction, seen from above
pp 60–61 breaking.of.the.fourth.wall
pp 62–63 Boiler Bay 4 (Music Stage)
pp 64–65 Grand Staircase under construction
p 67 Worker climbing a shipping container
pp 68–69 The auditorium of the Hearn Theatre
pp 70–71 Worker pulling a shipping container wall
p 72 The set of *The James Plays* under construction
p 73 The Music Stage from the side
pp 74–75 *Situation Rooms* from above under construction
pp 76–77 The Turbine Hall from above
pp 80–81 *Situation Rooms* under construction
pp 84–85 First open side bay in the Turbine Hall with first emergency staircase
pp 86–87 View from backstage of the Music Stage audience area under construction
pp 90–91 First open side bay in Turbine Hall with *Circa 1948* by Stan Douglas under construction
pp 92–93 *Situation Rooms* under construction
p 94 Executive Producer Clyde Wagner in production trailer
pp 98–99 Hearn Theatre during *James III: The True Mirror*
pp 100–101 Shooting range of *Situation Rooms* under construction
pp 102–103 Boiler Bay with sound insulation
pp 106–107 Water puddles between the Turbine Hall and Boiler Hall with crane
pp 108–109 Audience path in Boiler Hall under water
p 110 Future audience path in Boiler Hall after a rainstorm
pp 114–115 The Hearn Generating Station smokestack seen from the Port Lands
pp 116–117 Window in the Control Room
pp 118–119 The Boiler Hall
pp 120–121 *1000 Speculations* on the ground in Turbine Hall
pp 122–123 Side Bay in Turbine Hall with OCAD U (artist Bonnie Tung)
pp 124–125 Architectural model in PARTISANS' pop-up architecture studio in the Boiler Hall
pp 126–127 Applying the festival logo to the first arch in the Turbine Hall
pp 128–129 The crane in the Turbine Hall with *1000 Speculations*
pp 130–131 View from the mezzanine into the Turbine Hall with works by Jordan Söderberg Mills
p 133 A table in Le Pavillon in the Control Room
pp 134–135 A Member of Team FX jumping from the smokestack on opening night
pp 138–139 Monkey Vault rehearsing on the Music Stage
pp 140–141 The bar and barstools at Le Pavillon
pp 142–143 Fight rehearsal for *James II: Day of the Innocents*
p 144 Audience during Unsound Toronto at the Music Stage
p 147 Selfie with *1000 Speculations*
p 148 Roly Porter and MFO (Unsound)
pp 150–151 Couple kissing in Boiler Hall during Unsound Toronto
pp 152–153 The Biergarten at night
p 154 Tim Hecker
pp 156–157 Kid Koala's *Music to Draw To* participants in the Side Room
pp 160–161 Seating at the Music Stage
pp 164–165 Margaret-Anne O'Donnell, Producer for *The James Plays* and Luke Kernaghan, Assistant Director for *The James Plays*
pp 166–167 The Airstream of the Artistic Director with the main entrance in the background
p 169 "Don't Look Back" (Hommage to Bert Neumann) at main entrance
pp 170–171 The technical team for *The James Plays*
p 172 Audience waiting at main entrance
p 175 Installation of *Trove: A View of Toronto in 50 of its Treasures* in The Jackman Gallery
pp 178–179 The smokestack and east side of the Hearn
pp 180–181 Yes Yes Y'all and Dudebox on the Music Stage
pp 182–183 Unsound Toronto on the Music Stage
p 186 *Chamber Music* by the Toronto Symphony Orchestra in the Side Room
p 187 The smokestack illuminated at night
p 201 The Toronto Symphony Orchestra rehearsing on the Music Stage
pp 202–203 Dancing Phil and the Ten Queens
p 205 Rufus Wainwright performing *Rufus Does Judy Again* on the Music Stage
p 206 Rufus Wainwright rehearsing *Rufus Does Judy Again*
pp 208–209 Rufus Wainwright rehearsing *Rufus Does Judy Again*
pp 210–211 Le Pavillon
p 213 Kid Koala DJing at Le Pavillon
pp 216–217 The kitchen counter at Le Pavillon
pp 218–219 Kid Koala's *Music to Draw To* in the Side Room
p 221 Wall with images from *Trove: A View of Toronto in 50 of its Treasures*
p 224 Highway billboard with image from *Trove: A View of Toronto in 50 of its Treasures*
pp 226–227 Fred Morin's camper trailer with the Portlands Energy Centre
p 232–233 Boiler Bay
p 236 Reflection of the Boiler Hall in a water puddle
pp 240–241 Truck in the Turbine Hall leaving the Hearn
p 243 Striking the Hearn Generating Station
p 244 Striking the Hearn Theatre
p 246 Airstream seen through the main entrance
p 247 Striking barrels
pp 254–255 The roof

30 JUNE

© 2017 Black Dog Publishing Limited, London, UK, the authors and the artists. All rights reserved.

Black Dog Publishing Limited
308 Essex Road,
London, N1 3AX
United Kingdom

+44 (0)20 7713 5097
info@blackdogonline.com
www.blackdogonline.com

Designer: Clara Emo-Dambry
Editor: Jörn Weisbrodt
Editorial Assistant: Nicole Hurtubise

All opinions expressed within this publication are those of the authors and not necessarily of the publisher or the Luminato Festival.

British Library in Cataloguing Data
A CIP record for this book is available from the British Library

ISBN 978-1-911164-29-6

No part of this publication may be reproduced, stored in a retrieval system, or transmitted, in any form or by any means, electronic, mechanical, photocopying, recording, or otherwise, without prior permission of the publisher.

Every effort has been made to trace the copyright holders, but if any have been inadvertently overlooked the necessary arrangements will be made at the first opportunity.

Black Dog Publishing Limited, London, UK, is an environmentally responsible company. *Into the Culture Cave: Generator of Art, Community, Emotions and Ideas* is printed on sustainably sourced paper.

Cover: Photograph by Jonathan Castellino